Ideas and Ideologies
General Editor:
Eugene Kamenka

Intellectuals and Revolution

Socialism and the Experience of 1848

Edited by Eugene Kamenka
and F. B. Smith

St. Martin's Press
New York

© Edward Arnold (Publishers) Ltd 1979

All rights reserved. For information write:
St. Martin's Press, Inc., 175 Fifth Avenue, New York, N.Y. 10010
Printed in Great Britain
First published in the United States of America in 1980

ISBN 0–312–41893–0

Library of Congress Cataloging in Publication Data

Main entry under title:

Intellectuals and revolution.

(Ideas and ideologies)
Bibliography: p.
Includes index.
1. Europe—History—1848–1849—Addresses, essays.
lectures.   2.   Socialism in Europe—History—Addresses,
essays, lectures.   I.   Kamenka, Eugene.   II.   Smith,
Francis Barrymore.   III.   Series.
D387.I57   1980   940.2´84   79–21903
ISBN 0–312–41893–0

Contents

Introduction

For two hundred years now the idea of revolution has loomed large in human consciousness. The eighteenth century, in an important sense, invented the idea, together with that of happiness. The nineteenth and twentieth centuries have seen more great social and political upheavals, and more enthusiasm for and fear of them, than any other period in recorded history. Two of the greatest, most 'world-historical', of such upheavals—the French Revolution of 1789 and the Russian Revolution of 1917—have become for most students and practitioners of revolution classical paradigms on which to base their analyses and tactics, their hopes and their fears.

There is a third, equally important, paradigm, which is in many ways more ambiguous but also more instructive and 'relevant': that of the revolutions of 1848. It was on behalf of those revolutions and in the course of them that Marx and Engels first worked out, in specific and practical terms, the tactics and strategy that became the legacy of communist revolutionary movements everywhere. It was in 1848, rather than in 1789 or in 1917, that revolutions spread like wildfire and with remarkable family resemblance in trends and response throughout the whole of Europe—except Spain, Great Britain and Russia, which remained the cornerstones of stability and helped, by containing war, to defeat those revolutions. It was in 1848 that the middle classes and the proletariat first came fully to recognize each other as historic forces and to gauge each other's comparative strength and roles, initially as allies and then as actual and potential enemies. It was in 1848 that the peasants formed a third force and that nationalisms confronted each other in all their internal and external complexities and their ambiguous (and ambivalent) relation to both socialism and democracy.

Outside France, liberals, democrats, students and workers may have thought, at first, that they were fighting together against historic anachronisms, against survivals of an *ancien régime* which had lived

viii   *Intellectuals and Revolution*

on too long. But they were doing so in new conditions, in conditions which in many respects had more in common with the world of today than had Paris in 1789 or St Petersburg and Moscow in 1917. The events of 1848 and the lessons that contemporaries and their successors drew and have drawn from them cannot be left out of the theory of revolution or out of the attempt to understand the modern world. The chapters that follow seek to illuminate, in a concrete context, the role in revolution of great social movements, ideologies and estates —liberalism, socialism, nationalism and communism, the workers, the intellectuals and middle classes, and the peasants. Their existence, interests and concerns span the nineteenth and twentieth centuries and make these centuries part of one complex, developing and yet uncertain and unfinished history.

The present volume arose out of a weekend seminar on 'The Revolution of the Intellectuals—Men and Ideas of 1848', held in 1974 in the History of Ideas Unit of the Institute of Advanced Studies of the Australian National University in Canberra. It incorporates some of the papers presented there. To those others who also read or circulated papers and to Dr Smith, who helped plan the seminar and has joined me as co-editor, I owe much. The President and Fellows of Trinity College, Oxford, the German Academic Exchange Service (DAAD) and the Max Planck Institute for Foreign Private and Private International Law in Hamburg, as well as the generous research provisions of my own university, made it possible to complete this and other work in ideal research conditions in the Europe that is still the indispensable centre of great libraries, great scholarship and great ideas.

Mrs E. Y. Short has put a great deal of work into this volume, assisting me with research, compiling the chronology and index, translating Professor Bodi's Heine quotations, checking all the manuscripts and proofs. I am very grateful to her.

Hamburg, January 1979

Eugene Kamenka

I

Europe in upheaval

Eugene Kamenka

The revolution of 1848, Sir Lewis Namier has reminded us, 'was universally expected, and it was super-national as none before or after; it ran through, and enveloped, the core of Europe, "the world" of the continental Europeans, which extended from the Channel ports to the frontiers of Russia, from Paris to Vienna.'[1] Insurrection at Palermo, barricades in Paris, Vienna and Berlin; disturbances in Cologne; street riots, National Guards, 'Academic Legions', Committees of Public Safety; Metternich's house in flames and the prince himself forced to flee; revolution in Hungary, Bohemia, Milan, Venice, the Kingdom of the two Sicilies, the minor German states, Denmark and Holland; ministers dismissed, constitutions granted, national assemblies, democratic and supra-national congresses convoked; kings and emperors, Pope and princes trembling and uncertain. Progress, it seemed in the first few months of 1848, was on the march: constitutional democracy and the principle of national self-determination, as steps toward the conversion of all men from subjects into citizens and from serfs or oppressed and despised workers and nationalities into free men and free nations, could not be resisted.

The revolution that was so universally expected and that appeared to rest so firmly on every principle that enlightened, progressive Europeans held dear, proved, within one year, to be a momentous failure. The overthrow of Louis Philippe's bourgeois monarchy in France in February 1848 was followed by a crushing defeat, first for both democratic and revolutionary socialism and then for republicanism. The working-class revolt was suppressed; the victory of the 'party of order' in June 1848 ended, by 1852, in the elevation of Louis Napoleon, through universal or at least greatly extended suffrage, to plebiscitory dictator and emperor of France. The German-speaking lands, despite or because of their welter of diets, assemblies, parlia-

---

[1] Sir Lewis Namier, *1848: the Revolution of the Intellectuals* (Oxford, 1946, reprinted from *Proceedings of the British Academy*, xxx), p. 3.

ments and congresses, came out of their upheavals neither unified nor democratized, neither as Little Germany nor as Greater Germany. Poland remained divided under foreign rule, the remaining western and southern Slavs unfree and Italy fragmented; the Roman Republic collapsed and the Pope returned to Rome less liberal than he had left it; the Austrian Empire, like the Russian, lived on in fact if not quite in name into the twentieth century. Revolution had called forth successful counter-revolution: by 1852, Switzerland was the only democratic republic in Europe, and Sardinia—whose king, Charles Albert, had skilfully averted internal revolution by granting a liberal constitution, making nationalist war on Austria and abdicating, in defeat, in favour of his son Victor Emmanuel—the only constitutional and liberal state in Italy. The Dutch Netherlands, Denmark and Prussia had made some gains toward constitutional government compared with their situation before 1848, but the abolition of serf-dom in Hungary, Bohemia and Austria itself was the only immediate major and irrevocable gain of a revolution that had hoped to emancipate not only the backward peasant areas, but whole nations, cultures and classes. With very little cost—a few minor constitutional reforms here and there—the revolution that failed had made reaction secure for another generation. The twenty years after 1848 were to be, depending on one's point of view, periods of unparalleled peaceful progress or of reactionary stability; certainly they were not the products of revolutionary slogans or revolutionary achievement, a consummation of constitutionalism or a liberation of nations. The uprisings of 1848–9 had driven revolutionaries almost everywhere into exile and political outer darkness. They had retarded, in many ways, the development of democracy in Europe by revealing the weakness of its democrats and the competing allegiances of its middle classes.

How could so universally expected, so general and so timely a series of connected revolutionary upheavals have turned out to be a failure? That they were timely—manifestations of a growing and irresistible trend—was not only widely believed among contemporaries but forms remarkably common ground between Marxist and non-Marxist historians. It was Lord Macaulay, and not yet Karl Marx, who issued a warning in one of his great speeches in 1831 supporting the First Reform Bill. Throughout history, he maintained, we find that portions of the community which had been of no account expand and grow strong, whether they be merchants and manufacturers in Manchester, Birmingham and Sheffield or 'free people of colour' in Jamaica, and these cannot be denied those rights in politics that their power, influence and prestige have already won for them in social and economic life without fomenting revolution.[2] It was Tocqueville, and not only Marx, who warned the Paris Chamber of Deputies, a month

[2] T. B. Macaulay, *Speeches of Lord Macaulay* (London, 1860), pp. 8–9.

before the revolution, that 'a storm was brewing'. That storm was social but also nationalist. The liberation of the Greeks had earlier fired the sympathies of educated or progressive Europeans everywhere; now the liberation of Poland once again did the same, at least initially, in the first half of 1848. Constitutions, or demands for constitutions, were the order of the day. Nationalism and democracy seemed to march hand in hand.

For Marxists, the principle of progress and the influence and irresistible effect of economic and social change are writ large in history; they tend to elevate these with sweeping confidence. For them, these demands are inescapable results of the industrial revolution, of the new commercial-industrial economy. Thus E. J. Hobsbawm on the background, the underlying causes, of the events of 1848 and of the expectation that revolution would occur:

> In brief, the world of the 1840s was out of balance. The forces of economic, technical and social change released in the past half-century were unprecedented, and even to the most superficial observer, irresistible. Their institutional consequences, on the other hand, were as yet modest. It was, for instance, inevitable that sooner or later legal slavery and serfdom (except as relics in remote regions as yet untouched by the new economy) would have to go, as it was inevitable that Britain could not for ever remain the *only* industrialized country. It was inevitable that landed aristocracies and absolute monarchies must retreat in all countries in which a strong bourgeoisie was developing, whatever the political compromises or formulae found for retaining status, influence and even political power. Moreover, it was inevitable that the injection of political consciousness and permanent political activity among the masses, which was the great legacy of the French Revolution, must sooner or later mean that these masses were allowed to play a formal part in politics. And given the remarkable acceleration of social change since 1830, and the revival of the world revolutionary movement, it was clearly inevitable that changes—whatever their precise institutional nature— could not be long delayed.
>
> All this would have been enough to give the men of the 1840s the consciousness of impending change. But not enough to explain, what was widely felt throughout Europe, the consciousness of impending social revolution. It was, significantly enough, not confined to revolutionaries, who expressed it with the greatest elaboration, nor to the ruling classes, whose fear of the massed poor is never far below the surface in times of social change. The poor themselves felt it. The literate strata of the people expressed it. 'All well-informed people', wrote the American consul from Amsterdam during the hunger of 1847, reporting the sentiments of the German emigrants passing through Holland, 'express the belief that the present crisis is so deeply interwoven in the events of the present period that "it" is but the commencement of that great Revolution, which they consider sooner or later is to dissolve the present constitution of things.'

The reason was that the crisis in what remained of the old society appeared to coincide with a crisis of the new.[3]

In the 1830s and 1840s, Hobsbawm goes on to argue, the difficulties of the new economy seemed only to increase with its power to produce larger and larger quantities of goods by more and more revolutionary methods.

In fact, 1848 did not see that breakdown of capitalism which was being forecast by some of its most radical socialist critics, and hoped and worked for by the secret revolutionary societies, first the League of the Just and then Blanqui's Society of the Seasons and the Communist League. It was to be followed, instead, by the dawn of capitalism's most rapid and unchallenged period of expansion and triumph. Many would now say, and some have said, that socialists were confusing the birth-pangs of industrial society with the death-pangs of capitalism. Be that as it may, the new tensions, crises, antagonisms and fears of the 1840s, as sketched by Hobsbawm, were undoubtedly there, injecting new factors and new complexities into the age-old struggle against poverty, oppression and being treated as of no account. They gave new strength and new content to the unparalleled number of *idées forces* that the French Revolution of 1789 had cast into the world, almost before their time; they did indeed revive, and make once more 'relevant', in new forms, the great revolutionary tradition. For Tocqueville, as clearly as for Marx, 1848 was part of the *one* revolutionary process that had begun in 1789; for him, as for Marx, it had certainly *not* been halted by the setback of 1848, by the fact that socialism lay, at the end of that revolution, 'buried in contempt'.[4] Both expected further major institutional changes in society; only Tocqueville had a much better sense of their complexity and unpredictability.

Sir Lewis Namier's style—and sympathies—are markedly different from those of Marx and Engels; his eye, in general, is fixed on more particular events. When he steps back to assess the age, it is largely in political and cultural terms, and with a tendency not to take seriously the 'ideology' of revolutionaries or the 'ideas' of the poor and uneducated. Yet his account of the immediate background of the revolution and of the way it began is in content, if not in sympathy and terminology, very close to that given by Marx and Engels themselves, as participant-observers, and since copied by the more intelligent of their disciples. Emphasizing, like Marx and Engels and more recently Hobsbawm, the universal expectation of revolution in

[3] E. J. Hobsbawm, *The Age of Revolution: Europe 1789–1848* (London, 1962), pp. 304–5.
[4] Alexis de Tocqueville, *Recollections*, translated from French by G. Lawrence, edited by J. P. Mayer and A. P. Kerr (New York, 1970), pp. 95–6.

1847 and the strength of intellectual beliefs in reform, affecting the rulers themselves, Namier discerns, as at least part of the story, the same conjunction of crises and the same social forces as the Marxists do. He, too, stresses the universal expectation of revolution. He is not much given to the phrase 'it was therefore inevitable', and emphasizes rather the weakness of will of the rulers of Europe, apart from England and Russia, when confronted with the 'progressivist spirit'. But he also writes:

There was undoubtedly also an economic and social background to the revolution. Lean harvests in 1846 and 1847, and the potato disease, were causing intense misery in most parts of the Continent. Agrarian riots occurred in France where 1847 was long remembered as *l'année du pain cher*; there was a 'potato revolution' in Berlin (complete with barricades), bread riots in Stuttgart and Ulm, labour troubles in Vienna and in Bohemia, rank starvation in Silesia, etc. Count Galen, the Prussian Minister, wrote from Kassel on 20 January 1847: 'The old year ended in scarcity, the new one opens with starvation. Misery, spiritual and physical, traverses Europe in ghastly shapes—the one without God, the other without bread. Woe if they join hands!' Against this background, economic or social conflicts were assuming a bitter, acute character. In most parts of the Austrian Empire, but more especially in Hungary and in Galicia, a final adjustment between big landowners and peasants was overdue: seignorial jurisdictions, *corvées*, and other remnants of serfdom had to be cleared away, and the title of the peasant to the land which he worked on his own had to be established. Even in southwestern Germany, on the confines of France and Switzerland, feudal survivals were fomenting agrarian revolt. All over Europe independent artisans were fighting their drawn-out losing battle against modern industry, especially desperate in the case of hand-spinners and weavers, or of carriers and bargees facing the competition of railways and steamboats: hence the attacks against modern machinery and means of transport at the outbreak of the revolution. On the other hand, the new class of factory workmen was starting its fight for a human existence. And when in 1847–8 a severe financial crisis set in, widespread unemployment ensued both among artisans and workmen, and among the large numbers of unskilled labour engaged on railway construction. Here was plenty of inflammable matter in ramshackle buildings. [Namier, pp. 4–5.]

Neither does Namier have any more doubt than Marx and Engels about who sparked off the revolution—the workers of almost every large city in Europe—about how little initial resistance there was, and who it was that tried at first to profit from it:

The French Revolution of 1789 and the Russian of 1917 were made and sustained by the converging action of the two greatest revolutionary forces: the people of the capital, effective through concentration at the very centre of government, and the peasant masses, invincible through their numbers, their dispersion, and the primitive, practical character of their demands (they never seek by revolt to establish new and higher forms of production, but to free themselves of burdens, or seize more land in order to cultivate it in their traditional, inadequate manner). In 1848 it was the proletariate of the quickly growing modern capitals which brought the widespread discontents to a head: and 'accidents' and 'misunderstandings', epidemic in character—the 'fusillade' of the Boulevard des Capucins on 23 February, the salvo before the Vienna Landhaus on 13 March, and the 'two shots' fired in front of the Royal Palace in Berlin on the 18th—converted revolts into risings. For lack of support from other sections of the population, and of faith in themselves, the monarchical Governments collapsed under the impact of the working-class revolution. The conviction was universal that a change was long overdue. Aristocratic assemblies, such as the Hungarian Diet or the Bohemian Estates, were showing a progressive, oppositional spirit; in Italy, a liberal Pope, elected in 1846, set out to reform the administration of his States; in Prussia, the convocation of the United Diet in February 1847 (partially redeeming a promise of more than thirty years' standing) marked a step towards a constitutional régime. The abortive Polish revolution of 1846, the 'Sonderbund' War of 1847 in Switzerland, and, early in 1848, the oubreaks in Italy (or even the Lola Montez riots in Munich, an *opéra bouffe* suited to the place) were forerunners of a very much greater movement, symptoms of 'that mysterious force' which was to raise Europe. There was an intense consciousness of revolutionary tension, and no one seems to have had the strength, or even the will, to stand up to the storm when it broke. In exile Louis Philippe declared that he had given way to forces of a moral order—*á une insurrection morale*; and on the eve of the revolution his queen and sons pressed for a change of system. On 9 March 1848 King Wilhelm of Württemberg thus excused himself to Gorchakov, then Russian Minister in Stuttgart: 'Je ne puis pas monter á cheval contre les idées.' In Vienna members of the Court and the Government were convinced of the need of Metternich's resignation before the cry for it was raised in the streets. Frederick William IV of Prussia more than surrendered to the revolution: he made a half-hearted attempt to place himself at its head. The monarchs gave in because they themselves were affected by the *Zeitgeist*—the ideas of a period 'whose active religion was politics'; and the middle classes, the foremost exponents of the new political creed, let them reel but did not overthrow them: with the sole exception of the Orleans dynasty, none lost its throne in 1848. The monarchs had merely to turn 'constitutional' and receive liberal intellectuals into political partnership. The mob had come out in revolt, moved by passions and distress rather than by ideas: they had no articulate aims, and no one will ever be able to supply a rational explanation of what it was they fought for, or what made them fight. Proudhon writes: 'Le 24 février a été fait sans idée.' The working classes touched it off, and the middle classes cashed in on it. [Namier pp. 5–7.]

If 1848 was, in European terms, a 'universal' revolution, it was also an extremely complex one. The railways and the new electric telegraph brought news from one end of Europe to another with unprecedented speed; if this spread revolution and revolutionary ideas, it also spread complexity and complication. The complexity of the revolution of 1848 lies not only in the fact that a number of revolutions took place in a number of different regional and national settings, and that Germany had (and still has) no real capital, but in the fact that these all interacted, all had to and did take account of each other. For perhaps the first time revolutionaries were called upon, from the moment of assuming their unaccustomed positions of at least pretended power, to become international statesmen in the context of fragmenting empires and shifting federations. They had to look above all to their frontiers, their neighbours and their minorities. With the possible exception of the poet Lamartine, they failed dismally.

In general terms, Marx and Engels and Marxists since then see the revolution of 1848 as containing two revolutions. There is the defeated proletarian revolution in France, brutally massacred in the June Days; there is also the defeated bourgeois revolution in Prussia, the other German territories and the Austrian Empire. This was not massacred, but betrayed by the weakness and timidity of the bourgeoisie and petty bourgeoisie, by their dependence on the government and their fear of the proletariat which had sparked off the revolution and which, together with university students, constituted its only genuinely militant element, its only courageous material force. The national factor they treat as significant but epiphenomenal, confusing the 'real' issues. With the peasantry they are not at home. The political weakness and timidity of the German bourgeoisie, for Marxists, reflects its economic weakness, its character as a still undeveloped and unself-conscious class. The big bourgeoisie is still dependent on the royal and imperial households and the liberal revolution, as a result, is in the hands of professors, minor officials and the petty trading class of the cities—men who dare not speculate, who tremble for their minor property and position, who are totally removed from all real action and fear, above all, violence, disorder, the mob in the streets, the proletariat that has nothing to lose. A Parliament of Professors, that was the ill-fated Frankfurt Assembly; a revolution of the middle class, of pharmacists and schoolteachers, of what Namier calls the Intellectuals, that was why 1848, in Germany, ended as a débâcle. In revolution as in war, Engels writes,

> it is always necessary to show a strong front, and he who attacks is in the advantage; and in revolution as in war, it is of the highest necessity to stake everything on the decisive moment, whatever the odds may be. There is not a single successful revolution in history that does not prove the truth of these axioms.[5]

[5] Cf. Friedrich Engels, *Revolution and Counter-Revolution in Germany*, especially chapter 15, in Karl Marx and Friedrich Engels, *Selected Works* (3 vols, Moscow, 1969) I.

Professors, schoolteachers and pharmacists, shopkeepers and minor bureaucrats are not the people to display audacity, to make real war on their enemies. That, too, is precisely Namier's point.

Here is how Marx's writing in December 1848 characterizes the Prussian bourgeoisie that for nine months both hoped and feared to make a revolution:

> While the Revolutions of 1648 and 1789 had been inspired with a bound-less feeling of pride, standing, as they did, on the threshold of a new era, the pride of the Berliners in 1848 was based on the fact that they represented an anachronism. Their light was not unlike the light of those stars whose rays reach denizens of our earth 100,000 years after the extinction of the luminary which sent them forth. The Prussian Revolution of March represented in miniature—it represented nothing except in miniature—such a star in Europe. Its light was the light of a social corpse long since decayed.
>
> The German bourgeoisie had developed so languidly, so timidly, so slowly, that when it began to constitute a danger to feudalism and absolutism, it already found itself opposed on the other hand by the proletariat and all those strata of the city population the interests and ideas of which were identical with those of the proletariat. Its enemy included not only the class *behind* it but all of Europe *in front*. As distinguished from the French bourgeoisie of 1789, the Prussian bourgeoisie was not the class that would defend the whole of contemporary society against the representatives of the old order, the monarchy, the nobility. It had declined to the level of an estate which was in opposition to the crown as well as to the people, and it was irresolute in its relations to either of its enemies because it was always beholding both of them either before it or behind its back: it was inclined from the very start to betray the people and to make compromises with the crowned representative of the old society, for the German bourgeoisie itself belonged to the old society; it represented the interest not of a new order against the old, but interests within the old order, which have taken on a new lease of life; it stood at the helm of the revolution not because it was backed by the people, but because the people had shoved it to the front; it found itself at the head not because it took the initiative in favour of the new social epoch, but merely because it represented the discontent of the obsolete social epoch; it was a stratum of the old State which had not yet effected its emergence, but which was now flung to the surface of the new State by an upheaval; without faith in itself, without faith in the people, grumbling against the upper classes, trembling before the lower classes, selfish in its attitudes toward both, and aware of its selfishness, revolutionary with respect to the conservatives, and conser-vative with respect to the revolutionists, distrustful of its own slogans, which were phrases instead of ideas, intimidated by the world storm, yet exploiting that very storm, devoid of energy in any direction, yet resorting to plagiarism in all directions, banal through lack of originality, but original in its sheer banality ... without a universal historical calling, a doomed senile creature, devoted to the impossible task of leading and

manipulating the robust youthful aspirations of a new people in his own senile interests—sans eyes, sans ears, sans teeth, sans everything—such was the position of the Prussian bourgeoisie that had been guiding the destinies of the Prussian State since the March Revolution.[6]

And this is how Engels, four years later, characterizes the intellectuals and the petty bourgeoisie, the democratic extreme left of the Frankfurt National Assembly, the men who saw themselves as the élite of revolutionary Germany:

> These poor, weak-minded men, during the course of their generally very obscure lives, had been so little accustomed to anything like success, that they actually believed their paltry amendments, passed with two or three votes majority, would change the face of Europe. They had, from the beginning of their legislative career, been more imbued than any other faction of the Assembly with that incurable malady *parliamentary cretinism*, a disorder which penetrates its unfortunate victims with the solemn conviction that the whole world, its history and future, are governed and determined by a majority of votes in that particular representative body which has the honour to count them among its members, and that all and everything going on outside the walls of their house—wars, revolutions, railway-constructing, colonizing of whole new continents, California gold discoveries, Central American canals, Russian armies, and whatever else may have some little claim to influence upon the destinies of mankind—is nothing compared with the incommensurable events hinging upon the important question, whatever it may be, just at that moment occupying the attention of their honourable house. Thus it was the Democratic party of the Assembly, by effectually smuggling a few of their nostrums into the 'Imperial Constitution', first became bound to support it, although in every essential point it flatly contradicted their own oft-proclaimed principles, and at last, when this mongrel work was abandoned, and bequeathed to them by its main authors, accepted the inheritance, and held out for this *Monarchical* Constitution, even in opposition to everybody who *then* proclaimed their own *Republican* principles. [Engels, chapter 15, pp. 370–71.]

Namier's characterization of that middle class is not so significantly different:

> In France and Germany the middle classes comprised probably half the nation, and were ever ready to comport themselves as if they formed the whole. Self-assertive but timid, and individualistic in outlook, they were not given to mass action, and watched popular movements with misgivings. When in Vienna and Berlin they demanded 'arms for the people' (*Volksbewaffnung*), they meant for men of property or education, fit guardians of the existing social order as much as of the newly acquired

[6] Karl Marx, 'The Bourgeoisie and the Counter-Revolution' an article for the *Neue Rheinische Zeitung*, 15 December 1848. Cf. Marx and Engels, *Selected Works* I, pp. 140–41.

freedoms: in both cities workmen, day labourers, or journeymen were excluded from the National Guard. The terms 'Communists' and 'proletariate' (since embalmed in the Marxian nomenclature) were in general use, and evoked intense, exaggerated, fears. The very absence of a definite programme, perhaps not unjustifiably, tended to increase them: for it pointed to a class war of blind hatreds. On 13 March cases of murder and looting occurred in the Vienna suburbs, though the mob which attacked factories and destroyed their machinery carefully refrained from pilfering. Even when during the siege of Vienna, in October 1848, the nationalist radicals fought side by side with men from the working-class suburbs, distrust persisted. Smolka, a Pole who at that time presided over the Austrian Parliament, in a letter to his wife on the 30th, mentions fears of looting by the 'proletariate' as they were being forced back on to the Inner City. 'I was sure that this would not happen,' he writes; 'I have come to know the integrity and honour of the poor people of this town: their exemplary behaviour deserves the highest praise.' All over Europe the middle classes paid lip-service to the 'people' and its cause, but never felt altogether secure or happy in its company. They would emulate the humanitarian endeavours of the Convention of 1792 (described by one of its members as 'an assembly of philosophers engaged on preparing the happiness of the world') but they were determined to avoid the sequel. They had faith in democracy, parliamentary democracy, and trusted that the people whom they had enfranchised would return them in elections; and then it should stand behind them, and await the outcome of their deliberations. They wanted the revolution to enter like the ghost in Dickens's *Christmas Carol*, with a flaming halo round its head and a big extinguisher under its arm. [Namier, pp. 7–9.]

And after arguing that only the triumph of reaction in fact saved the reputation of the German revolution of 1848, made possible the myth of liberalism, instead of showing up the German middle classes as a cowardly and ineffective motley whose only abiding enthusiasm was German chauvinism—the desire to keep Poles and Czechs in order in the 'German' provinces, a desire for which they would and did sacrifice the revolution—Namier concludes by citing, with the same relish that Engels would have felt, the Russian revolutionary Alexander Herzen's contemptuous dismissal of the German revolution as a pathetically earnest playful cow:

The 'fighting Convention' assembled in St Paul's Church at Frankfort, and consisting of well intentioned professors, doctors, theologians, pharmacists, and philologists, *sehr ausgezeichneten in ihrem Fache* [very distinguished in their fields], applauded the Austrian soldiers in Lombardy and curbed the Poles in Posnania.... The first free word uttered after centuries of silence by the representatives of Germany seeking her own emancipation was in opposition to the oppressed and weak nationalities. This incapacity for freedom, these awkwardly revealed inclinations to retain what had been unjustly acquired, provoke irony: insolent pretensions are forgiven only when accompanied by vigorous actions, and those were lacking.

The revolution of 1848 was marked by lack of foresight and by precipitation, but in France and in Italy there was scarcely anything ridiculous about it; in Germany, everywhere except in Vienna, it had a comic character, incomparably funnier than Goethe's wretched farce, *Der Bürgergeneral*....

French weaknesses and shortcomings are palliated to some extent by their light and fugitive character. In the German the same defects assume a more solid and basic character, and hence are more striking. One must see for oneself these German efforts to play *so einen burschikosen Gamin de Paris* in politics in order to appreciate them. I was always reminded of the playfulness of a cow, when that excellent and respectable animal, adorned with domestic kindliness, takes to gambolling and galloping in the meadow, and with a serious face kicks up her hind legs or gallops sideways, whipping herself with her tail.[7]

'Insolent pretensions are forgiven only when accompanied by vigorous action.' That the German revolution was a revolution of talkers, Marx, Engels and Namier agree; they agree that revolutions require force and above all war: otherwise the forces divide, alliances crumble, 'parliamentary cretinism' takes over. This, perhaps the most famous passage of Namier's study of 1848, could have been written by Engels and certainly embodies what was regarded by Marx and Engels and, as we shall see, is still regarded by their revolutionary followers, as the main lesson of 1848:

In the interplay between constitutional and national movements on the European Continent, which opens in 1848, it is the latter that win: and they cut across into the international arena. A constitutional régime is secure when its ways have become engrained in the habits and instinctive reactions—*dans les mœurs*—of the political nation: it safeguards civilized life, but it presupposes agreement and stability as much as it secures them; and it can hardly be expected to build up, recast, or dissect the body in which it resides. (Hence the talk about 'missed opportunities' of uniting Germany by 'Parliamentary action' lacks substance.) States are not created or destroyed, and frontiers redrawn or obliterated, by argument and majority votes; nations are freed, united, or broken by blood and iron, and not by a generous application of liberty and tomato-sauce; violence is the instrument of national movements. Mass violence takes two forms, denoted as revolution and war; and there is close inter-action between the two—they shatter political structures, and open the way for each other. In 1848 the subversive social forces were not equal to the task, and war had to come first: hence the bellicose ardours of the social revolutionaries, and the prudent pacificism of the Conserva-

[7] *1848*, p. 124, Namier's translation from Herzen's *Byloe i dumy* in A. Herzen, *Polnoe Sobranie sochinenii i pisem*, edited by M. K. Lemke (22 vols, Petrograd, 1919–25) XIII, pp. 252–3.

tives—for once both sides understood their business (better, indeed, than many historians who have written about it since). The national revolutionaries, recruited mainly from the middle classes or the petty gentry, and, most of all, from the intellectuals, could not become effective except by laying hold of governments and armies: as in Piedmont and Hungary. But these were small States, the one hampered by hesitations and the other beset with difficulties, which still further reduced their strength, while Prussia's action in Slesvig-Holstein was less than half-hearted. Throughout 1848 the ultimate control of the state-machine, and still more of the armies of the Great Powers on the European Continent, remained with the Conservatives; and it is this which preserved peace in Europe. The 'Revolution of the Intellectuals' exhausted itself without achieving concrete results: it left its imprint only in the realm of ideas. [Namier, p. 31.]

Only in war, the war with Russia that Marx and Engels from June 1848 advocated so ardently as necessary to save the revolution, could the 'real' revolutionaries have gained and maintained popular support, and at least have had a chance of creating and then capturing a centralized state and powerful popular armies. Peace, as Namier says, is on the side of the conservatives and in politics, as in baseball, nice guys usually come last.

Revolutions, Marx and Engels believed, from 1845 onward at least, are made by classes and not by revolutionary societies or clubs. As such, they are part of the inexorable march of history and if they fail it is because they are, 'objectively', premature. On this view, 1848 is in a sense the first truly modern revolution, in which there is an active socialist and working-class element complicating the position of the bourgeoisie and a national and super-national interaction complicating the position of both. What seem to Marxists the comparative simplicities of the bourgeois revolutions in seventeenth-century England and eighteenth-century France cannot be repeated—a point that Marx underscores himself. And given the new world of nationalisms and aspiring nation states for which 1848 was also a great rehearsal—a world attributed by Marxists to the uneven development of capitalism, but certainly recognized by them—the tactics of the socialist revolutionaries become very much more complex than confronting outworn autocracies, bankers and captains of industry with the organized economic and political power of labour. Paradoxically, it is the evolutionary socialists, the social democrats, not the Marxist revolutionaries or the communists who take the uncomplicated view that progress is simple and bound to triumph.

It was in 1848 that the problems and the cunning of the modern revolutionary were born: the theory of permanent revolution, of united and democractic fronts to be used and dissolved; the appreciation of the political importance of war and the state and armies that could be built or captured, politically, through war; the distrust of universal franchise, of elections 'held too early' and of the conservative bias of the peasantry; the role, in revolutionary situations, of demands for nationhood and national liberation; the insistence that if revolution is an all-out struggle it can afford neither constitutionalism nor parliamentary 'cretinism'. Above all, the events of 1848 gave him a self-confident contempt for the 'enlightened' middle classes, with their longing for peace and order, their unease with enthusiasms and their aversion to blood. For the communist revolutionary has always known full well what Sir Lewis Namier had to bring out for the well meaning democrat: that 1848 was not a democratic and peace-loving 'springtime of nations' but the beginning of the great European war of every nation against its neighbours, that democratic forces could be, and were, infected with a bellicosity greater than that of obstinate reactionaries and that peace and restraint were the policies and bastions of conservatism.

2

Louis Auguste Blanqui: the Hamlet of revolutionary socialism?

Tony Denholm

'Let us have enough sense to wait a few days more—then the revolution will be ours.'[1] Such was Blanqui's advice to the revolutionary enthusiasts at the Club du Prado forty-eight hours after Louis Philippe had been swept from power in the February Days. Released from detention, this apostle of insurrection and veteran of the Society of Seasons and its attempted coup of May 1839, returned immediately to Paris. His reputation was such that all sections of political opinion expected him to establish revolutionary socialism with a *coup de main*. Instead, Blanqui counselled caution. For the three months he remained at liberty he failed to take advantage of the apparent opportunities that presented themselves. Circumstances certainly looked propitious for a coup. In February, an improvised provisional government clung precariously to power at the Hôtel de Ville, surrounded by thousands of revolutionaries whose expectations were almost limitless and who were determined not to be cheated of the fruits of victory, as they had been in 1830. The army was in disarray, the National Guard leaderless and outflanked by the popular forces. The new police chief was a tried republican with an impeccable secret society record. Nothing, it appeared, could stand in the way of a concerted *putsch*. Yet Blanqui, who in 1839 had taken his men out into the streets of Paris in almost suicidal conditions, now shrank from the deed. He continued to shrink from it even in March and April, when he had had time to marshal the forces of insurrection. He still seemed to be waiting 'a few days more'.

Crane Brinton has said that in revolutions 'the moderate is doomed by the internal dynamics of revolution.'[2] So too, perhaps, is the extremist who hesitates. Blanqui did not lack courage. His initial view of insurrection was as insistent as that of Engels: everything should

[1] In Roger Price, (ed.), *1848 in France* (London, 1975), p. 72.
[2] An idea developed at length in Crane Brinton, *The Anatomy of Revolution* (revised and expanded edn, New York, 1965), pp. 121–47.

be staked on the decisive moment, whatever the odds might be.[3] From February to the fiasco of 15 May, which put him back into prison, the odds could scarcely have been better—or could they? Blanqui, it is said, could have been the Lenin of 1848: after all he invented the 'dictatorship of the proletariat' even if he never actually called it that. Why didn't he launch a coup? Why, at every critical moment between February and May, did he urge delay and caution? Was he like Hamlet struck by some fatal flaw of indecision? He had, like Hamlet, 'the cause, and will and strength, and means to do't'. Did 'all occasions inform against' him, or did he fail by 'thinking too precisely on the event'?[4] If there were good reasons for waiting, what exactly was he waiting for? Clear answers to these questions are difficult to find but there are clues—in the events of the 1848 revolution itself, in Blanqui's previous insurgent history, and in his own theory of insurrection.

This is not the place for a full discussion of the origins of Blanqui's theory of revolutionary socialism. It is generally agreed that he owed something to Babeuf's Conspiracy of Equals, especially through Filippo Buonarroti,[5] for they both belonged to the Society of the Friends of the People in 1832. However, twenty years' experience in opposition to the régimes of Charles X and Louis Philippe, in the Carbonari and secret societies, in the streets, on the barricades and in the prisons, was probably as influential as his study of Hébertistes or Babouvistes in the making of Blanqui's philosophy. From his student days as a Carbonaro, the tightly controlled, disciplined, secret cell became his ideal instrument for revolutionary action. He participated in street battles in Paris against Charles X and was deeply impressed with the fighting qualities of the workers, whose doggedness and determination he set against the timidity of more bourgeois participants.

Blanqui fought on the barricades during the 'three glorious days' of July 1830 and was later decorated by the Orléanist régime. He drew up instructions for his fellow insurrectionists on barricade-building and on the many uses of *pavés* (paving stones). Sixteen to sixty-year olds were to place themselves under the command of veteran soldiers and arms and food supplies were to be organized by volunteer committees.[6] He despised the half-hearted response of his fellow journalists on the *Globe* to the outbreak of disturbances which

---

[3] Cf. Friedrich Engels, *Revolution and Counter-Revolution in Germany*, in Karl Marx and Friedrich Engels, *Selected Works* (3 vols, Moscow, 1969) I, p. 377.

[4] *Hamlet*, act IV, scene iv.

[5] Alan B. Spitzer, *The Revolutionary Theories of Louis Auguste Blanqui* (New York, 1957), pp. 125ff.

[6] Samuel Bernstein, *Auguste Blanqui and the Art of Insurrection* (London, 1971), p. 35.

he again contrasted with the enthusiastic heroism of the *peuple* in the thick of the fighting. If Blanqui came to idealize the Parisian workers, it was from his observation of them in combat and at close quarters. He was no armchair socialist. Blanqui quickly came into opposition with the July monarchy and he served two periods of imprisonment before 1837, once for arousing class hatred and another, after his foundation of the Society of Families, for the illegal possession of arms. Released by amnesty in 1837, he promptly founded another secret society, the Society of Seasons, along with Armand Barbès and Martin Bernard.

This society, largely fashioned by Blanqui, came closest to his ideal. Bernstein describes its pyramidic structure and ranks:

> The lowest, known as the *Week*, had seven members, counting Sunday, the head. A *Month* had four *Weeks* or twenty-eight members, twenty-nine with the leader, *July*. Three *Months* made up a *Season* which, with the top man, *Spring*, added up to eighty-eight members. The highest division, a *Year*, had four *Seasons* totalling three hundred and fifty-three men, including a responsible revolutionary agent. [Bernstein, p. 79.]

One week was unknown to another week and this secrecy continued up the hierarchy, thus ensuring maximum security should one part fall victim to police penetration. Obedience to immediate superiors, and through them to Blanqui, was the key to the effectiveness of the society. The secrecy, the strong chain of command, tight discipline, determined, knowledgeable, deeply committed membership made it a formidable force, even if the practice rarely measured up to the theory.

These revolutionary cells formed the élite which, when the time was right, would launch an insurrection. They would determine tactics, issue arms, and provide leadership for the masses, whose involvement was essential. They were the shock troops who would establish a revolutionary dictatorship on behalf of the masses. Such a dictatorship was necessary to educate the masses to an understanding of their true role and position. Having been so preconditioned by bourgeois society, Blanqui knew 'how difficult it is for the proletariat to open their eyes against their oppressors.'[7] Parisian workers, dissident intellectuals and other *déclassés* were, by virtue of their exposure to the realities of class war, their intelligence and freedom from superstition (i.e. catholicism), the most 'advanced' part of the proletariat. They embodied the 'General Will' of France. They would seize the state by force; to them fell the task of disarming the possessing classes and arming the masses. They were the planners for, and educators of, the proletariat. In the making of insurrection this pre-

[7] Cited in J. P. Mayer, *Political Thought in France, from The Revolution to the Fourth Republic* (revised edn, London, 1949), p. 41.

revolutionary preparation of the élite was more important than any Marxist 'objective conditions'.

Who were the proletariat, according to Blanqui? At his trial in 1832 Blanqui described himself as a 'proletarian ... one of thirty million Frenchmen who live by their labour' [Spitzer, p. 6]. No distinction was made between mental and manual workers. This great majority of Frenchmen were united because they were oppressed by a minority of capitalists—bankers, merchants, 'notables', or what Marx called the 'finance aristocracy'.[8] The masses had been kept in ignorance by the state and the church, but initially under the leadership of the élite and later with universal secular education they could be brought to see the light. Religion enslaved the mind as capitalism enslaved the body: both had to be destroyed. Gradually, then, the masses, conditioned as they were by the struggle between oppressed and oppressors, would understand the processes of history—processes leading ultimately to the triumph of equality. As their understanding increased, so too would their revolutionary potential, which depended much more on their state of mind than on their material conditions. Revolution had to be made in the head of the proletariat before it could be translated into action on the streets. The élite fostered permanent insurrection, as an example to the masses and because, if the élite failed to fight the state, knowing its true oppressive nature, then it effectively legitimized it.

Blanqui's socialist vision is not easy to discern. Though he scorned contemporary utopians, he owed something to them, especially to Saint-Simon and Fourier. In the distant future a reign of equality would be established by a revolutionary dictatorship. Characterized by 'the common ownership of the means of labour, including land', it would create a 'social system, where thine and mine were unknown' [Bernstein, P. 61]. Spitzer is even less specific. 'It is clear,' he says, 'that Blanqui fought for something other than capitalist democracy and that the goals of his revolutionary endeavour included some sort of egalitarian and collectivist economic system' [Spitzer, p. 95]. Whatever the ultimate socialist vision, Blanqui was quite clear that to be a socialist meant being a revolutionary. It was illusory to hope for the emancipation of the proletariat through capitalist institutions. Capitalism would not create the political and economic machinery which would lead to its own destruction. Insurrection remained inevitable because class struggle was inevitable. If Blanqui's definitions of class lack Marx's precision, the classes are for him at least equally irreconcilably antagonistic. The state acts as the agent for the bourgeoisie and the church. Whatever social and political reforms it

---

[8] Karl Marx, *The Class Struggles in France 1848–1850*, chapter 1, in Marx and Engels, *Selected Works* I, p. 206.

may see fit to make will not alter the fact that capitalism will always be preserved by the coercive power of the state.

Armed with this doctrine Blanqui took the Society of Seasons on to the streets in May 1839 and led them to utter disaster. In 1839 France suffered a cyclical economic crisis which hit Paris badly; production was low and unemployment high. After the resignation of Molé on 8 March, there ensued a political crisis of unprecedented duration and proportions, at least for the July monarchy. Paris seethed with rumours of the imminent collapse of the régime. Spurred on by his enthusiastic followers, impatient for the real thing after so much preparation and practice, Blanqui reluctantly decided the time had come, and finally settled on Sunday, 12 May as the day. Fresh troops, unfamiliar with the city, had just relieved the old Paris garrison, and a race meeting at the Champ de Mars arranged for that day provided a diversionary bonus since it took police and officials away from central Paris. Blanqui, Barbès and Bernard led their vanguard in attacks on vital points—the Hôtel de Ville, the Palais de Justice, and the Préfecture of Police. Success in taking the first two led to a proclamation of a provisional government in traditional style from the balcony of the Hôtel de Ville. Barbès, who read the proclamation, condemned the monarchy for allowing people to starve and announced the arrival of equality and the appointment of Blanqui as commander-in-chief. However, the workers from the Faubourg Saint-Antoine and the rabbit warrens of the Marais failed to rise in numbers. A brief barricade resistance collapsed the next day. Barbès and Bernard were soon arrested, though Blanqui evaded capture until October. Blanqui's sentence of death, like that of his fellow conspirator Barbès, was commuted to life imprisonment. His terrible suffering in prison at Mont St Michel, aggravated by the death of his beloved wife Amélie, unbalanced him for a while. Nevertheless his confinement here and later at Tours gave him ample opportunity to ponder the mistakes of May 1839. Had he misread the signs? Had he been pushed into a premature move by the enthusiasm and impatience of his men? Were his lieutenants, however popular and able, any real asset? Should not the society have been more broadly based? Should not the masses have been better prepared? These questions must have preoccupied his thoughts during the eight long years of his imprisonment and surveillance.

The February revolution brought Blanqui scurrying to Paris, excited and eager no doubt, but a stranger to the peculiar circumstances that had produced the successful uprising, and a greater stranger to the men who had captured power. The question of the hour, for Blanqui and the new provisional government alike, was whether he would attempt an immediate coup, relying on his formidable reputation among the Parisian workers. This was more than an academic question. Already one radical, François Raspail, himself an old leader of the Society of the Rights of Man, had forced the declaration of the republic from the timid members of the government besieged in the Hôtel de Ville. On the afternoon of 25 February, and speaking in the name of the Paris proletariat, Raspail warned Lamartine and his colleagues that, unless the republic were declared, he would return with 200,000 men to enforce his demand. Raspail may have overestimated the numbers he could command but no one doubted the reality of the threat. As Marx said:

> The bodies of the fallen were scarcely cold, the barricades were not yet cleared away, the workers not yet disarmed, and the only force which could be opposed to them was the National Guard. Under these circumstances the doubts born of considerations of state policy and the juristic scruples of conscience entertained by the Provisional Government suddenly vanished. [Marx, p. 211.]

Marx undoubtedly enjoyed describing the discomfiture of the bourgeois politicians but they were clearly vulnerable to any attempted *coup de main*.

Surrounded by milling crowds in the Place de Grève and even in the Hôtel de Ville itself, Lamartine later the same day resisted the adoption of the red flag to replace the tricolour. A compromise formula that a red rosette be fastened around the flagstaff was eventually agreed, but here was a cause and an opening for Blanquist action. Public order was kept by armed revolutionaries. Marc Caussidière, the newly appointed police chief, had hardly had time to muster enough force to provide safety for the government and was in any case recruiting his force from among the insurgents. The army and National Guard had dissolved into the people. The crowds were still volatile, the revolutionary *élan* still abroad. Here was a heaven-sent opportunity for Blanqui. Everyone knew it, and the rumours of an imminent communist coup had even reached the twitching ears of the British ambassador.[9] Such was Blanqui's reputation that, had he given the signal, a new insurrection would have begun at once, though with what success is of course entirely conjectural. Instead, at a meeting of revolutionaries at the Prado, Blanqui warned against frightening the provinces and the bourgeoisie, who might bring back the king. The men at the Hôtel de Ville were impotent, he said. 'Their feebleness is a sure sign of their fall. Their power is but ephemeral: we—we have the people and the clubs, where we shall organize them in revolutionary fashion, as was the way of the Jacobins of old' [Price, p. 72].

Did Blanqui hesitate because he had not had time to organize his

[9] C. H. Phipps, marquis of Normanby, *A Year of Revolution: From a Journal Kept in Paris in 1848* (2 vols, London, 1857) I, pp. 112–13.

own club as a reliable power base? Did he expect a better moment in the future when he had re-established his position? Did he have difficulty finding allies? We do know that Caussidière rejected his overtures [Bernstein, pp. 137–8]. To act from fear of the provinces and the bourgeoisie was not only uncharacteristic but a denial of his own theory of permanent insurrection. Did the short-lived fraternity among all classes throw him off guard? Had this 'pleasant abstraction from class antagonisms, this sentimental reconciliation of contradictory class interests', as Marx [p. 215] called it, undermined the mass movement that Blanqui considered essential for a successful coup? Evoking the experience of the first revolution, Blanqui told his followers that another 10 August 1792 was necessary, together with the mass support of the people and insurgent *faubourgs*. If they were to move now it would be as thieves in the night, but under his conditions they would have 'le prestige de la force révolutionnaire'.[10] Whatever the reasons, Blanqui seems to have lowered his sights, at least for the time being, and set himself the task of exerting pressure on the government, and preventing a counter-revolution. When asked by a politician whether he intended to overthrow them, Blanqui replied: 'No! But to bar the road behind you' [Spitzer, p. 147, n. 39].

The instrument of this policy was the club Blanqui founded, the Central Republican Society, one of over 140 established in Paris by the end of March. Blanqui's club differed in many important respects from his old Society of Seasons. It was operating in a republican, not a monarchical, setting and was primarily a political party contending with other clubs to influence government policy. Though many of its personnel were old revolutionaries, whose presence made it an object of fear to the possessing classes, its mode of operation was open and democratic and its meetings noted more for stormy debate than the plotting of insurrection. As Amann says:

> ... though tourists visited the Central Republican Society to watch an emaciated, black-gloved Blanqui preside, icily passionate, the sessions were not simply Blanqui's show: they were filled with the rowdy give-and-take of debates ... in which Blanqui intervened, but which he made no attempt to dominate.[11]

The contrast between this political club and the secret, authoritarian structure of the Society of Seasons could not be clearer. The Central Republican Society had several powerful rivals, notably the Club of the Revolution sponsored by Ledru Rollin, the minister of the interior, who hoped to use it to block Blanquism. Ledru Rollin made a distinc-

[10] Suzanne Wassermann, *Les Clubs de Barbès et de Blanqui en 1848* (Paris, 1913), p. 50.
[11] Peter H. Amann, *Revolution and Mass Democracy: the Paris Club Movement in 1848* (Princeton, 1975), p. 62.

tion between 'good' and 'bad' clubs, but he still had an anti-republican policeman spy on them all [Amann, p. 75]. The Club of the Revolution was associated with Barbès, Blanqui's fellow conspirator of 1839 but now his enemy and arch-rival for the favours of the Paris *menu peuple*. Other influential clubs were Cabet's Central Fraternal Society, and Raspail's Society of the Friends of the People.

Blanqui's first task was to mobilize opinion and specifically to have the national elections for a constituent assembly, scheduled for 9 April, delayed or postponed. Along with other tried republicans, Blanqui realized that France as a whole would vote conservative. The achievements of the Parisian workers would be swamped by the rural vote. The French people could not be expected to cast off the political shackles of fifty years overnight. Time was needed to familiarize them with republican values and ideas. In the first two weeks of March clubbists of all persuasions kept up pressure on the provisional government. Their chief demands were for a free press, which was granted on 6 March, the postponement of elections to the Paris National Guard, the removal of troops from Paris, and above all the adjournment of the elections for the constituent assembly. This was the background to the *journée* of 17 March, a day of massive popular demonstration which one recent historian has described as 'a major turning point precisely because, when the point was reached, no turn was made' [Amann, p. 110]. There were two reasons for this: first, the radicals within the provisional government, led by Louis Blanc, failed to use this mass demonstration of popular support to purge the government of Lamartine and the moderates; and second, Blanqui either would not, or could not, turn the mass demonstration of 17 March into an insurrection.

In many ways Blanqui made the running in the planning of this manifestation. He urged unity with other democratic clubs and on 13 March his club voted to join with other republicans in a show of strength. A committee was set up to organize a demonstration which would petition the government for the removal of troops from Paris and the postponement of the elections. Blanqui wanted the elections postponed *sine die* to allow for the proper education of the electorate. He argued that the forces of counter-revolution had indoctrinated the people for fifty years. Was it too much for the republicans to have just one? He was forced however to modify this demand in the interests of broadening the base of the demonstration.

Around 9 a.m. on 17 March crowds began gathering in the Champs Elysées, the starting point of the march. They moved off in columns, each club bearing its own flags and banners. They were joined by others en route to the Hôtel de Ville where delegates from the clubs were received by the provisional government. According to Lamartine, Blanqui was the spokesman for them all. Blanqui demanded the removal of troops and the adjournment of the elections and, according to Lamartine, the government's

> implicit obedience to the dictatorial will of the multitude as expressed by the clubs—in other words, the enslavement of the government, the outlawry of all persons throughout the nation, save only the populace of Paris, and an indefinite dictatorship imposed on the government, on condition that the government should submit, and itself ratify the dictatorship of sovereign demagoguism.[12]

Though, by this time, a coup was out of the question, the confrontation in the Hôtel de Ville, with the supporters of the clubs in virtual occupation of the building, made a purge of the government possible. It needed only the support of Louis Blanc, but Blanc feared Blanqui more than he hated Lamartine, and he shrank from the opportunity to remove the moderates and set up a Committee of Public Safety, a government which would guarantee his brand of socialism. Blanc joined with Lamartine and Ledru Rollin. Without the petition being actually rejected, the proposals were talked out, no assurances were given, and the government demanded the right to make decisions free from harrassment. The deputation led by Cabet left, Blanqui made no move, and from the balcony of the Hôtel de Ville Blanc addressed the throng urging them to disperse peacefully. After much cheering the demonstrators moved off in the direction of the Bastille.

If Blanqui had thoughts of using this demonstration as a springboard to power, or simply to purge the government, he was hampered by its very success. Some 150,000 to 200,000 people took part in the march and club control of such a huge number was difficult, especially as Caussidière had secured the front place in the demonstration for supporters of the government. Blanqui denied that he intended any mischief on 17 March and claimed that, when his proposals for the *indefinite* postponement of the elections were rejected by the planning committee, he had lost interest and had gone along only for the ride. Bernstein suggests that the experience of that day led Blanqui to a reappraisal of his tactics. The republic as well as the monarchy could oppress the proletariat, the time had come to do away with 'sterile formulas' [Bernstein, p. 152] and really change things. Though the provisional government made minor concessions—the national elections were postponed for a fortnight, chiefly for technical reasons—the massive demonstration frightened conservatives both in and outside government. Lamartine was unable to reinforce Paris with troops, but the army of the north under Négrier had explicit orders to march on Paris at the sign of an insurrection.

Between 17 March and the next *journée* on 16 April, Blanqui's

[12] Alphonse de Lamartine, *History of the French Revolution of 1848*, translated from the French (London, 1888), pp. 392–3.

position was gravely weakened by his failure to organize a federation of clubs dedicated to *social revolution*, and by the corresponding success of the anti-Blanquists in organizing a Club of Clubs to electioneer on behalf of *social reform*. Above all else, Blanqui's credibility as a popular leader was brought into question by the damaging allegations that he had betrayed his fellow conspirators in 1839. The Taschereau affair, as it came to be known, broke on 31 March, and Blanqui spent much time in the next two weeks drawing up an answer to his accusers. Though his reply satisfied most of the chief club leaders, some mud stuck. Considering Taschereau's connections with Ledru Rollin, and Lamartine's avowed aim to split the club movement, the authenticity of the document 'proving' Blanqui's guilt must be highly suspect. At the time, however, it did its work and some clubs, previously supporters of Blanqui, went over to the Barbès-backed Club of Clubs. Blanqui's own electioneering activities were curtailed and undermined and Paris became alive with speculation and rumour of the wildest kind. Talk of insurrection was on everyone's lips, not least when, one week before the elections and one day before a new demonstration, Blanqui was known to have had a meeting with Lamartine. Invariably Blanqui was cast in a Satanic role whose new terror would make that of 1793–4 pale into insignificance. Even Blanqui's appearance told against him: the pallor of his complexion contrasted with the inevitable black clothing and his lean, hungry look and piercing eyes completed the image of a ruthless, power-crazed conspirator. His friends gave him respect rather than love, but he had more enemies than friends in Paris in mid-April and most of them expected the worst.

There can be little doubt that Blanqui's position was so weakened by the Taschereau affair that he did not plan to launch a coup of 16 April. On this day workers gathered at the Champ de Mars to elect officers to the National Guard and then, after a march to the Hôtel de Ville, to present a petition to the government on behalf of Blanc's principles. Rumours were rife that Blanqui intended a coup but it was in fact his club rivals, Barbès and Sobrier, who came closest to illegality by urging Ledru Rollin to put himself at the head of a Committee of Public Safety in order to block a Blanquist *putsch* [Amann, pp. 183–4]. When the minister of the interior eventually refused, and on the day finally called out the National Guard, Barbès and Sobrier could do nothing but act as government agents. Colonel Barbès appeared at the head of his Twelfth Legion.

When 40,000 unarmed, peacefully petitioning demonstrators arrived at the Hôtel de Ville, they were greeted by ranks of armed guards and shouts of 'A bas les communistes' and 'A bas Blanqui'. The workers were humilitated and angry, the National Guard triumphant, and Lamartine beside himself with joy. He described 16 April as the happiest day of his political life [Lamartine, p. 466]. Blanqui claimed that he only went to the Champ de Mars to distribute copies of his reply to Taschereau. Whether the Central Republican Society intended a coup or not is difficult to prove, for the *rappel*, calling out the National Guard, was beaten before any insurgency had time to gel [Wasserman, p. 128]. The most that can be said is that, by going to the Champ de Mars, Blanqui was in a position to take advantage of any unforeseen opportunities, either there or en route to the Hôtel de Ville. This tactic would certainly be in keeping with the traditional secret societies[13] but, as we have seen, the Central Republican Society was not organized in that way. It was an open club and it went unarmed. Even so, a warrant was issued for Blanqui's arrest, though it was not subsequently pursued.

16 April was a blow, not only to Blanqui but to radical republicanism in general. The massive show of strength by civilian guardsmen loyal to the government, and the abuse hurled at socialists and clubbists, heralded the counter-revolution. That certainly was the way Blanqui saw it, for that same evening he proposed to his assembled club that they re-form themselves as a secret society. Even though Blanqui did not deny that a conspiratorial organization was launched in a secret session of the Central Republican Society on 17 April [Spitzer, p. 149], he still advocated defence of the provisional government and democratic procedures. Perhaps he still pinned some hopes on the elections. If so he was wrong.

About eighty-five per cent of adult Frenchmen voted on 23 April and they returned a national constituent assembly unsympathetic to socialism and radical republicanism. Only about one third of the deputies were genuine republicans, the rest disguised royalists. It met on 4 May and reconstituted the government. Ledru Rollin only kept his place at Lamartine's insistence. Louis Blanc was of course dropped, and a week later his proposal for a ministry of progress virtually hooted out of the Assembly. The forces of bourgeois order were now stronger than at any time since February: the Assembly gave them legitimacy and Paris had been reinforced. The clubs had failed as election agencies and a decline in their numbers was already visible by early May [Amann, p. 196]. Paradoxically, the weakness of the club movement early in April obscured some growing strengths. Defeated in the elections, outflanked by the Assembly, the more radical clubs drew closer together, especially in their common condemnation of the action of the Rouen National Guard in cutting down nearly a hundred workers who had protested the defeat of their radical candidates. Club ranks closed further, early in May, in support of

[13] Marc Caussidière, *Memoirs of Citizen Caussidière* (2 vols, London, 1848) I, p. 33. Caussidière claimed that it was the tactic of the secret societies to attend a 'place of meeting, without arms, in small detachments, and to take advantage of circumstances'.

the Polish resistance to Austrian and Prussian military operations. Events rushed to a new climax when news reached Paris, on 10 May, that the Prussians had crushed the Polish rising over Posen. The clubs called for intervention on behalf of the Poles to keep faith with traditional republican assistance to peoples throwing off monarchical régimes. Additionally, some clubs divined that a French army sent to help the Poles would produce a European war. This could well turn out to the advantage of the radicals by giving them an opportunity to further the revolutionary impulse, as war had aided the Jacobins in 1793. The link between war and the furtherance of revolutionary aims was well known to the clubbists. With the Polish cause they hoped to reverse Lamartine's pacific, non-interventionist foreign policy, in the expectation that subsequent events would allow Paris to resume the leadership of the revolution. Whatever their motives, some club leaders were determined to have a demonstration on the Polish issue, which would take the form of a petition to the Assembly calling for action. After much disagreement and hesitation, they called Parisians out on to the streets on 15 May for what was to be the last demonstration of club power in 1848. On that day thousands of club-bists and workers filed from the Bastille to the Madeleine, down on to the Place de la Concorde. Here they were to halt while the petition was presented, but an ill-defended bridge allowed the crowds to burst across and into the Assembly which, after tumultuous scenes, was declared dissolved. A short-lived government was set up at the Hôtel de Ville, but the National Guard mustered and by evening the insurgents were in Vincennes and the deputies back on their benches. What part did Blanqui play in this day's events?

Blanqui and the Central Republican Society were incensed by the massacre of workers in Rouen and they demanded not only the dissolution of the National Guard there and the punishment of the officers responsible but, foreseeing a similar situation arising in Paris, the removal once again of troops from the capital. On the Polish question Blanqui was at odds with his club.[14] It was they who insisted on joining a demonstration and Blanqui (though sympathetic to the cause) who advised against it. As he said at his trial, he suspected a plot and warned his membership that they should be wary of foolish tricks [Wasserman, p. 172]. Blanqui was not involved in planning the demonstration and Sobrier and Huber appear to have been chiefly responsible for the organization. However, as usual, it was generally feared that Blanqui would use the manifestation for an attempted coup. Blanqui tried to restrain his club, arguing that the forces of reaction were dominant for the moment but, he promised, 'attendez, attendez cinq à six semaines, et alors les vents et les flots seront pour

---

[14] Wasserman, p. 171. As Blanqui said, 'Le club, ordinairement docile à ma voix, s'est regimbé.'

nous' [Wasserman, p. 170]. Blanqui was unquestionably right in having nothing to do with the organization of this *journée*. It is difficult to imagine anything more ill-conceived.[15] But was his reference to five or six weeks a prophecy that the time for action was indeed coming, or yet another example of his indecision?

While Blanqui clearly opposed the demonstration, his role during the day itself is not clear. Waiting at the Gaiety Theatre with his club for the column coming from the Bastille, he told one man advocating violence that he was a false brother [Wasserman, p. 173, n. 2]. However, Blanqui appeared to give some leadership to the demonstrators when the situation on the Place de la Concorde offered scope for the successful invasion of the Assembly [Wasserman, p. 174]. Similarly, once inside the Chamber, he took the opportunity to address it. De Tocqueville's famous description bears repeating:

> I saw a man go on to the rostrum, and, although I have never seen him again, the memory of him has filled me with disgust and horror ever since. He had sunken, withered cheeks, white lips, and a sickly, malign dirty look like a pallid mouldy corpse; he was wearing no visible linen; an old black coat frock covered his lean emaciated limbs tightly; he looked as if he had lived in a sewer and only just come out. I was told that this was Blanqui.[16]

Though Blanqui spoke of Poland, amid the din and utter confusion, he spent more time demanding revenge for the Rouen massacre and discussing the plight of the poor. He spoke of work and food but, far from exciting the crowds further, he tried to calm them. After Huber declared the Assembly dissolved, and the enthusiastic Barbès had gone off to establish his very brief provisional government at the Hôtel de Ville, Blanqui dispersed his club and went off to a café in the Rue Saint-Denis [Wasserman, p. 181]. His name, however, appeared as a member of the new government and two of his associates, Flotte and Lacambre, were arrested at the Hôtel de Ville that same evening. Though Blanqui avoided arrest until 26 May, his club had been closed four days earlier. Thus ended Blanqui's 'revolutionary' career in 1848. On 2 April 1849 he was sentenced to ten years imprisonment for the 'part' he had played on 15 May. At his trial Blanqui denied planning a coup. He said he knew that most Parisians did not want to turn out the assembly, and that the National Guard, most workers, and the department would be indignant at such an attempt. Moreover, he knew that any chance or surprise government would not last eight days.

[15] Amann, pp. 205–47, tells the full, sorry story and argues that Sobrier's entourage was probably involved in some sort of plot.

[16] Alexis de Tocqueville, *Recollections*, translated from the French by G. Lawrence, edited by J. P. Mayer and A. P. Kerr (New York, 1970), pp. 118–19.

On 15 May Blanqui was carried along by the stream; his non-involvement in the planning, his warning to his club, the absence of significant numbers of armed men, his refusal to be drawn to the Hôtel de Ville, or to implement the known defence strategy, indicate that he thought the move premature. Blanqui's explanation for his inaction is similar to that which he advanced on 25 February. As Wasserman said: 'As on 25 February, as on 17 March, as on 16 April, at the moment for action Blanqui stole away, not finding the occasion favourable' [Wasserman, p. 181].

Why did this arch-conspirator apparently let so many chances slip from his grasp in 1848? Was he waiting for some 'objective conditions' to appear before making his move? Answers to these questions lie foremost in the events of 1848 themselves. Blanqui was no trigger-happy bandit taking to the streets at any time against any odds. It may be true in revolutions as in love that only the brave deserve the fair, but equally important in both situations there are times when nothing should be done. Having misjudged the decisive moment in 1839, Blanqui was determined to avoid the same mistake again. The conditions would have to be just right—then and only then was the time for bravery.

The February revolution took everyone by surprise—a 'happy surprise' Blanqui called it [Price, p. 72], soon after his arrival back in Paris. Though there is evidence that men of the secret societies helped organize the insurrection in February, the movement was essentially broadly based, involving all classes, and its success produced an intense feeling of fraternity and goodwill. Blanqui's reputation was high, the sufferings of 'l'Enfermé' well known, but he had no Society of Seasons to return to, no revolutionary élite awaiting his call, trained in his methods or disciplined by his precepts. The mass proletarian support that he now realized was necessary had been diluted by blossoming fraternity. The essential preconditions for a successful coup—the élite shock troops and a supportive mass movement—were non-existent in the case of the former, and very doubtful in the latter. The logic of Blanqui's position in February would suggest that he should build up an élite and await a favourable moment when he could be sure of popular support. He certainly adopted the wait-and-see tactic, but the Central Republican Society was not a revolutionary organization until after 16 April, and only then in part.

The problem, of course, was that Blanqui was operating in an unexpected and unfamiliar milieu. A republic committed to universal suffrage and social reform was quite different from a corrupt monarchy exploiting France in the interests of a handful of *haute bourgeois*. However sceptical Blanqui was about the intentions of the men at the Hôtel de Ville, however insightful into the ultimate consequences of their actions, this very different enemy complicated matters. Distinctions between good and bad were not easily made. Caussidière's men had been drawn from the barricades and the underground opposition to Louis Philippe. Louis Blanc was a socialist and patron of a working-man's parliament at the Luxembourg. Both these men were now part of the establishment. These were not his only problems.

Blanqui's opportunities were limited by the fact that he was only one of a number of club leaders all competing for the hearts and minds of the Parisian multitudes. The influence of the clubs was vital in securing mass support and without this a coup was hazardous— hence Blanqui's attempts to unite clubs sympathetic to his cause. Cooperation between clubs was impeded by the mutual antipathy of Barbès and Blanqui, the rumour-mongering, and later the Taschereau accusation. The government's skill in sowing discord among the clubs, the elaborate spy system, and the press-inspired image of Blanqui as the incendiary prince of darkness, all added to Blanqui's difficulties.

Given these circumstances, it is difficult to see how Blanqui could have organized a coup, especially in the relaxed liberal atmosphere of the post-February days. His one hope was to wait until all the illusions had been shattered and the bourgeois republic revealed as a sham for proletarian aspirations. While the Paris worker was stricken with the romantic malaise, the belief in what Marx called the 'imaginary abolition of class relations' [Marx p. 215], he was obviously in no condition to help make a proletarian revolution for the whole of France. The days of 17 March and 16 April gave him injections of realism but the fevered lyrical illusion persisted, until the elections had done their work and produced a conservative assembly. Then the Rouen massacre and the Assembly's scornful dismissal of Blanc's ministry of progress jolted the patient to full recovery. As McKay said, 'the first ten days of May form a watershed in the history of the Revolution of 1848,'[17] for the workers realized they were being deceived and betrayed by the Assembly. On 13 May the first steps were taken towards the dissolution of the National Workshops, though how well known this was outside the ranks of the executive commission is uncertain.

What is certain is that the ground suddenly became familiar, the enemy more sharply defined, and the battle lines clearer. There was a polarization of opinion and feeling, based unequivocally on class differences. Both Tocqueville and Marx agree. Tocqueville wrote:

> Society was cut in two: those who had nothing united in common envy; those who had anything united in common terror. There were no longer any ties of sympathy linking these two great classes, and a struggle was everywhere assumed to be inevitable soon. [Tocqueville, p. 98.]

[17] D. C. McKay, *The National Workshops* (Cambridge, Mass., 1965), p. 66.

Marx concluded:

> The National Assembly gave vent to its determination to force the pro-
> letariat into a decisive struggle. The Executive Commission issued a series
> of provocative decrees, such as that prohibiting congregations of people,
> etc. The workers were directly provoked, insulted and derided from the
> tribune of the Constituent National Assembly. [Marx, p. 224.]

The old conditions were returning. Wait a while longer and the Paris
workers would be totally disillusioned as the Assembly went about
its work. Meanwhile keep the powder dry, plan and organize. It is
most likely that this is what Blanqui had in mind when he asked his
club for five or six weeks just before the 15 May demonstration. The
June Days, with the clubs united against a common enemy and
supported by the dismissed National Workshop men, would have been
a great threat indeed. The outcome might or might not have been
the same but, with Blanqui and other club leaders free, the event would
have been very different. The conditions in June were certainly closer
to Blanqui's requirements: the 100,000 National Workshop men who,
under the direction of Emile Thomas, had been kept loyal to the
government in March and April, were now radicalized by the dismissal
of Thomas and the plans to dissolve them. Blanqui, however, was
denied his own decisive moment. Instead, he allowed himself to be
drawn reluctantly into the demonstration of 15 May, with disastrous
consequences.

It is said that Leninism is 'Marxism plus Blanquism'.[18] It is therefore interesting to compare Blanqui's tactics in 1848 with Leninist
doctrine for insurgency. Lenin outlined three conditions for a successful insurrection. First, it 'must rely not upon conspiracy and not upon
a party, but upon the advanced class'. Second, it 'must rely upon
a revolutionary upsurge of the people'. Third, it 'must rely upon that
turning point in the history of the growing revolution, when the activity
of the advanced ranks of the people is at its height, and when the
vacillations in the ranks of the enemy and *in the ranks of the weak,
half-hearted and irresolute friends of the revolution* are strongest' [taken
from Bernstein, p. 87]. On the first point, Blanqui considered
conspiracy and party as essential as an 'advanced class'. However,
this class was emerging, disillusioned and polarized in May and June
1848, but its 'advanced' character was determined not simply by its
relationship to the means of production. Blanqui argued that, before
men could be organized for a revolution, they had to be drawn out
of their 'lethargy' and activated by 'an electric current of ideas'
[Spitzer, p. 142]. He was right in identifying the end of the workers'
'lethargy' with the Rouen massacre and their reaction to the Assem-

---

[18] K. J. Kenafick, *Michael Bakunin and Karl Marx* (Melbourne, 1948), p. 277.

bly's dictates. A new 'revolutionary upsurge' could thus be expected, as the Assembly filled the cup of bitterness. As the 100,000 workshop men became radicalized, Lenin's third point would also be met, at least in part. The activity of the advanced ranks, the Paris proletariat, would reach a new height as it did in June. While the 'vacillations' of the enemy were certainly *not* at their strongest, the 'half-hearted, irresolute friends' had long since gone. Moreover, who could deny that a 'turning point in ... the growing revolution' was at hand, with the Assembly hell-bent on dismembering what remained of the social revolution? As we have seen, an inevitable struggle between the classes was expected in all quarters.

If Blanqui was waiting for this most propitious moment, and all his actions in 1848 suggest that he was, not only was he closer to Lenin than at first appears, but in practice he had moved away from the simple conspiratorial methods of the Seasons. Blanqui's caution in 1848 stemmed less from 'occasions' informing against him, or even simply from thinking 'too precisely on the event'; it stemmed more from a vital lesson he had learnt in 1839—no coup could succeed without the support of the Paris masses, *their* readiness determined the decisive moment. Unfortunately for Blanqui, when the moment finally arrived on 23 June, he was not there. In Vincennes he would have heard the gunfire, and perhaps the tumult, but he was not free to direct the insurrection he had been waiting for. Like Hamlet, Blanqui had the 'cause, and will and strength and means to do't', but his tragic fatal flaw was not indecision. His weakness, in 1848 as in 1839, was to surrender the insurgent strategy of his intellectual convictions to the exuberant enthusiasm and foolish impatience of his supporters. Perhaps, after all, he was a man of his time, and like them, a romantic revolutionary.

3

Louis Blanc: the collapse of a hero

R. B. Rose

The 1848 revolution ruined many reputations, but few so suddenly and disastrously as that of Louis Blanc. At the beginning of the year, the chosen spokesman of the revolutionary masses and doyen of the democratic and social republic; by the end of the year, 'Louis Blague', Louis-the-joke, a discredited exile without a country and without a party.

Blanc, of course, offered his own explanation, in the *Historical Revelations*, published ten years after the event. It was a question of timing: the backward masses of rural France were not ready for socialism in 1848 and drowned the 'democratic and social republic' beneath the overwhelming flood of universal suffrage. The mistake therefore was to hold elections too early, before the people had been properly enlightened.

Other explanations have been subsequently canvassed. For the Marxist, Jean Vidalenc, the crux is the inexorable dialectic of objective forces. 'Blanc's solution of the social question might have been adequate for the needs of the times in 1840 but it had become anachronistic even before the revolution broke out in 1848.' Consequently, as a revolutionary, Blanc was doomed from the start.

Yet others have seen the matter in more voluntaristic terms. Louis Blanc failed because he shared a fatal flaw common to many well meaning moderates. 'In the final analysis', writes Leo Loubère, Blanc's American biographer, 'he reminds one of those moderate revolutionaries, the Marquis de Condorcet, Friedrich Ebert, Alexander Kerensky, J. Ramsay Macdonald, Léon Blum, who ultimately failed because they were not prepared to undertake the brutal means that their opponents, either of the right or the left, willingly resorted to.'

Blanc failed, then, in 1848 because he was not able enough and ruthless enough to seize power. The débâcle of Blancism was no more pre-ordained by the iron laws of history than was the success of individualistic capitalism. 'One cannot claim that Blanc's system was a success or a failure,' protests Loubère, 'since there was no experiment in the Jacobin Socialism he championed, but only the creation of a few isolated cooperatives launched like fragile boats in times of storm. What, one must ask, would have been the fate of capitalism had it not encountered the benevolence of feudal monarchs and the active assistance of mercantile states?'

Perhaps other inevitabilities than Marxist ones were working themselves out? With Alphonse de Lamartine, Louis Blanc may be identified without difficulty as Crane Brinton's archetypal moderate: the 'man in the middle' who in the first phase of a revolution struggles desperately to create a new stable basis for the orderly government which will consolidate the gains of the revolution. The moderate strives to reconcile the opposites—the extremists who wish the revolution to go further, and the conservatives, who would like it to take a step or two backward if possible. In Crane Brinton's model, the moderate is doomed by the internal dynamics of revolution. The revolution must follow its course to the climax. The reign of terror must succeed the rule of the moderates before Thermidor becomes possible. And so the Lafayettes, the Kerenskys and the Louis Blancs find their position undermined by the steady desertion of the opposing parties they must try to hold together. At the last minute they themselves desert to the right, but too late to regain the confidence of the conservatives. Whether the left wins or loses in the next stage is immaterial: the moderates are finished.

There is no doubt that something like this happened in Blanc's case. The question of whether Brinton's pattern itself is inevitable nevertheless remains one that demands closer investigation.

Louis Blanc was born in 1811 and lived until 1882, that is for seventy-one years. What is the significance of this information? Firstly, he belonged to a generation for whom the French Revolution of 1789 was a living memory, and in Blanc's case a personal reality in the sense that any period must be for a historian who sets out to write an account of it. He belonged to a generation that experienced the first impact of the industrial revolution in France and the growing division of classes which that revolution caused. As a Parisian, Blanc personally witnessed the three revolutions of 1830, 1848 and 1871 in which the praxis of class struggles and political and historical conflicts forced its way brutally into the human consciousness. As a young man in the 1830s and the 1840s he belonged to the same generation of alienated romantics as Lamartine and Lamennais, Fourier, Buchez and Cabet, and his most significant works were written in this period: the *History of Ten Years 1830–1840* (1841–4) and *The Organization of Labour*, first published in 1839.

Blanc's upbringing and education seem improbable for a future socialist revolutionary. He was certainly very far from being a proletarian. At the time of his birth, his father was an official in the Napoleonic administration of Joseph Bonaparte in Spain. But the family tradition was frankly counter-revolutionary. In the eighteenth century the Blancs had been wealthy merchants and shipowners in the south of France and the grandfather had taken part in the royalist uprising at Lyons in 1793 and had been guillotined in 1794. In fact Blanc's education was paid for partly by a pension granted his father in 1821 in recognition of his grandfather's services to royalism and partly by a scholarship to the *collège* at Rodez awarded largely for similar reasons. His upbringing was therefore royalist rather than Bonapartist and certainly not revolutionary. It is not, in fact, until after 1830 that there is any trace of revolutionary or working-class sentiment.

What brought about this change of heart? Perhaps it was a realistic assessment of the change in patronage in Paris. In July 1830 Louis and his brother had set out for Paris in the dawn of the July Days with the same itch that drove all talented Frenchmen then and now to seek to make a name for themselves in the capital, the centre of the civilized world. But the July revolution upset their reckoning. The family pension was stopped and in Louis Philippe's Paris there were no openings for legitimists. However, through family connections Louis was able to get an appointment as a family tutor with the Hallette family of Arras. The Hallettes were an interesting family. They were ironfounders and manufacturers in the forefront of the industrial revolution, with a foundry employing 600 workmen and turning out steam locomotives and other advanced machinery, the symbols of the new age. One biographer, Vidalenc, tells us that, while working as a tutor at Arras: 'It was easy for Louis Blanc to visit workshops, to enter into contact with workers like himself', but neither he nor Loubère offers any evidence that Blanc ever did visit the works. So the question of whether Blanc had any first-hand knowledge of the shape of modern industry remains open until somebody again looks into Blanc's papers and correspondence.

What we do know is that while at Arras Blanc came under the influence of a radical lawyer and newspaper editor called DeGeorge, and that his own political sympathies became radicalized. Already, too, he was following up an interest in the French Revolution and showing signs of partiality towards Arras' most famous son, Maximilien Robespierre. By 1834 he felt himself ready to have another crack at the capital, and he got an introduction from DeGeorge to the editor of the *National*, a radical paper. Unfortunately the *National* was going through difficult times and Louis had to scratch around a bit until he found himself a job on another even more radical publication, *Bon Sens*, as assistant editor at 2,000 francs a year. This

was a good salary that enabled Blanc to live a very comfortable bourgeois life. It was, for purposes of comparison, about ten times the
current wage of a primary schoolteacher.

Working on *Bon Sens* certainly brought Blanc into contact with
the proletariat, but perhaps in a less immediate and less real sense
than his stay at Arras. *Bon Sens* was a journal which took a deliberately
pro-worker line, opening a *tribune des prolétaires* for letters from the
workers and publishing pamphlets on 'the worker question'. Yet there
were strict limits to this social radicalism.

As editor after 1836 of *Bon Sens*, Blanc took a line opposed to
subversive secret societies, trade unions and strikes, critical of the
republican and working-class revolts of Paris and Lyons which had
taken place in the early 1830s. The message of *Bon Sens* was one of
patience: there would be, in time, a complete revolution in society,
but a peaceable one, prepared by the propaganda of an enlightened
élite, not by a sudden seizure of power; the revolution would open
the gates, not to the vengeance of the oppressed but to the fraternity
of all classes—the dawn of a new era. Meanwhile Blanc counselled:
'Patience is a *republican* virtue ... it is the nature and glory of élite
minds to precede their epoch, but violence is not permissible.' *Bon
Sens* was hardly a working-class mass circulation newspaper; Blanc
eventually managed to help push its circulation to about 1,650. This
is not so insignificant as it sounds. *La Réforme*, the most powerful
journal of left republicans, on which Blanc was also to serve as editor,
had at the most 2,000–3,000 subscribers. *L'Atelier*, another journal
of radical socialist nuance, could claim a circulation of about 1,500.

What can we build on such figures? First, that the public for
advanced socialist ideas in the 1830s was both narrow and middle
class, a contention which will surprise few people. Second, that a vast
gulf existed between the narrow fringe group of socialist intellecuals
on the left of the revolutionary and republican movement, and the
masses of artisan and proletarian Paris, to whom they were in the
habit of handing down ready-made solutions of 'the social question'.
Of all the competing creeds of the epoch perhaps Louis Blanc's
doctrine of Jacobin Socialism came closest to bridging that gulf, by
linking socialist objectives and mass democratic means.

But first it was necessary for practical political experience to add
a practical bite to Blanc's theoretical Jacobinism. In 1838 a controversy erupted which revealed Louis Philippe's outwardly progressive
monarchy in a strikingly unflattering light and forced Blanc into a
profound reappraisal of his political alignment. The issue was the
beginning of railway building on a large scale in France and government proposals to leave this in the hands of private companies while
promising extensive subsidies. Both Blanc and Lamartine (who was
by no means a socialist) saw this as an open invitation to speculators

to rob the community at will and a confirmation of a fundamental immorality at the heart of Louis Philippe's system. In January 1839 Blanc joined Jacques Dupont in founding a new opposition paper, the *Revue du Progrès*, which had a distinctive Jacobin socialist orientation. Over the next two years Blanc developed his fundamental ideas in the new paper.

Blanc's doctrine was an optimistic derivative of Rousseau. Men were originally good, but became evil as a result of their environment. Moral: reform the environment and all will be well. In the contemporary conflict between the bourgeoisie and 'the proletariat', Blanc's sympathies were with the proletariat. Not, however, with the proletariat as it was, but with the proletariat as it might be. Politically, the key to 'reforming the environment' was democracy. Thus Blanc preached universal male suffrage (women, being too dominated by the priests and too naturally conservative, were not included); a decentralized political administration, with local, elective municipal government but with the state still holding the reins at the centre; majority rule, one-chamber government, with basic liberties to be preserved behind the bulwark of a supreme court. And the purpose of all this? To redress the balance between the classes, in Blanc's own words 'to re-establish the equilibrium between the strong and the weak'.

This then was the 'Jacobin' half of Jacobin socialism, the creed with which Blanc's name became associated. The other half, Blanc's socialism, was centred on the notion of the creation by the state of 'social workshops', self-governing associations of working producers.

In 1840 Blanc revised his *Revue du Progrès* articles on the social question and published them in a book entitled *L'Organisation du travail* in an edition of 3,000 copies. The police immediately tried to stop the circulation, but it was too late. *The Organization of Labour* met a need of the times, and by 1847 it was into its fifth edition.

Why *was* Louis Blanc's pamphlet at once so frightening to the police and so popular with the public? Probably because it was based on the one simple but powerful idea that it was the duty of the state to ensure the provision of employment and a minimum of the amenities of life to the citizens. This idea was doubly powerful because it was launched at a time when France was really beginning to feel for the first time the effects of serious population pressures and of the industrial revolution. In the 1840s, Paris in particular was the goal of uprooted peasants and hand-workers from the provinces for whom capitalism had not yet found and could not find jobs, at a time when France was ruled by a régime convinced that the state had no responsibility for its citizens apart from encouraging them to enrich themselves. In 1841 the one piece of social legislation of the July monarchy, for restricting child labour, left its policing to voluntary inspectors appointed by the factory owners. It is unlikely that the uprooted peasants themselves read *The Organization of Labour*. But some of the literate diehards of the Paris *faubourgs* doubtless did so. There is evidence in the slogans of 1848—'The right to work', the state as the 'banker of the poor', 'the organization of labour'—that during the 1840s Blanc's basic ideas had become familiar to a wide section of the Paris working class.

In the 1848 elections more than 120,000 Parisians voted for Blanc. By 1871 his name was able to rally more than 200,000 votes in the Seine Département. What were Blanc's basic ideas? First, there was a general critique of the existing competitive economic order, which was shown to be disastrous for all classes. Among the proletariat the competition of wage-earners for jobs forced down wages and led to continual and intensifying poverty. As for the employing class, competition between different manufacturers and merchants, by price-cutting, steadily and inevitably drove the least fortunate into bankruptcy, with a consequent increase in unemployment and yet more suffering for the proletariat. This vicious circle had to be broken. But how? Not by bloody revolution, but through a gradual peaceful transformation of society. Once the political battle had been won, and the proletariat was in control of the state, through universal suffrage, the state would make capital available for the expansion of a new cooperative mode of production free from the defects of the old competitive mode. A network of *ateliers sociaux* would be founded— workshops conducted by the workers themselves—with a national or central workshop responsible for the rational coordination of production and distribution on a voluntary basis. All this would be accomplished painlessly, without conflict or bitterness. The capital, for example, would be provided by a voluntary credit institution, the 'People's Bank' and not by taxing the rich. Blanc even hoped (like Fourier before him) that benevolent capitalists would invest money in his social experiment. For a time there would be a mixed economy, with private and cooperative enterprise existing side by side. Ultimately, provided that the government acted as a neutral umpire to ensure fair conditions, the competition of the cooperative sector would drive the other enterprises out of business, and the result would be the fraternal absorption of the capitalist class by the people. Meanwhile the cooperatives would move steadily towards socialism for the social welfare provisions they would finance, coupled with the elapse of time, would steadily diminish the legacy of human selfishness inherited from the old régime.

Initially, Blanc had accepted the need for wage differentials, for compromise over incentives. But in the 1848 edition of *The Organization of Labour* he extolled the ultimate ideal of proportionate equality: 'Let each produce according to his aptitudes and strength; let each consume according to his need.' In 1840 he had foreshadowed a not too remote future 'when it will be recognized that he who has received greater strength and greater intelligence from God owes more to his fellow men. Then it will behove the genius, and that is worthy of him, to declare his legitimate authority, not by the importance of the tribute he will levy on society, but by the greatness of the services he will render. For it is not in the inequality of remuneration that the inequality of aptitudes should end, it is in the inequalities of duties.'

We may sum up the essentials of Louis Blanc's political philosophy on the eve of the 1848 revolution, then, in these terms: the solution to the manifest ills of the contemporary world, poverty, moral disorder and class hatreds, lay in the progressive construction, on the foundation of voluntary working-men's cooperatives, of a fraternal socialist commonwealth of complete equality. The first and essential step was the achievement of a democracy, based on universal suffrage. Both the immediate political reform and the ultimate social transformation were seen not as the product of violent revolution and the exercise of power by sectarian or sectional groups, but as the product of a universal consensus and a reconciliation of the classes.

It was because he remained faithful to such preconceptions that Louis Blanc cut such a poor figure as a revolutionary leader in 1848. Thrust forward repeatedly by powerful political forces representing the radical artisans of Paris, he was as repeatedly unable to consummate the revolution they wished for, the practical seizure and exercise of political power. Instead he spent his time mediating between the parties, urging patience and reconciliation, while less scrupulous revolutionaries outflanked and outmanoeuvred him.

The process began in the first few days of the revolution. On 24 February, along with the other radicals, Flocon and Albert, Blanc was pushed into the new provisional government by popular pressure. The supporters of this group expected rapid and decisive action. On 25 February a deputation of workers invaded the council room where the provisional government was meeting, and its leader, Marche, pounded the table with a musket and demanded 'the Organization of Labour' within one hour. According to Garnier-Pagès, Blanc, Flocon, and Ledru-Rollin actually did draw up a programme for the state organization of workers' cooperatives but, when they found the other members of the provisional government in firm opposition, they accepted a weak compromise formula. This, the proclamation of 25 February, certainly pledged the government 'to guarantee work to all citizens' and 'recognized that the workers should associate themselves to enjoy the legitimate profits of their labour', but it was a paper proclamation which was never even signed. Similarly, within a few days Blanc accepted another defeat, the refusal of the government to place him at the head of a ministry of labour (which would make a start with the social revolution), and instead agreed to preside over the Luxembourg Commission to enquire into the problems of labour. It was a time of symbols, and the symbol of Blanc's predicament was his confrontation on 26 February with Auguste Blanqui, when the latter arrived at the Hôtel de Ville with his private army of militants to demonstrate for the adoption of the red flag, something to show that the democratic and social republic meant business. Blanc stood out for the fraternal tricolour, albeit with red ribbons on the flagpole, and saved the provisional government in a tight spot. During the next crucial weeks, instead of attempting to organize a powerful workers' party based on the Luxembourg, we find Blanc mediating between employers and workers, settling strikes, deliberately blunting the edge of a proletarian militancy. On the very first day of the Luxembourg assembly of the delegates of the Paris workers' organizations, 29 February, Blanc supported Arago when he turned down demands from the floor for shorter hours and the end of *marchandage*, the hated system of contracting labour through commission-taking middlemen.

In his most weighty address to the Luxembourg delegates, made in early March, Blanc counselled patience, urged class harmony, and warned his hearers that the only real amelioration of their position would come from the progressive lightening of toil through the introduction of machinery.

Politically, the same ambiguity was always manifest. On 17 March the Luxembourg democratic and socialist clubs and the workers' union stages a great mass demonstration to demand a postponement of the promised national elections, to allow time for the radicals and socialists to organize and propagandize. 150,000 Parisians surrounded the Hôtel de Ville, the meeting place of the provisional government. They gave Blanc a tumultuous welcome as he arrived from the Luxembourg. It was the apogee of Blanc's popularity: at that moment he possessed more than enough power to overthrow the provisional government. Proudhon was astonished and Marx scathing at the missed opportunity to set up a personal dictatorship. For missed it was; Blanc's chosen role, instead, was to act as a lightning-conductor, to soothe the crowd with soft words, to send them away without an answer to their petition yet somehow convinced their demands would be met. But not all of them. According to Loubère, as the crowd was dispersing, a partisan of Blanqui seized Blanc by the arm and hissed close to his face, 'So you're a traitor, you too.'

Blanc's personal refusal to respond to the challenge of revolutionary power meant the collapse of the dream of Jacobin socialism. Instead of the People's Bank and the social workshops, the opponents of socialism in the provisional government were free to create the parody of the Organization of Labour that went under the title of the National Workshops. The National Workshops were little more than aggregations of destitute men and women herded together on relief works under a semi-military discipline by Emile Thomas and his Polytechnic students, yet by many they were disastrously identified as models of socialism in practice, and their failings attributed to Louis Blanc.

By 16 April the balloon of Blanc's popularity had burst. Another Luxembourg-led demonstration rallied scarcely more than 20,000 demonstrators. One more act of the comedy was still to be played out. On 15 May the left mounted its last challenge. The elections of the end of April, by universal suffrage, had been an almost universal disaster for the socialists and the radicals. Blanc, though elected to the National Assembly, was out of the government, and socialism was at a discount.

The leaders of the clubs and the Luxembourg staged yet another march on the Assembly, ostensibly to demand French intervention on behalf of Polish liberation. On the way they 'captured' Louis Blanc, draped him in a Polish flag, and forced him to address the column. He then had to join the demonstration and witness the forcible dissolution of the Assembly that resulted. The rebels would have liked Blanc to lead them to the Hôtel de Ville too, to join in proclaiming their short-lived new provisional government. But this was too much for this revolutionary leader *malgré lui*, who managed to escape in a cab opportunely produced by his brother. Perhaps not even a Lenin could have saved that revolution; Blanc did not begin to try. His world was collapsing irretrievably, his entire political platform in ruins. Universal suffrage, the king-pin of his system, had turned out, in Proudhon's aphorism, to be 'counter-revolutionary'. The bourgeoisie was already showing itself more interested in class discipline than in class reconciliation.

In June the insurrection of the Faubourg Saint-Antoine and its repression delivered the final crushing blow—an orgy of class hatred unparalleled in modern history, with Blanc a helpless witness outside the struggle. Before long the victors of the June Days took their revenge on those who had turned the heads of honest workers with socialist nonsense and Louis Blanc was forced into exile. Thus he survived to face the same dilemma at the time of the Paris Commune in 1871 when, a deputy again, he completed the moderate pattern by publicly denouncing the violence of the Communards, while remaining silent on the violence of the Versaillais.

I began by asking the question: was Blanc's failure inevitable? Politically, it is clear that there were occasions, in February and March, if not in May and June, on which Blanc could have made other choices than the ones he did make, could have put himself at the head of an insurrectionary movement and could, at least temporarily, have grasped political power. In order to have done so, however, he would have had to cease to be Louis Blanc. He would, that is, have had to cease to believe in gradual and non-violent change, in democratic majority rule, and in reconciliation between classes. The lesson of 1848 was that socialism and these three things were incompatible and to this extent, at least, Louis Blanc's failure was clearly inevitable.

Was it inevitable, too, in the wider sense indicated by the Marxists? In the *Communist Manifesto* Blanc's contemporaries, Marx and Engels, criticized Blanc's illusions along with those of other utopians. Class reconciliation was an objective impossibility; instead class conflict must intensify as capitalism developed. The state could not hold the ring in the conflict between classes, but must act as the agent of the dominant class. For the achievement of socialism the support of only one class could be counted on: the industrial proletariat, the product of capitalism, steam-power, the factory system, and modern industry. The experience of 1848 certainly seemed to give powerful support to these Marxist conclusions about class war. Yet, ironically, in the long run social democracy, in advanced countries, has won its successes through appeals to moral idealism across class barriers rather than through class war. And so it is arguable that Blanc's doctrines were 'premature', rather than 'anachronistic'. Jacobin socialism, although not so named, had a long course yet to run.

The same is not, however, true of the basic institution of Blanc's socialist order, the cooperative workshop. A reading of *The Organization of Labour* leaves one with the conviction that Blanc's understanding of the structure of industry was based on his observations of early nineteenth-century France, before the industrial revolution had begun to take firm root. He was familiar with the small-scale, artisan production that predominated in most trades and his vision of social workshops was the coming together of bands of artisans in traditional trades and not the founding of complex, highly capitalized factories —the tailors' cooperative of Clichy, his one successful experiment in Paris in 1848, rather than the Hallette locomotive yard under worker management. Revealingly, in *The Organization of Labour*, Blanc talks of the need to ensure to the worker 'les outils du travail' (working tools), rather than 'the means of production'.

In such a context the organization of voluntary producers' co-operatives did not seem to contemporaries to be an economic operation of any particular difficulty, and the notion was popular with Proudhonists, as well as other French socialist groups, but above all with the English Christian Socialists. Was it not Charles Kingsley who in *Politics for the People* (1848) asserted that the French cry, 'Organization of Labour,' is worth a dozen of the People's Charter? Like Blanc in Paris, the Christian Socialists had some success in organizing the London tailors. But when they ventured into something more complex and more heavily capitalized like the cooperative ironworks at Southwark or Greenwich, they met with failure. The reasons for the collapse of the Christian Socialist experiments are intricate and controversial. One explanation is a significant transformation of working-class attitudes after the end of the 1840s, reflecting the changing composition of the proletariat as new-style industry took hold.

The reasons for the failure of productive cooperatives in France were simpler: they faced the hostility of orthodox bourgeois governments and were finally squeezed out by Napoleon III's police. It is perhaps not very profitable to speculate, with Loubère, on their chances of survival had the governmental winds instead been favourable. We can say, however, that they were not necessarily an anachronism for many years after 1848. As late as 1865 a contributor to the *Revue des Deux Mondes* was still able to write: 'What above all else characterizes Parisian industry is the extreme division of labour, the variety and small scale. Large factories are few and far between, small workshops are very numerous; there is nothing to resemble the character of factory towns where several large factories each employ hundreds and thousands of workers.' Parisian industry was still predominantly artisan for a generation at least after 1848. Vidalenc is wrong, therefore. If Blanc's solution was at all appropriate in 1840, it was no less appropriate in 1870. There was certainly no overwhelming socio-economic reason why Blanc's experiment could not have been begun in 1848, provided that effective government support had been made available.

It was Blanc's own axiom that 'the seed-bed of socialism can only be fertilized by the winds of politics.' His failure in 1848, as he himself recognized, was a political failure, and not one determined by the objective forces of history.

The consequences of the evident bankruptcy of Jacobin socialism for French history were momentous. For a brief period, in the 1840s, the two streams of political democracy and social utopianism had flowed together in one powerful current. After 1848 the streams parted once more, and remained separate for a generation. In their despair after the June Days, the politically conscious elements among the French working class rejected the vision of fraternal socialism fostered by a democratic state. Of the two political creeds that replaced Blancism, the Proudhonists renounced the state altogether, veering towards anarchism. The Blanquists, on the other hand, retained the state, but rejected democracy. Socialism would come, they believed, when it came, only by way of violence and dictatorship. The road back to democratic socialism, in France, was to be long and hard.

Appendix: Statistics from Troyes illustrating Louis Blanc's conception of the social structure of industrial France

We have ourselves had occasion to study the influence of the present social system on the fate of the working class at Troyes. . . . We shall let the figures we personally gathered speak for themselves. . . . We have not included in the table professions occupying only a very small number of workers [Louis Blanc].

Trade	Masters	Workers	Workers per master
Bonnetiers (hosiers)	400	300	.75
Charpentiers (carpenters)	25	250	10
Cordonniers (shoemakers)	200	300–400	1.75
Maçons (masons)	20	150	7.5
Menuisiers (joiners)	150	700	5
Plafoniers et peintres en bâtiments (plasterers and painters)	100	300	3
Serruriers (locksmiths)	80	250	3
Tailleurs d'habits (tailors)	120	200–250	2
Tanneurs et corroyeurs (tanners and leather dressers)	25	50–60	2
Tisserands (weavers)	?	500–600	?
Total (excluding the weavers)	1120	2580	2.3
		(approx)	

Adapted from *L'Organisation du travail* (5th edn, Paris, 1848), pp. 41–3.

Apart from the workers in the building industry, Blanc's researches at Troyes familiarized him with an industry of small masters, self-employed, or employing one or two workers, and domestic handicraft workers.

4

Heinrich Heine:
the poet as *frondeur*[1]

Leslie Bodi

Heinrich Heine played an enormous and hitherto not always recognized role in the shaping of the imagination of German intellectuals in the decades preceding the revolution of 1848. From *Reisebilder* to *Zeitgedichte* and *Deutschland: ein Wintermärchen* he gave poetic expression to the political dreams and aspirations of his age, based on a unique synthesis of the German literary and philosophic tradition with Saint-Simonian ideas and supported by a lucid analysis of the turbulent political life of Louis Philippe's Paris. Heine saw a close parallel between the development of German classical philosophy and the course of the French Revolution; his incessant questioning of the relationship between 'deed' and 'thought', his satirical attacks on all the ills of a feudalistic Germany aggravated by the belated development of capitalism and the prevailing philistinism of the country are expressed in forceful poetic images which came to dominate the thinking and the imagination of his best German contemporaries.[2] His predictions about the coming of a communist revolution in the articles of the Augsburg *Allgemeine Zeitung* from 1840 to 1843 had a tremend-

---

[1] This chapter is a continuation of my articles, 'Heine und die Revolution', in *Dichtung, Sprache, Gesellschaft: Akten des IV. Internationalen Germanisten-Kongresses 1970 in Princeton*, hrsg. von V. Lange und H. G. Roloff (Frankfurt, 1971), pp. 169–77; and 'Kopflos—ein Leitmotiv in Heines Werk', in Internationaler Heine-Kongress 1972, *Referate und Diskussionen: Heine-Studien*, hrsg. von M. Windfuhr (Hamburg, 1973), pp. 227–44, 254–7. Of the extensive secondary literature on Heine, I have mainly used books and articles by A. Betz, J. Dresch, B. Fairley, L. Hofrichter, H. Kaufmann, L. Kreutzer, G. Lukács, S. S. Prawer, A. Vallentin. Fritz Mende's *Heinrich Heine: Chronik seines Lebens und Werkes* (Berlin, 1970) gives a very useful chronological guide to this topic.

I should like to express my appreciation to Mrs E. Y. Short who, with great care, has rendered Heine's almost untranslatable prose into English for this chapter.

[2] See mainly the statement by F. Engels on Heine's role in recognizing the 'revolutionary' function of German philosophy, in the second paragraph of *Ludwig Feuerbach und der Ausgang der klassischen deutschen Philosophie* (1886): 'What, however, neither the government nor the liberals saw, one man at least saw as early as 1833, and his name was Heinrich Heine.'

ous impact on the thinking of young Marx and Engels, which was then reinforced by their personal contact with the poet in the decisive years of their ideological development between 1843 and 1845. The utopian vision of unalienated man contrasted with the misery of German reality, which is the essence of *Deutschland: ein Wintermärchen*, certainly influenced the development of German socialism. The compelling influence of Heine's satire on German political style can be well seen in the great number of acknowledged and unacknowledged quotations in the early writings of Marx and Engels and in their articles in the *Neue Rheinische Zeitung* of 1848–9.[3] Some of the writings of Marx and Engels in the years immediately following the revolution are inconceivable without Heine's influence. I am convinced that forceful political satires like *Die grossen Männer des Exils* or *Der achtzehnte Brumaire des Louis Bonaparte* could never have been written without the impact of Heine's *oeuvre*.[4]

Unlike the ideological leaders of the German radicals and the poets of 'Young Germany' however, Heine could never conceive of the coming of revolution, and especially of a German revolution, without strong intellectual and emotional misgivings.[5] He believed in the historical necessity of revolutionary change; emotionally, however, he was torn between Promethean enthusiasm and an insight into the horrors, the irrationality and the inhumanity inherent in political action. He saw the contrast between an abstract revolutionary programme and the human misery and bloodshed it necessarily implied and he knew that—notwithstanding all his predictions about an imminent revolutionary situation in his homeland—German society would never be able to achieve revolutionary rebirth in a destruction of all the obstacles to freedom, democracy and national unity. His poems against the illusions, the emotionalism and the stupidity of the German radical *Tendenzdichter*, and especially his *Atta Troll*, identified placid philistinism and empty revolutionary rhetoric as coming essentially from the same source; he always equated bad poetry with bad politics.

In a great variety of thematic images his book on *Ludwig Börne* of 1840 aimed at showing the impossibility of a German revolution ever coming to a victorious end. The ironic summary of the book is the sentence: 'A revolution is a misfortune but a failed revolution is a disaster.'[6]

Considering all this, it is worth giving a brief account of what

[3] A good summary in Nigel Reeves, 'Heine and the Young Marx', *Oxford German Studies* VII (1972–3), pp. 44–97.

[4] *Op. cit.*, pp. 74–8; see also R. Livingstone's 'Introduction' to Karl Marx and Frederick Engels, *The Cologne Communist Trial* (London, 1971), p. 32.

[5] See L. Bodi, 'Heine und die Revolution'.

[6] *Heinrich Heines sämtliche Werke*, edited by E. Elster (7 vols, Leipzig and Vienna, n.d., hereafter *Werke*) VII, p. 84.

happened to Heine when confronted with the reality of the revolutions of 1848. Such a survey might be regarded as a case history of the German intellectual and artist in an extreme political situation and could, in a broader sense, also serve as a model for the problematic relationship of literary engagement and political action. Heine's situation, admittedly, was a very special one: he had lived in exile for almost two decades at the time of the outbreak of the revolution; he had achieved a high reputation as a truly European figure and held a central position in the French as well as in German intellectual and artistic life. The poet's health had already deteriorated catastrophically by February 1848, but even so it remains highly characteristic that his activities as an engaged political writer came to an almost complete halt during these decisive years.

In early February 1848 Heine was committed to a nursing home. On 23 February, after a visit to his Paris flat, his carriage got in the way of a demonstration, was overturned and used for the building of a barricade. During the next three weeks Heine wrote a number of articles for the Augsburg *Allgemeine Zeitung*, the South German liberal paper which he had earlier so often used as a forum to speak to his German readers.[7] The first article, dated 1 March, opens with the following words:

> I have not yet been able to write to you about the events of the three great February Days, for my head was quite deafened. A continual beating of drums, noise of shots and the Marseillaise. The latter, that unending song, nearly split my brain, and alas! the most seditious rabble of thoughts, which I had kept locked up there for years, suddenly broke out again.[8]

The words closely tie up with the style used earlier to describe the drumming of the friend of his youth, Le Grand, which had conveyed to him the imagery and the melodies of the great French Revolution and the Napoleonic age,[9] and also with his enthusiastic *Letters from Heligoland* of July and August 1830, which were later incorporated into his book on Börne.[10] The parallel is obvious to Heine. He immediately asks:

---

[7] The series was first published under the title *Die Februarrevolution*, in *Werke* VII, pp. 377–85.

[8] *Werke* VII, p. 377: 'Ich habe Ihnen über die Ereignisse der drei grossen Februartage noch nicht schreiben können, denn der Kopf war mir ganz betäubt. Beständig Getrommel, Schiessen und Marseillaise. Letztere, das unaufhörliche Lied, sprengte mir fast das Gehirn und ach! das staatsgefährlichste Gedankengesindel, das ich dort seit Jahren eingekerkert hielt, brach wieder hervor.'

[9] *Ideen: das Buch Le Grand*, in vol. II of *Reisebilder* of 1826 (*Werke* III, pp. 127–94).

[10] *Werke* VII, pp. 42–66. A similar style is used in connection with the events of 1830 in the 'Spätere Nachschrift' in *Die Stadt Lucca* (*Werke* III, pp. 428–30); the 'Schlusswort' in *Englische Fragmente* (*Werke* III, pp. 501–3); and a number of articles of *Französische Zustände*, mainly in 'Vorrede', Artikel III, VI, IX and 'Tagesberichte' (*Werke* V, pp. 24–5; 46–54; 90–94; 131–48; 156–89).

Is the great author repeating himself? Are his creative powers failing? Wasn't the play, presented to us last February with such pride, the same as he produced eighteen years ago in Paris under the title of 'The July Revolution'? But one can always see a good piece twice. At any rate, it has been improved and expanded and the conclusion in particular is new and was received with thunderous applause.[11]

He then talks about the almost magic skill of the French in the building of barricades and extolls the bravery, honesty and altruism of the *ouvriers* who have brought the revolution to victory, giving at the same time a picture, Brechtian in its irony, of the rich and wealthy of the *juste milieu*, who were not only afraid of any revolution but also experienced a terrible shock when they realized that the harsh treatment meted out to thieves by the rebellious people of Paris might well turn against the rich themselves. The article ends with a sentimental anecdote about a thirteen-year-old boy who at the sacking of the Tuileries took only a jar of marmalade for his sick grandmother. The thought of the sweetness of the 'confections of Louis Philippe' leads him to think of the bitter taste of the 'sweets of exile' which the dethroned king will now have to consume in cold, foggy England.

The next article, dated 10 March, gives a sentimental and slightly ironic picture of the dethroned 'citizen-king' and states that the French have finally grown out of royalism and romanticism, and that the republican blouse has now become the only garment giving suitable freedom of movement to the whole nation. The article is mainly devoted to Lamartine. Heine recapitulates his earlier criticism of that poet's 'spiritualist' Petrarchism, but says that his attitude to Lamartine has now completely changed. He emphasizes that Petrarch was not only the platonic lover of Laura, but also a friend of the rebellious Cola di Rienzi. The enthusiastic Promethean language of his first article breaks through again when speaking of Lamartine's book on the Gironde (1847) which, in a strange association, is compared to a relief on an antique sarcophagus:[12]

> for here we see the fantastic bacchanals of the French Revolution, thyrsus-waving corybants of freedom and equality, terrorist cymbal-players and moderantist flute-players, goatfooted satyr-figures, patriotic blackguards, maenads of the guillotine with streaming locks, crowds

[11] *Werke* VII, p. 377: 'Wiederholt sich der grosse Autor? Geht ihm die Schöpfungskraft aus? Hat er das Drama, das er uns vorigen Februar zum besten gab, nicht schon vor achtzehn Jahren ebenfalls zu Paris aufführen lassen unter dem Titel: "Die Juliusrevolution"? Aber ein gutes Stück kann man zweimal sehen. Jedenfalls ist es verbessert und vermehrt, und zumal der Schluss ist neu und ward mit rauschendem Beifall aufgenommen.'

[12] The image of a bacchantic feast as presented on an ancient sarcophagus accompanied Heine to his very last days; see the poem 'Für die Mouche' (*Werke* II, pp. 45–59).

drunk with divine madness, reeling along in the most amazing and incredible attitudes, at sight of whom a terrible destructive intoxication seizes us too—*Evoe Danton! Evoe Robespierre!*[13]

The chain of associative images establishes an equation between the events of 1789 and those of 1848, and an identification of revolutionary action with full artistic, sensual and erotic freedom. Dance and terror, ancient religious frenzy and modern politics merge into a grotesque and highly ambivalent prose poem.

Heine then remarks that Lamartine has now surpassed his fame as a writer by having become one of the great heroes of the new revolution, a *gonfaloniere* of the tricolour, which he has succeeded in protecting from the danger of being turned into the red flag of a socialist republic, the blood-red banner . . . from which may Heaven long preserve us'. At the end of his article Heine scribbled the following personal message to his friend Gustav Kolb, the editor of the *Allgemeine Zeitung*: 'Dearest Kolb, I cannot see at all now and cannot take even two steps. Your unfortunate friend H. Heine.'[14]

The third article remained a fragment. It was dictated to a French secretary, his 'dictator', as Heine calls him. This word immediately triggers off a sequence of thoughts about the dangers of egalitarian radicalism for the writer and poet which, as Heine earlier so often stressed, will put an end to all art: 'In a republic no citizen need write better than any other. Not only freedom of the press but also sameness of style must be decreed by a truly democratic government.'[15] He concedes that the revolution needs new men who have to come from the lowest strata of society, and that it needs new brooms to clear away the rubbish of old times: 'New times, new brooms!' The last sentence is a melancholy statement: 'Our carnival was very sad.'

The last of the articles, dated 22 March, was written under the impact of the rapid spread of the revolutionary movement in

---

[13] *Werke* VII, pp. 381–2; 'wir sehen hier nämlich die abenteuerlichen Bacchantenzüge der französischen Revolution, thyrsusschwingende Korybanten der Freiheit und Gleichheit, terroristische Zimbalschläger und moderantistische Doppelflötenspieler, bocksfüssige Satyrgestalten *bougrement patriotiques*, Mänaden der Guillotine mit flatterndem Haar, von dem göttlichen Wahnsinn berauschte Scharen, in den unerhörtesten und unglaublichsten Posituren dahintaumelnd, und bei deren Anblick uns ebenfalls eine grauenhafte, zerstörungssüchtige Trunkenheit ergreift—*Evoe Danton! Evoe Robespierre!*'
[14] *Werke* VII, 382: 'Jene rote Blutfahne . . . vor welcher uns der Himmel noch lange bewahre', and at p. 607: 'Liebster Kolb! Ich kann gar nicht mehr sehen u[nd] keine zwey Schritte mehr gehen. Ihr armer Freund H. Heine.'
[15] *Werke* VII, pp. 382–3: 'In einer Republik braucht kein Bürger besser zu schreiben wie die andre. Nicht bloss die Freiheit der Presse, sondern auch die Gleichheit des Stils muss dekretiert werden von einer wahrhaft demokratischen Regierung.' This is one of the most important arguments used by Heine when explaining his fear of a communist revolution.

Germany, and especially its victory in Vienna and Berlin. It seems to Heine to be a fairytale, surpassing those of the *Arabian Nights*— but then he raises again the ironic question 'But how did this come about? Are the affairs of this world really directed by rational opinion, by thoughtful intelligence? Or are they only ruled by a laughing rascal, the god of chance?' The victory of the revolution was a historic necessity, but the timing of its outbreak was reduced by the working of chance which, for once, really acted in favour of the French people: 'The nation, that great orphan, has drawn winning numbers in Fortune's lottery this time.'[16] The article again ends with an anecdote: at the election of the provisional government the names of the ministers were scribbled on a paper and handed on to the speaker in the Chamber of Deputies on the points of bayonets. Half ironically, Heine hopes that the new government will successfully be able to fulfil its functions.

Of these articles only the first was published on 9 March. In mid-May Heine asked Kolb to return the other three articles which by then were superseded by the flow of events. It is interesting to note that scarcely anything of Heine's works was published in Germany over the next months. In April, the 1832 'Introduction' to his *Französische Zustände* appeared in Leipzig as a small booklet under the title *Heinrich Heines politisches Glaubensbekenntnis oder: Epistel an Deutschland*. And in early May one of Heine's most biting satires on the monarchic principle, his *Schlosslegende* of 1847, was reprinted in a Leipzig newspaper (*Kritische Blätter*).[17]

During the first two months of the revolution, Heine's letters were dominated by his shock at having had his name exposed in a list of writers, artists and emigré politicians who had been receiving a secret pension from Louis Philippe's government since 1836. This news item soon found its way into the German newspapers and was extremely harmful to his reputation. With the loss of this pension, the losses suffered by the collapse of the Paris stock exchange and the impossibility of earning money through publishing in Germany, Heine's financial position became catastrophic. Throughout his correspondence we find a strange mixture of complaints about his quickly progressing illness, his financial difficulties and comments on the revolutionary scene. The first letter to his mother after the outbreak

---

[16] *Werke* VII, pp. 383–4: 'Doch wie ist das gekommen? Werden die Angelegenheiten dieser Welt wirklich gelenkt von einem vernünftigen Gedanken, von der denkenden Vernunft? Oder regiert sie nur ein lachender Gamin, der Gott-Zufall? . . . Das Volk, das grosse Waisenkind, hat dieses Mal sehr gute Nummern aus dem Glückstopfe gezogen.'

[17] 'Schlosslegende' was banned in Germany for a long time; it could only be reprinted in later Heine editions. E.g., *Sämtliche Werke*, edited by O. Walzel (Leipzig, 1913) III, p. 370, where it appears under the alternative title, 'Wälsche Sage'.

of the revolution (30 March) expresses some concern for what is happening in Germany, but is dominated by sentences like 'The whole world is gaining freedom and going bankrupt.'[18] The poet ironically speaks about the difficulties of having to write without the 'benevolent' control of censorship[19]; he is disgusted by the rhetoric of the German radical revolutionaries.[20]

Heine now started working on a projected new edition of his complete *oeuvre*. He bitterly complains to his publisher Campe: 'My head is free, mentally clear, even cheerful. My heart too is sound, almost wild for life, strong and lusty—but my body so crippled, so wasted. I'm buried alive.' In the same letter he stresses, however: 'I have never changed my convictions and thus have nothing to alter in my books, even after the February revolution.'[21] A public statement (*Erklärung*) was written by Heine on 15 May about his pension, emphasizing that he had by no means sold himself to French political interests when accepting it, but that it was granted him by Guizot's government as a part of 'the large charity which the French nation offered to so many thousands of strangers who, by their zeal for the revolutionary cause in their homeland, were more or less gloriously compromised and sought sanctuary at the hospitable hearth of France'.[22] He emphasized that it was of special importance to him to accept the money because the decree of the German Diet of 1835 had made his existence as a German writer completely impossible.

In the days between the writing of this *Statement* and its publication in the *Allgemeine Zeitung* on 23 May, Heine went out for the last time. He collapsed in the Louvre and had to be brought home, never to be able to walk again. He stylized this experience into a beautiful romantic story which he must have told many times to his friends and which three years later gained symbolic significance in the Postscript to *Romanzero*. It identifies the collapse into his final

---

[18] *Heinrich Heine: Säkularausgabe*, edited by F. H. Eisner (Berlin and Paris, 1970–72), xx–xxiii, hereafter *Briefe* xxii, p. 270. 'Die ganze Welt wird frey und bankrott.'

[19] *Gespräche mit Heine*, edited by H. Houben (Frankfurt, 1926, hereafter *Gespräche*), pp. 603–4.

[20] *Briefe* xxii, p. 271: 'Auch war es sehr lästig, als ich rings um mich lauter alte Römergesichter sah, das Pathos an der Tagesordnung war.' ('It was very annoying, too, that pathos was the order of the day, while all around me I saw countless ancient Roman faces.')

[21] *Briefe* xxii, pp. 272–3: 'Mein Kopf ist frey, geistesklar, sogar heiter. Auch mein Herz ist gesund, fast lebenssüchtig, lebensgierig gesund—und der Leib so gelähmt, so makulaturig. Bin wie lebendig begraben. . . . Ich habe nie meine Gesinnung geändert und habe also auch seit der Februar Revoluzion nichts in meinen Büchern zu ändern.'

[22] *Briefe* xxii, p. 275: 'das grosse Allmosen, welches das französische Volk an so viele Tausende von Fremden spendete, die sich durch ihren Eifer für die Sache der Revoluzion in ihrer Heimath mehr oder wenig glorreich kompromittirt hatten und an dem gastlichen Heerde Frankreichs eine Freistätte suchten.'

illness with the collapse of his sensualist creed and, implicitly, with the first defeat of the revolution in France in May 1848:

> It happened in May 1848, on the day when I went out for the last time, when I bade farewell to the fair idols I worshipped in my times of happiness. Only with difficulty did I drag myself as far as the Louvre and I almost broke down as I entered the lofty gallery where the most blessed Goddess of Beauty, Our dear Lady of Milo, stands on her pedestal. Long did I lie at her feet and wept so bitterly that a stone must have been moved to pity. The Goddess too looked down in compassion, but at the same time so sorrowfully as if to say: do you not see that I have no arms and therefore cannot help you?[23]

Heine moved to a summer residence in Passy and wrote his testament; his letters are full of semi-political jokes and allusions to his completely paralysed state: 'My legs have not outlived royalty. I am carried around like a baby.... Brotherly greetings. Heinrich Heine.'[24]

After the workers' revolt and its brutal repression by the French army he wrote to his mother on 26 June:

> Since another great bloodbath has taken place in Paris, you are sure to be very anxious about me and I therefore make haste to let you know that we spent the three terrible days in great safety here and that meanwhile I am waiting here in the greatest peace and comfort for the end of the affair.... The world is full of misfortune and one even forgets oneself.[25]

A letter to Campe dated a week later reiterates Heine's complaints about his financial difficulties and his terrible illness. He finishes the letter with the often quoted words:

> Concerning current events I will say nothing; it is universal anarchy, the world turned upside-down, divine madness made visible. The Old

---

[23] *Werke* I, p. 487: 'Es war im Mai 1848, an dem Tage, wo ich zum letztenmale ausging, als ich Abschied nahm von den holden Idolen, die ich angebetet in den Zeiten meines Glücks. Nur mit Mühe schleppte ich mich bis zum Louvre, und ich brach fast zusammen, als ich in den erhabenen Saal trat, wo die hochgebenedeite Göttin der Schönheit, Unsere liebe Frau von Milo, auf ihrem Postamente steht. Zu ihren Füssen lag ich lange und ich weinte so heftig, dass sich dessen ein Stein erbarmen musste. Auch schaute die Göttin mitleidig auf mich herab, doch zugleich so trostlos als wollte sie sagen: siehst du denn nicht, dass ich keine Arme habe und also nicht helfen kann?' Heine's earlier rendering of the story is recounted by Karoline Jaubert. (*Gespräche*, pp. 624–5.)

[24] *Briefe* XXII, p. 283: 'Mes jambes n'ont pas survexcu [sic] à la royauté. On me porte commune un petit enfant ... Salut et Fraternité. Henri Heine.'

[25] *Briefe* XXII, p. 285: 'Da wieder in Paris ein grosses Blutbad angerichtet worden, so bist Du gewiss meinetwegen in Sorgen, und ich eile daher Dir zu melden dass wir hier in grosser Sicherheit die drey schrecklichen Tag verlebt und ich auch vor der Hand hier in behaglichster Ruhe das Ende der Dinge abwarte.... Die Welt ist voll Unglück und man vergisst sogar sich selbst.'

One must be shut away if this continues. This is the fault of the atheists who so greatly enraged him.[26]

Heine's letters prove that his 'return' to the God of the Old Testament and his break with enlightened materialism and neo-Hegelian atheism were closely connected with his traumatic experiences during the first great victories of the counter-revolution in May and June 1848. An important passage in his later conversations has escaped the attention of most Heine critics. Talking to a young German writer, Ludwig Kalisch, in January 1850, Heine said:

> I have not become a follower of the Nazarene . . . but the classical world, lovely and bright as it is, is no longer enough for me, since I myself am no longer lovely or bright [handsome or cheerful]. I was living in Passy when my severe illness began. While I tossed and turned on my bed, the terrible battle of June raged outside. The thunder of cannon deafened me. I heard the screams of the dying; I saw Death with his merciless scythe cutting down the youth of Paris. In such hideous moments pantheism is not enough; one has to believe in a personal God, in a life after death.[27]

In the letters of the following months the motif of his return to a 'personal God' is added to the ever-recurring topics of sickness and financial difficulties, but they are also interspersed with troubled innuendoes about the course of the revolutionary events in France and Germany. In mid-September, Heine sent his friend Gustav Kolb the last manuscript pages of *Zur Geschichte der Religion und Philosophie in Deutschland*, which contained the sum total of his revolutionary credo of the early thirties, his ultimate statement about German philosophy leading to German revolution, thought leading to action [*Werke* IV, pp. 292–6]. This horrifying and highly ambivalent piece

---

[26] *Briefe* XXII, p. 287: 'Ueber die Zeitereignisse sage ich nichts; das ist Universalanarchie, Weltkuddelmuddel, sichtbar gewordener Gotteswahnsinn!
Der Alte muss eingesperrt werden, wenn das so fort geht.—Das haben die Atheisten verschuldet, die ihn toll geärgert.'
[27] *Gespräche*, p. 668. 'Ich bin nicht Nazarener geworden . . . aber das Griechentum, so schön und heiter es auch ist, genügt mir nicht mehr, seitdem ich selbst nicht mehr schön und heiter bin. Ich bin in Passy gelegen, als meine böse Krankheit anfing. Während ich mich krampfhaft auf dem Lager wälzte, wurde draussen der entsetzliche Junikampf gekämpft. Der Kanonendonner zerriss mein Ohr. Ich hörte das Geschrei der Sterbenden; ich sah den Tod mit seiner unbarmherzigen Sense die Pariser Jugend hinmähen. In solchen grässlichen Augenblicken reicht der Pantheismus nicht aus; da muss man an einen persönlichen Gott, an eine Fortdauer jenseits des Grabes glauben.' This seems to prove conclusively that Heine's attitude to the 1848 revolution was not determined by that of the wealthy bourgeoisie, who saw the June uprising in terms of a 'base revolution' as opposed to the 'fair revolution' of February. This statement by Marx is made in an article in *Neue Rheinische Zeitung* of 29 June 1848 (MEGA, Abt. I, Bd. VII, p. 116) and has been used by DDR Heine-scholars to explain Heine's ambivalent attitude to the revolution.

uses the strongest revolutionary imagery, drawing an alarming picture of the followers of Kant and Fichte assuming the guise of radical fanatics. It evokes the threatening prospect of Schelling's *Naturphilosophie* turning into demonic destruction and an aimless natural force identified with the senseless fury of the heroes of ancient Teutonic myths. The passage ends with a warning to the French and to the whole civilized world to beware of the anarchic nationalist forces that a German revolution might unleash.[28]

This passage had been deleted by the censor when *Zur Geschichte der Religion und Philosophie* was first published in 1834 and was unavailable in its original German form to the German reading public. With its publication in September 1848, Heine clearly wanted to establish his role as a prophetic visionary in view of the impending defeat of the revolutionary movement in Germany. It also acquired new significance for Heine who, in these weeks, repeatedly warned his French friends about the dangers of German chauvinism and 'Teutomania'.[29] It was, however, too late. On 19 October, Heine asked Kolb with a slighly melancholic irony to return the manuscript:

> Three or four weeks ago I sent you a prophecy, written fifteen years ago, concerning the German revolution, together with a few words of introduction; I thought that you might use it in the *Allgemeine [Zeitung]* for topical interest or for curiosity's sake; since this has not been done, I beg you to return the manuscript to me.

The brief letter ends with the question of Job which was to become one of the ever-recurring motifs of Heine's later poetry: 'Why must the just suffer so greatly on earth? That is the question which constantly torments me on my bed of pain. It is true that pain purifies the soul, but I feel I could have done without this cure.'[30]

The letters of the following months demonstrate Heine's complete loneliness in the restless atmosphere of a metropolis still alive with

---

[28] *Werke* IV, p. 295. It is highly characteristic of the ambivalence of Heine's ironic style that over the past hundred years this statement could well be interpreted as a prophecy both of the inevitability of a socialist revolution in Germany and of the coming of Hitler's rule.

[29] Letters to Edouard de la Grange, 25 August 1848 (*Briefe* XXII, pp. 284–5) and to Jacques-Julien Dubochet, 29 August 1848 (*ibid.*, pp. 289–90).

[30] *Briefe* XXII, pp. 298–9. 'Vor 3 oder 4 Wochen schickte ich Ihnen eine vor 15 Jahren geschriebene Weissagung über die deutsche Revoluzion nebst einigen einleitenden Worten; ich dachte, dass Sie in der Allgemeinen davon Gebrauch machen würden, der Actualität oder auch der Kuriosität wegen; da dieses nicht geschehen ist, so bitte ich mir das Manuskript zurückzuschicken.... Warum muss der Gerechte so viel auf Erden leiden? Das ist die Frage, womit ich mich beständig auf meinem Marterbette herumwälze. Es ist wahr, dass der Schmerz ein seelenreinigendes Medicament ist, aber mich dünkt, ich hätte doch dieser Kur entbehren können.' On the use of biblical language in Heine's works see Margaret A. Rose, *Die Parodie: Eine Funktion der biblischen Sprache in Heines Lyrik* (Meisenheim am Glan, 1976).

the extremes of political action. He found special pleasure in repeating in letters to French and German friends an ironic *bon mot* on the realization of communism which had, after all, 'triumphed' already both in France and Germany:

> Everything is quiet here, for we have got what we wanted and even an old Bonapartist like me may at all events be pacified when he hears the shout 'vive Napoléon'! Communism too is doing well, though complaining of bad times. We have none of us any money any more, so communist equality exists *de facto*. We have community of women too, only the husbands don't know this yet.[31]

The only new poem published by Heine in the first ten months of 1848 was a satire on Giacomo Meyerbeer; the only prose work a brief public statement connected with Heine's fight for the maintenance of the pension paid to him on the basis of his wealthy uncle's will. The *Berichtigung* of April 1849 contains the first public statement of the change in Heine's religious attitudes, a renunciation of neo-Hegelian anthropocentric views and Goethe's artistic 'sensualism':

> I am no longer the Great Pagan no. 2, whom people used to compare to Dionysus crowned with vineleaves, while my colleague no. 1 [i.e. Goethe] received the title of a Weimarian grand-ducal Jupiter. I am no longer a somewhat stout Hellene, full of the joy of life, smiling down at the melancholy Nazarenes—I am now just a poor, mortally ill Jew, an emaciated picture of misery, a wretched creature![32]

The next sentence already shows an unmistakable touch of Heinean irony ('So much for my state of health from the well of true suffering'), while the end of the statement indicates that Heine is fully aware of what is happening in Germany in these months of the victorious counter-revolution: 'To the hearts which are bleeding to death in the Fatherland, greetings and tears!'[33]

---

[31] Letter to G. Kolb, 17 April 1849 in *Briefe* XXII, p. 309. 'Hier ist Alles still, denn wir haben, was wir wollen und sogar ein alter Bonapartist wie ich bin, mag allenfalls zufrieden gestellt seyn, wenn er vive Napoléon rufen hört! Dem Kommunismus geht es auch gut, obgleich er über schlechte Zeiten jammert. Wir haben alle kein Geld mehr und somit existirt de facto die communistische Gleichheit. Auch haben wir Weibergemeinschaft; nur die Ehemänner wissen es noch nicht.' A similar statement also in a French letter to François Mignet in January 1849, *ibid.*, p. 306.

[32] *Briefe* XXII, p. 311: 'Ich bin nicht mehr der grosse Heide Nr. II, den man mit dem weinlaubumkränzten Dionysus verglich, während man meinem Collegen Nr. I den Titel eines grossherzoglich weimar'schen Jupiters ertheilte; ich bin kein lebensfreudiger etwas wohlbeleibter Hellene mehr, der auf trübsinnige Nazarener herablächelte—ich bin jetzt nur ein armer todtkranker Jude, ein abgezehrtes Bild des Jammers, ein unglücklicher Mensch!'

[33] *Briefe* XXII, p. 311: 'Den Herzen welche verbluten im Vaterland, Gruss und Thräne!'

Throughout the period of the active revolutionary fight in Germany, Heine wrote a number of satires. There is only one poem in which the mood, style and imagery of a Promethean revolutionary attitude become apparent. It is *Im Oktober 1849* [*Werke* I, pp. 426–7 and p. 558]. The genesis of this poem is well documented. On 16 November 1849 Heine again complained to his publisher Campe about his financial difficulties and said:

> The expenses of my agony, dearest Campe, would amaze you. It is dear enough just to live in Paris; but to die in Paris is infinitely dearer. And yet I could be hanged so cheaply at home in Germany or in Hungary just now! I wrote the accompanying poem four weeks ago; I beg you to publish it over there in my name as a flysheet or in a newspaper, so that it reaches the public; since several inaccurate versions are already circulating here, we must get in ahead of any corrupt publication. Besides, it is a truly topical poem, portraying a mood of the moment.[34]

Heine's interest in the Hungarian revolution and the national struggle for independence had been awakened through his acquaintance with Karl Maria Kertbeny, whom he had known since spring 1847 and who had drawn his attention to the poetry of Petöfi. In mid-August 1849 Kertbeny sent translations of poems by Petöfi to Heine. Heine answered in a letter expressing his joy and comparing Petöfi with Burns and Béranger, calling him a surprisingly 'healthy' artist, far removed from the sickly emotionalism and the abstract speculations of German poets. He summarizes: 'I myself found but few such natural notes in which this country boy is as rich as any nightingale.'[35]

The Hungarian revolution had been the topic of an article in the last number of the *Neue Rheinische Zeitung* (19 May 1849), in which Engels, though strongly critical about the previous phases of the Hungarian revolution, stressed the importance and the 'European character' of the Hungarian war of independence.[36] Soon after the suppression of their paper, Marx and Georg Weerth visited Heine

---

[34] *Briefe* XXII, p. 322: 'Die Kosten meiner Agonie, liebster Campe, dürften Ihnen fabelhaft erscheinen. Es ist schon theuer genug, in Paris zu leben; aber in Paris sterben, ist noch unendlich theurer. Und dennoch könnte ich jetzt daheim in Deutschland oder in Ungarn so wohlfeil gehenkt werden! Beyfolgendes Gedicht habe ich vor vier Wochen geschrieben; ich bitte Sie, geben Sie es dort in Druck mit meinem Namen, als fliegendes Blatt, oder in einem Journal, wodurch es ins Publikum kömmt; da es nemlich hier in einigen unkorekten Abschriften cursirt, müssen wir jeder corrumpirten Publikazion zuvorkommen. Ausserdem ist es ein wahres Tagesgedicht, eine momentane Stimmung schildernd.'

[35] *Briefe* XXII, p. 320: 'Ich selbst fand nur wenige solcher Naturlaute, an welchen dieser Bauernjunge so reich ist wie eine Nachtigall.'

[36] Karl Marx and Friedrich Engels, *Werke* (39 vols, Berlin; 1960–68) VI, p. 507. See also K. Obermann, *Die ungarische Revolution von 1848/49 und die demokratische Bewegung in Deutschland* (Budapest, 1971).

in Paris. The fate of Hungary was at that time the topic of the day, and stood in the centre of many conversations on the future of the revolution. It cannot be established if Heine knew that Petöfi had disappeared at the end of July in the fight against Russian cavalry at the battle of Segesvár; he must certainly have been fully informed, however, about the final defeat of the Hungarian forces and the capitulation of the army at Világos on 13 August.[37] *Im Oktober 1849* has a special place in the poetic *oeuvre* of Heine. It is the third piece in a lyrical chronology—starting with *Anno 1829*, a satire attacking 'the countinghouse morality' of the Hamburg bourgeoisie and German philistinism. *Anno 1839* expresses Heine's homesickness for Germany, but at the same time stresses the complete and utter stagnation in his homeland. The first stanzas of *Im Oktober 1849* show that Germany has returned to the conditions of 1829 and 1839. They present a parodistic idyll of a country that, after the thunderstorm of the revolution, has again returned to Biedermeier happiness, philistine Christmas trees, *Gemütlichkeit* and the bliss of family life. The peaceful romantic moonshine is, however, broken by the sound of gunfire; Heine for a moment thinks of a friend who might have been shot because of his unwise persistence in revolutionary activities, but then of fireworks celebrating the centenary of Goethe's birth, or the reappearance on stage of a famous singer. A few bitter satirical lines are devoted to Franz Liszt, the bragging virtuoso, and lead on to the four central stanzas of the poem. They contain an unreserved glorification of the Hungarian revolution, identifying its heroes with those of the *Nibelungenlied*, whose fight also ended in tragic defeat. However strongly revolutionary emotions may act, heroic action is always doomed to failure. A satirical comparison follows between the defeat of Germany and that of Hungary; the heraldic beasts that overcame the Hungarian revolution were stronger than the wolves, pigs and dogs that have won the victory in Germany. The poem evokes the sound of revolutionary armies and battles reminiscent of Heine's famous early Napoleonic ballad *Die Grenadiere*; in the final version he even changes the word 'ringing' to 'clashing' to bring this association more strongly to mind.[38] In the last stanzas, the sound of weapons and heroic battles is replaced by animal sounds, and the last two lines carry an ironic admonition to the poet to be reasonable and to overcome his untimely revolutionary ardour:

[37] In October–November 1849, he was visited by one of the leaders of the defeated Hungarian army, Sándor Asztalos. See M. Werner (ed.), *Begegnungen mit Heine* (2 vols, Hamburg, 1973) II, p. 140.
[38] 'Viel Schwerter klirren und blitzen' 'Die Grenadiere', *Werke* I, p. 40: 'Many swords clash and flash'; and 'Es klirrt mir wieder im Gemüt/Die Heldensage, längst verklungen' 'Im Oktober 1849', *Werke* I, p. 427: 'Once again there clashes in my soul/The tale of heroes, long died away'.

Such howling, baying, grunting—I can hardly stand the smell of the
victors. But hush, poet, this exhausts you—you are so ill, it would be
wiser to say nothing.[39]

The poem was first published in a Stuttgart periodical in September
1850. By this time Europe had become altogether quiet. Heine's
political interest is mainly evident in a number of biting satires later
to be incorporated into the *Romanzero* and *Gedichte 1853–54*. Some
were unpublishable in the climate of post-revolutionary repression.
They attack the abysmal stupidity and philistinism of the German
radicals and their counter-revolutionary opponents. *Erinnerung aus
Krähwinkels Schreckenstagen* [*Werke* II, pp. 207–8] is one of the
strongest indictments of law-and-order terrorism in German literature. The satires against Herwegh dealing with his ill-fated meeting
with Friedrich Wilhelm IV in 1842 (*Die Audienz*) and his slightly
pathetic role as one of the leaders of the Baden adventure of radical
emigrés (*Simplicissimus I*)[40] are of special importance when trying to
define Heine's attitude to revolutionary action. He attacks in Herwegh
a poet who confuses literature with life and cannot distinguish between
true poetry and the rhetoric of revolutionary action with all its heroic
posturing.

During 1849 and 1850, Heine's activities as a creative writer were
mainly devoted to the third great collection of his poems, the
Romanzero, which is pervaded by a mood of utter pessimism and the
questioning of an evil world order which makes the bad triumph and
the good suffer; but the *Romanzero* shows few signs of open political
engagement. His letters and conversations, however, were still
strongly centred on the question of the revolution. In the autumn
of 1850 a great deal of his correspondence was devoted to his angry
reaction to a book by his old friend, Heinrich Laube, on the history
of the Frankfurt Parliament.[41] Heine finally confesses to Laube that
the book had increased his illness considerably; as the work is very
well written, Heine fears that its 'stupid' political line could well be
ascribed to opportunism. He writes:

I can understand that you, with your talent for pungent satire, should

---

[39] *Werke* I, p. 427: 'Das heult und bellt und grunzt—ich kann
                      Ertragen kaum den Duft der Sieger.
                      Doch still, Poet, das greift dich an—
                      Du bist so krank und schweigen wäre klüger.'
[40] 'Die Audienz' (*Werke* II, pp. 208–10); 'Simplicissimus I' (*Werke* II, pp. 189–91).
In an article on 'Georg Herwegh and the Aesthetics of German Unification', *Central
European History V* (1972), pp. 99–126, William J. Brazill gives a good summary of
Herwegh's political views, completely missing, however, the main point of Heine's
attack.
[41] Heinrich Laube, *Das erste deutsche Parlament* (3 vols, Berlin, 1849).

have mocked the heroes of your former party—(perhaps you have forgotten that you once belonged to the revolutionary party and as a leading member of it had to suffer enough)—and have made fun of the hollow liberals, the republican men of straw, the rotten remnant of a great idea—at any rate you had an easy task, for you only needed to make accurate copies of these people, since Nature had been before you and delivered them as ready-made caricatures to your pen—you were guillotining headless men. But I cannot understand how with stoic persistence you could praise those even worse and more mediocre, those heroes scarcely worthy to unloose the shoestrings of their despised opponents.[42]

Here Heine draws the clearest dividing line between himself, and Laube and all those former German radicals who sided with the powers of restoration after the defeat of the revolution. He himself had never hesitated to treat the German liberals and radicals as objects of satire, but had always felt himself as a member of the 'party of revolution' and would never have praised the conservative and reactionary enemies of the 'movement'.

Notwithstanding his sickness and the change in his religious views, Heine remained faithful to the ideals of his youth. In his letters he still saw himself in the role of a tortured Prometheus [*Briefe* XXIII, p. 112], and in August 1851 he confessed to Campe: 'You know, it is a terrible thing about politics; one can't quite rise above these superstitions.'[43] He tried again and again to clarify and to define his own position in view of the defeated revolution. In November 1851 he told Georg Weerth in connection with his Postscript to *Romanzero* that he would die as a poet whose concerns could not be identified with any closed ideological system:

The poet very clearly understands the symbolic idiom of religion and the abstract intellectual jargon of philosophy, but neither the lords of religion nor those of philosophy will ever understand the poet, whose language remains Greek to them.[44]

[42] *Briefe* XXIII, p. 54: 'ich begreife wie Du die Helden Deiner ehemaligen Parthei—(Du hast vielleicht vergessen, dass Du zur revolutionairen Parthei gehört hast und als ein Koryphäe derselben genug erduldet hast)—wie Du hohle Lieberale, strohköpfige Republikaner und den schlechten Schweif einer grossen Idee, mit Deinem prickelnden durchhechelnden Talente lächerlich machen konntest—leichtes Spiel hattest Du jedenfalls, da Du diese Personen nur treu abzukonterfeien brauchtest, und die Natur Dir hier zuvorgekommen, indem sie Dir die Karrikaturen bereits fix und fertig vorgeführt, an die Feder geliefert—Du hast kopflose Menschen guillotinirt. Aber ich begreife nicht, wie Du mit einer stoischen Beharrlichkeit der Lobpreiser jener Schlechtern und noch Mittelmässigeren sein konntest, jener Heroen, die kaum werth sind, ihren geschmähten Gegnern die Schuhriemen zu lösen.'

[43] *Briefe* XXIII, p. 117: 'Es ist doch eine schreckliche Sache mit der Politik; man kann sich über diesen Aberglauben nicht ganz hinaussetzen.'

[44] *Briefe* XXIII, pp. 147–8: 'Der Dichter versteht sehr gut das symbolische Idiom der Religion und das abstracte Verstandeskauderwelsch der Philosophie, aber weder die Herren der Religion noch die der Philosophie werden jemals den Dichter verstehen, dessen Sprache ihnen immer spanisch vorkommen wird.'

This credo is followed in the same letter by an account of a boring conversation on German politics with one of Heine's visitors, which is highly characteristic of the poet's epistolary style. The passage can well be read as a sophisticated ironic arabesque, illustrating Heine's previous statement that for the creative writer all abstract reasoning will immediately turn into literature—in this case a satiric identification of the stupid German with the 'stupidity' of Germany.

> The man saw everything in shades of gray, his own colour; he said Germany was standing on the edge of an abyss—in that case it is as well that Germany is no wild steed but a sensible ass, not growing giddy at sight of the abyss but wandering peacefully along its rim.[45]

In October 1850, Heine is reported to have been extremely pleased on receiving a letter from his old friend, Varnhagen von Ense, who assured the poet of his lasting loyalty to the ideals of the pre-revolutionary period. Varnhagen wrote: 'For your consolation I will say, however, that I am and remain what I was and as you knew me. We are forced to be *frondeurs* [in the sense of irreconcilable outsiders and rebels]—let us remain *frondeurs!*'[46] It is probably this definition of the writer and intellectual as a *frondeur* which influenced Heine when in *Enfant perdu* [*Werke* I, p. 430] the last poem of the *Romanzero*'s 'Lazarus'-cycle (1851), he stylized himself in the role of the lonely sentry on duty in a lost position, expressing the sum total of his stance as an engaged poet.

The last important phase of the European revolutions of 1848 was the takeover by Napoleon III in France. For Heine this was a horrifying and shocking spectacle, especially as he could never quite discard his childhood fascination with the figure of the great emperor. His earlier prophecies of the coming of the new Napoleon in France now changed to bitter irony. To his friend Alfred Meissner in 1849 he said: 'Paris, believe me, is truly napoleonic—I think the gold napoleon rules here.'[47] At an early stage he was already predicting that Louis Bonaparte was heading towards his 18th Brumaire, and many of his satirical statements on the change from revolutionary tragedy to its own parody are strongly reminiscent of Karl Marx's *Der achtzehnte Brumaire des Louis Bonaparte* of 1852.

---

[45] *Briefe* XXIII, p. 148: 'Der Mann sah alles grau in grau, was auch seine eigne Farbe ist; er sagte, Deutschland stünde an einem Abgrund—nun da ist es gut, dass Deutschland kein wildes Ross ist, sondern ein gescheutes Langohr, dem es vor dem Abgrund nicht schwindelt und an dem Rand desselben ruhig hinwandeln kann.'

[46] 'Ihnen zum Troste will ich aber sagen, ich bin und bleibe, der ich war und als den Sie mich gekannt haben. Man zwingt uns zum Frondieren,—bleiben wir Frondeurs!' Reported by Fanny Lewald, *Gespräche*, pp. 768–9.

[47] *Gespräche*, p. 638: 'Paris, glauben Sie mir, ist gut napoleonistisch—ich meine, hier herrscht der Napoleon d'or.'

The victory of Louis Bonaparte meant the ultimate and complete collapse of all revolutionary dreams for Heine. This experience could not at that time of utter political hopelessness, take the form of a poem; a passage in a letter to his friend Gustav Kolb on 13 February 1852, however, expresses in beautiful rhythmical prose the annihilation of all the revolutionary hopes of Heine's generation under the impact of the *coup d'état*:

> But my heart still bled, and my earlier Bonapartism has not held out against the grief which overwhelmed me when I realized the consequences of that event. The noble ideals of political morality, legality, civic virtue, freedom and equality, the rose-coloured daydreams of the eighteenth century for which our ancestors so heroically faced death, and in which we, no less eager for martyrdom, copied them—there they lie at our feet, shattered, destroyed, like shards of porcelain, shot-down weaklings —but I will keep silence and you know why.[48]

In this study of Heine's reactions to the course of the revolutions of 1848–51 I have tried to examine how one of the greatest political poets of European literature reacted to the most important political event of his lifetime. Heine's attitude to the revolution of 1848 was strongly coloured by his personal circumstances. By May 1848 he was incurably paralysed by his fatal illness, forced into complete physical inactivity, and experiencing grave financial difficulties. He was entirely isolated from events in Germany and could only passively observe the course of the revolution in France. Scarcely any of his works were published in Germany during 1848–9.

Heine's basic attitude to the events of the period was that of a sceptical observer and satirist, seeing art and poetry threatened by the emergence of dogmatic political ideologies, and recognizing the irreconcilable conflict between the revolutionary demands of 'freedom' and 'equality', between democratic liberty and radical terrorism.[49] He was deeply suspicious of all revolutionary rhetoric, of the heroic gesture parading in the costume of past revolutionary ages, and of any attempt to confuse utopian hopes with the realities of

---

[48] *Briefe* XXIII, p. 181: 'Aber mein Herz blutete dennoch, und mein alter Bonapartismus hält nicht Stich gegen den Kummer, der mich überwältigte, als ich die Folgen jenes Ereignisses übersah. Die schönen Ideale von politischer Sittlichkeit, Gesetzlichkeit, Bürgertugend, Freyheit und Gleichheit, die rosigen Morgenträume des achtzehnten Jahrhunderts, für die unsere Väter so heldenmüthig in den Tod gegangen, und die wir ihnen nicht minder martyrthumsüchtig nachträumten—da liegen sie nun zu unseren Füssen, zertrümmert, zerschlagen, wie die Scherben von Porzellankannen, wie erschossene Schneider—doch ich will schweigen, und Sie wissen warum.'

[49] This conflict remains the most dominant aspect of Heine's ambivalent attitude to communism in the last years of his life; it gains its most beautiful expression in the 'Préface' to the French edition of *Lutezia* dated 30 March 1855 (*Werke* VI, pp. 568–74).

political life. Heine was, moreover, afraid that a German revolution might turn into an uncontrollable outbreak of chauvinism—and he saw his worst fears confirmed when the French revolution again ended in a Bonapartist dictatorship.

Throughout the whole period, however, Heine showed concern, involvement and solidarity with the forces of the left. Notwithstanding the basic ambivalence in his attitude to the revolution, he was carried away by revolutionary emotions on first being confronted with the overpowering feeling of liberation and of dreams come true in his articles welcoming the events of the spring of 1848. It is highly significant, however, that even here his revolutionary enthusiasm is controlled by ironic ambivalence. The same applies to the only 'revolutionary' poem of this period, *Im Oktober 1849*. Only the defeat of the revolutionary movement in a far-away country enabled him to write some non-ironic stanzas on revolutionary action, embedded, however, in a poem otherwise full of satiric resignation. This is not dissimilar to the attitude of politically engaged writers of our own age who project their utopian hopes into the revolutionary struggles of exotic peoples in Asia, Africa or the Americas.

In many ways, Heine reacted to the events of the revolution by trying to stylize himself in the role of the prophetic visionary who had long ago sensed the inevitable corruption of all utopian projects if tested on the scene of political action. He also used the final outbreak of his fatal illness to give artistic expression to his helplessness in the face of powers beyond his control; his 'return' to the God of the Old Testament in many respects served a similar purpose. Heine's last visit to the Louvre in May 1848 becomes a symbolic event equating the personal tragedy of the poet with the tragic defeat of the European revolutions. This became one of the dominant underlying themes of Heine's poetry and prose in the last eight years of his life.

In his quest for an attitude that would permit a maximum of political engagement without loss of artistic integrity, Heine might well have found in Varnhagen's definition of the writer and intellectural as a *frondeur* the most acceptable description for his own stance. The attitude of the poet as a lonely guerilla on a forsaken post gains beautiful expression in *Enfant perdu*, and is a strikingly modern formulation of the paradoxical position of the engaged intellectual and writer of our own times.[50]

---

[50] In contemporary Marxism, this view has come to be regarded as one of the most dangerous deviations from the Leninist postulate of the 'party-poet' in the discussions about Lukács' definition of the relationship between literature and party politics: 'Der Parteidichter ist niemals Führer oder einfacher Soldat, sondern immer Partisan.' G. Lukács, *Schriften zur Ideologie und Politik*, edited by P. Ludz (Neuwied and Berlin, 1967), p. 44.

5

The view from the middle class: the German moderate liberals and socialism

G. A. Kertesz

I

'The history of all hitherto-existing society is the history of class struggles', begins the *Manifesto of the Communist Party*, and Marx and Engels certainly saw the revolutions of 1848 in terms of class conflict. Others, whose view of the situation and of the solution was different, thought in similar terms. Several chapters in this collection deal with such men who presented a radical critique of society and, consequently, proposed a radical restructuring of its social, economic or philosophical foundations, in most cases from the point of view of the working classes.

No one would deny the importance of these socialist or radical thinkers, yet it must be remembered that in 1848 the radical or socialist left was, even in France, a fairly small minority, and that it was the liberals who emerged at the head of the revolutionary movement, particularly in Germany. There is ample contemporary evidence to show that the moderate liberals received widespread popular support both in the years before the revolution and in 1848.[1]

This is not entirely surprising: the liberals believed, in Paul Pfizer's words, that they expressed goals 'which the entire nation wants, or must want in its rational interest',[2] and which were the 'living expression of the spirit of the time [*Zeitgeist*]' [*RW2* VIII, p. 534]. The liberals, and the middle class who provided most of the members of the liberal movement, were 'the core of the nation', that is, 'the moral location of those who represented the best for society as a whole'[3]— and a large proportion of the people accepted these views.

[1] Much has been written about this question. A recent article marshals the evidence well: James J. Sheehan, 'Liberalism and Society in Germany, 1815–48', *Journal of Modern History* XLV (1973), pp. 583–604.

[2] In C. von Rotteck and C. Welcker (eds), *Staats-Lexikon, oder Encyklopädie der Staatswissenschaften* (15 vols, Altona, 1834–43, hereafter *RW*); 2nd edition (12 vols, Altona, 1845–8, hereafter *RW2*). See *RW2* VIII, p. 524.

[3] Sheehan, p. 602 and literature cited.

But not all members of the middle class were liberals. Many were democrats,[4] others socialist. In retrospect Engels saw 'Socialism in 1847 [as] a bourgeois movement, Communism a working-class movement',[5] though in 1845 he referred to the 'Communism of the German educated bourgeoisie'.[6] There was, then, a section of the middle class which claimed that it represented primarily the interests of the working class, the majority of the people.

What the left, and particularly Marx and Engels, thought of the German liberal middle class is well known. It is not so clear, however, what the German liberals thought of socialism and communism. What did they understand by these terms? How did they view these movements and the social and economic changes which gave rise to them? Why did they disagree with the socialist solution? What solution did they themselves propose? These are the questions which this chapter will seek to answer.

To make the investigation practicable, I have decided to centre my interest on a comparatively small group of men, members of the right centre and left centre groups[7] in the Frankfurt Parliament, and particularly on their leaders. They were the men who set the tone of liberalism in this period. We are well served by sources relating to them: biographies, recollections, editions of letters and papers are abundant, many have written voluminously, the shorthand reports of the proceedings of the Frankfurt Parliament contain a large amount of their speeches, and for most of the period many of them are associated with a daily newspaper, the *Deutsche Zeitung*.

This newspaper was founded in 1847 by a group of liberal leaders in the southwestern states, predominantly Baden, to be the national organ of moderate liberalism. The long and detailed programme of the *Deutsche Zeitung* set forth the outlines of liberal policy, and its daily leading articles expressed the views of these men, among whom we can name—to confine the list to those who became members of the national and Prussian governments of 1848–9—Heinrich von Gagern, Robert von Mohl, Hermann Beckerath, Arnold Duckwitz, Max von Gagern, Friedrich Daniel Bassermann, Karl Mittermaier, Karl Mathy, Johannes Fallati, David Hansemann, Alfred von Auerswald and Maximilian von Schwerin-Putzar. From the time it began publication on 1 July 1847 to the time of Georg Gottfried

[4] Cf. Lenore O'Boyle, 'The Democratic Left in Germany, 1848', *Journal of Modern History* XXXIII (1961), pp. 374–83.

[5] Preface to the 1890 German edition of the Communist Manifesto, Karl Marx and Friedrich Engels, *Selected Works* (2 vols, Moscow, 1951) I, p. 31.

[6] Preface to the first German edition of his *The Condition of the Working Classes in England* (London, 1969), p. 18.

[7] I am concerned mainly with the Casino, Württemberger Hof, Augsburger Hof, Landsberg and Weidenbusch groups.

Gervinus's resignation as its editor in July 1848, the *Deutsche Zeitung* can be regarded as the organ of these men; but even later, after its move to Frankfurt in September 1848, it remained in close association with prominent members of the Casino and, later, the Weidenbusch groups.[8]

The *Deutsche Zeitung*, and particularly its leading articles, will thus be important for identifying liberal views, and will be supplemented, wherever possible, by the shorthand reports of parliamentary debates. To establish a framework of liberal theory I shall rely to a large extent on the successive editions of the Rotteck-Welcker *Staatslexikon* and on the volumes of *Die Gegenwart*.[9]

There are two major liberal writers on the social question, founders of what Lorenz von Stein called the 'science of society',[10] whose ideas I shall exclude from this discussion as they were not directly influential in 1848. They are Stein himself, and Robert von Mohl, who were the most advanced, systematic and original social thinkers among the liberals. Their views have been written about in such detail that a discussion of their ideas here would not be profitable.[11] Attention will be centred on the more clearly political majority of moderate liberals.

II

What did non-socialists and non-communists mean when they spoke of socialism or communism? One wonders if they knew what the words meant.[12] Windischgraetz called Schwarzenberg a communist because, after the revolution, he would not restore the privileges of the landowning aristocracy, and many bureaucrats called anyone who concerned himself with the social question a socialist.[13] Middle-class

---

[8] There is still no full-scale study of the *Deutsche Zeitung* (hereafter *DZ*), a gap I hope to fill with a book I am working on.

[9] *Die Gegenwart: eine enzyklopädische Darstellung der neuesten Zeitgeschichte für alle Stände* (12 vols, Leipzig, 1848–56, hereafter *GW*).

[10] In 'Der Socialismus in Deutschland', *GW* VII, pp. 517–63 at pp. 560–62. Stein is identified as the author of the article in H. K. P. Krause, '*Die Gegenwart* ...: eine Untersuchung über den deutschen Liberalismus' (dissertation, Berlin, 1935), pp. 113–14.

[11] Cf. Erich Angermann, 'Zwei Typen des Ausgleichs gesellschaftlicher Interessen durch die Staatsgewalt: ein Vergleich der Lehren Lorenz Steins und Robert Mohls', in W. Conze (ed.), *Staat und Gesellschaft im deutschen Vormärz* (Industrielle Welt, Bd 1), 2. Aufl. (Stuttgart, 1970), pp. 173–205, 275–6.

[12] Cf. A. E. Bestor, 'The Evolution of the Socialist Vocabulary', *Journal of the History of Ideas* IX (1948), pp. 255–302.

[13] W. Mommsen, *Grösse und Versagen des deutschen Bürgertums*, 2. Aufl. (Münster, 1964), p. 150.

liberals were no clearer: Camphausen, in a speech in the United Diet of 1847 saw 'the concepts which relate to the slogans of our time, to the words pauperism, proletariat, communism, socialism, organization of work' as 'dark and confused'.[14] Demands for the establishment of savings banks, for the abolition, without compensation, of the right to hunt on property not one's own, for a progressive income tax were all, at various times, labelled as communism [Mommsen, p. 150]. When, in March 1848, Trefurt proposed a 'voluntary' income tax of five to ten per cent, in order to assist the poor by providing interest-free loans to artisans and peasants, by establishing institutions to keep the unemployed busy and fed, and by financing the emigration of those without means, the *Deutsche Zeitung* headed its leading article criticizing the motion, 'A socialist proposal' [*DZ* no. 80, 20 March 1848].

But vagueness in the use of words does not necessarily mean that there was ignorance of the field to which they related. There is no doubt whatever that there was, among the liberal middle class, widespread awareness of and concern with not only the social question, but also socialist theories. No good purpose would be served by listing even the most important works, since Lorenz von Stein in 1852, Mombert in 1921 and Veit Valentin in 1931 survey the field very thoroughly.[15]

Books and pamphlets are, however, not necessarily the most effective means of communication. Although some books on French socialism, particularly on Saint-Simon's doctrine, were published in the early 1830s one is inclined to credit Heine's claim[16] that it was he who introduced the idea of socialism into German political consciousness through his reports from Paris to the *Allgemeine Zeitung* of Augsburg, at that time the most widely circulated and most highly regarded newspaper in Germany.[17] Heine's claim is borne out: Gustav Mevissen, a liberal industrialist in the Rhineland, had his interest in Saint-Simon aroused by these articles.[18]

It seems that German literature kept up with French socialist publications; the thought not only of Saint-Simon, but also of Fourier, Louis Blanc, Cabet and others was soon translated or analysed in

---

[14] Veit Valentin, *Geschichte der deutschen Revolution von 1848–1849* (2 vols, Cologne, 1970, originally published 1931) I, p. 77.

[15] For Stein see note 10 above; P. Mombert, 'Aus der Literatur über die soziale Frage und über die Arbeiterbewegung in Deutschland in der ersten Hälfte des 19. Jahrhunderts', Grünberg's *Archiv für die Geschichte des Sozialismus und der Arbeiterbewegung (Archiv)* IX (1921), pp. 169–236; Valentin I, pp. 279–80.

[16] I owe my knowledge of this to a friendly communication from Professor L. Bodi.

[17] See E. Heyck, *Die Allgemeine Zeitung 1798–1898* (Munich, 1898).

[18] Donald G. Rohr, *The Origins of Social Liberalism in Germany* (Chicago, 1963), p. 140.

Germany.[19] It was in works about French socialism that the words *Sozialist* and *Sozialismus* were first used, in 1840 and 1842 respectively.[20] From the appearance of the most important work in this field, Lorenz von Stein's *Der Sozialismus und Communismus des heutigen Frankreichs* (Leipzig, 1842), to the revolution, we have an increasing number of works, books as well as articles, popular as well as scholarly, on the social question and on socialism. Mohl's and Fallati's articles in the Tübingen *Zeitschrift für Staatswissenschaft*, Biedermann's in his periodicals *Unsere Gegenwart und Zukunft* and *Deutsche Monatsschrift* [Stein, pp. 547ff.] might be mentioned, and, of course, the various articles in the first two editions of the Rotteck-Welcker *Staatslexikon*.

The first edition of the *Staatslexikon* does not cover the field as well as might be expected. The only really relevant article is on Fourier's theory of society, with some comparisons with Owen and Saint-Simon, written by Wilhelm Schulz (*RW* v). There is no article on socialism, but it is doubtful whether this was a policy decision. The material for the *Staatslexikon*, originally expected to fill five to eight volumes, kept expanding because of Welcker's lax editing; in the end, to complete the work in fifteen volumes, the material under the letters S–Z was greatly compressed, with much omitted.[21]

Socialism fared much better in the second edition, with a long article on communism by Schulz (*RW2* III, pp. 290–339), one on the proletariat by Struve (*RX2* XI, pp. 210–17), on 'Eudämonismus und Egoismus' in relation to socialist and communist theories by Abt (*RW2* IV, 520–26) and on workers' riots by Oppenheim (*RW2* I, pp. 612–15). Even in this edition, there was no article on socialism: when the revolution broke out in 1848, it was decided to print, without revision, the material on hand for the last three of the twelve volumes (*RW2* XII, pp. 846–7). Thus the balance of the material of this section, already skimped in the first edition, still leaves a great deal to be desired.

It is interesting to note that the writers of these articles were, on the whole, on the left wing of the liberal movement. Until 1846, in

---

[19] 'Wegweiser auf dem Gebiete der sozialdemokratischen Literatur Deutschlands', first published in 1850 and included in Paul Wentzcke, 'Bibliographische Beiträge zur Geschichte des deutschen Sozialismus in der Bewegung von 1848', *Archiv* XI (1925), pp. 196–214 at pp. 199–207.

[20] For detailed discussion see C. Grünberg, 'Der Ursprung der Worte "Sozialismus" und "Sozialist"', *Archiv* II (1912), pp. 372–9, and E. Czóbel, 'Zur Verbreitung der Worte "Sozialist" und "Sozialismus" in Deutschland und in Ungarn', *Archiv* III (1913), pp. 481–5.

[21] H. Zehntner, *Das Staatslexikon von Rotteck und Welcker: eine Studie zur Geschichte des deutschen Frühliberalismus* (Jena, 1929), Chapter 1 *passim*.

many cases up to the revolution, radicals and moderates worked together even to the extent that some, like Schulz, wrote for the *Deutsche Zeitung*, [22] which was founded at least partly to defend true liberalism from the aberrations of the radicals [*DZ, Ankündigungsblatt*, 8 May 1847]. Because of the cooperation, and because the views of the two wings about socialism and the social question largely coincide, material from both will be used in this chapter. After the meeting of the Frankfurt Parliament, however, it is necessary to differentiate between the two groups. The left-wing liberals are better described as democrats or the parliamentary left, and the moderates as liberals or the parliamentary centre.

Those wanting to inform themselves about the social question, socialist (or communist) theories or movements, could, then, find ample opportunity in the literature. But it could often be done even more easily. Karl Biedermann, for instance, lectured on 'socialism and social questions' in the winter of 1846–7, first in Leipzig, then in Dresden, and in each place had an audience of from two hundred and fifty to three hundred people, including members of the first chamber, aristocrats and high-ranking bureaucrats. His lectures were equally popular when they were published as *Vorlesungen über Sozialismus und soziale Fragen* (Leipzig, 1847), and were banned in Prussia.[23] They express well the tone of liberal thinking in this period. The social question arose because of the growth of the proletariat, a class of people who were poor because the economic system made them so. Population growth aggravated the situation, but the underlying causes were, first, economic developments which, by separating capital and labour, made it impossible for workers to own the raw materials or tools they used, and, second, the industrial system which even separated skill and labour and required only the latter. Through the system of free competition even employers concerned about the welfare of their workers could not pay more than a minimum wage, and where the system was abused, where free enterprise became debased into a scramble for riches, the social question became acute [Rohr, p. 151].

These views are by no means isolated. Robert von Mohl's analysis is similar, though more penetrating; Mathy's picture of the causes is not greatly different.[24] Struve's description of the growth of the proletariat, if expressed in much more emotional terms, covers very

[22] L. Bergsträsser, 'Die Heidelberger "Deutsche Zeitung" und ihre Mitarbeiter', *Historische Vierteljahrschrift* XXXI (1937), p. 359.

[23] K. Biedermann, *Mein Leben und ein Stück Zeitgeschichte* (2 vols, Breslau, 1886) I, pp. 159–63. For a summary of the lectures see Rohr, pp. 150–54.

[24] See E. Angermann, *Robert von Mohl* (Neuwied, 1962), pp. 225ff. and his article 'Karl Mathy als Sozial- und Wirtschaftspolitiker', *Zeitschrift für die Geschichte des Oberrheins* CIII (n.s. LXIV, 1955), pp. 518–24.

similar ground [*RW2* XI, pp. 210–17]. Yet these are also the socialists' and communists' views as summarized by Abt [*RW2* IV, p. 524] and Schulz [*RW2* III, pp. 291–2], who wrote about the polarization of society, about the population increase and the introduction of machines. Socialists went further than liberals in seeing society in a state of conflict between rich and poor but, even so, most liberals agreed with the substance of the socialist analysis. As late as July 1849 the *Deutsche Zeitung* admitted the correctness of the socialist critique ['Zur socialen frage', *DZ* no. 199, 2. Beilage, 21 July 1849]. There were, of course, liberals who saw the situation differently, who regarded poverty and unemployment as self-inflicted, who thought that individualistic, *laissez-faire* economics—and economics alone— was the answer. But such men are far fewer than socialist and communist literature would lead us to believe.

If the mainstream liberals agreed with the socialist *analysis* of the social problem, they certainly did not agree with the *solutions* provided in socialist and communist theories. But before going on to discuss their criticism, it is necessary to establish what liberals understood by socialist policies. However vague the general usage of the words socialism and communism was, there must have been a core of meaning attached to the words, a meaning which would also show what socialist and communist policies were. Let us look at some liberal definitions of socialism and communism.

Biedermann, in 1847, argued that socialism sought to regulate individual relationships in the interests of fairness, in order to balance work done and rewards received, upon the principle that 'the individual would give to society what he produced and would receive back from society what he needed'. He saw communism, by contrast, as merging individual interests in the general interest; both systems, in his view, rested on the proposition that free competition and private property had to be abolished or at least drastically curtailed [Rohr, p. 152].

Schulz, in his article on communism [*RW2* III, p. 291], had a vaguer view of socialism, as a movement endeavouring to change society in the direction of greater social justice, and he described communism as a variety of socialism, the essence of which was the abolition of private property, general, permanent and hence enforced community of property, at least of immovable goods.

The best definitions I have found come, not surprisingly, from the pen of Lorenz von Stein in 1848 [*GW* I, p. 93]: 'Socialism consists of such theories as have as their main aim the domination of labour over capital, and through this domination a realization of the idea of equality through a distribution of goods according to work performed. Communism consists of such theories as strive to achieve this equality through the abolition of the principle of personal property, and the consequent introduction of absolute community of property.'

The simplest, and probably the most superficial, objection to socialist and communist policies related to their impracticability. During the initial discussions about the *Deutsche Zeitung*, Hecker 'expounded his communistic views with his customary impudence.... He was, however, silenced by the simple dry remark of Gervinus: that he would like to hear how they thought these often heard phrases could be translated into real life through practical political institutions.'[25]

Certainly the institutions introduced in France after the February revolution—and the theories underlying them—appeared impractical. They were not immediately or completely rejected, however. The *Deutsche Zeitung* was interested to see whether they would work out in the praxis of republican life; French developments would at least show whether direct action by the state was better than indirect ways of solving or mitigating the social problem. Yet the schemes were bound to fail because of the individual selfishness and laziness of men who would not work unless they had to: the schemes would 'promote indolence, man's animal nature will become predominant' [*DZ* no. 63, 3 March 1848, pp. 501–2 on 'Frankreich' and no. 78, 18 March 1848, leading article]. Very similar views were expressed in the great Frankfurt debate on the social question in February 1849 by a number of liberal deputies, most clearly perhaps by Moritz Mohl who, though he did not belong to a club, nevertheless stood quite close to the Württemberger Hof.[26]

If individual selfishness was used in the argument, class selfishness was even more important. Louis Blanc was singled out for criticism because he emphasized the interests of the fourth estate against the third; the domination of one class by another was firmly rejected: 'The classes cannot be separated and their interests even less. They are forever linked together' [*DZ* no. 283, 21 October 1848, leading article]. According to the report of the Economic Committee of the Frankfurt Parliament on Article 30 of the Fundamental Rights, 'laws protect the worker no less than they do the employer' [*St. B.* VII, p. 5102].

The liberals almost universally saw socialism and communism as a despotism worse than any other. This is true of Mathy [Angermann, 'Karl Mathy', p. 519], Welcker, Schulz, Abt, the writers of the *Deutsche Zeitung* [for example, *DZ* no. 193, 13 July 1848, leading article], to give only a few examples. These doctrines were imposed

[25] F. D. Bassermann, *Denkwürdigkeiten ... 1811–1855* (Frankfurt, 1926), p. 18.

[26] *Stenographischer Bericht über die Verhandlungen der deutschen constituirenden Nationalversammlung zu Frankfurt am Main ...* hrsg. von F. Wigard (9 vols, Leipzig, 1848–50, hereafter *St.B.*), VII, pp. 5100–121, 5127–47 and at p. 5109.

on human nature, they disregarded or oppressed individualism, individual freedom, which had to be distinguished from egotism. Schulz saw community, equality and individuality as the main features of human nature, and criticized communism for imposing community alone at the expense of the other two. A similar point was made by Abt: socialism rejected individualism and subjected it to an abstract generality (*Allgemeinheit*). Biedermann went further than most in the socialist direction when he described men as neither purely social nor purely individual beings, but even he saw in independence and self-reliance the 'vital principle, the essential key-note of human nature'.[27]

Socialist interference with, and communist abolition of, private property were very strongly objected to, as the right to property was generally regarded as one of the most basic rights and freedoms. Rotteck, Welcker and Schulz were quite agreed on this, although they would not go quite so far as the French politician Ducoux, who claimed that property made man into an ethical being (*sittliches Wesen*) [*cf. DZ* no. 193, as above].

That the sanctity of property as the basis of society should be emphasized by middle-class writers is not at all surprising. We would expect them to hold this view, as they did when the Prussian goverment declared an amnesty for the theft of goods under the value of five *Thaler* in cases of extreme need. A writer in the *Deutsche Zeitung*, probably John Prince-Smith, argued very forcefully that property had to be protected at all times, particular in times of great need [*DZ* no. 117, 25 October 1847, p. 391, 'A Berlin'; Bergsträsser, p. 347]. It is far more surprising that the strong views expressed in this article seem to be an exception.

Rotteck, for instance, believed that the safeguarding of the property rights of the citizen, rights which were founded on the law of reason and which existed before the state, were the rational justification of the state [*RW2* IV, pp. 211–16]. He admitted that inequalities—unavoidable inequalities—existed, yet for the state to violate the sanctity of the property of the rich in order to assist the poor would cause more evils than it would cure: the end would be poverty for everyone. The state must, nevertheless, abolish privileges which promote an unequal distribution of wealth, free industry from restrictions and provide education even for the lowest classes; legal equality should be introduced. These measures would not abolish but they would largely mitigate the evils which arise from economic inequality [Rohr, p. 110]. Welcker went further. He defended property rights against threatening communist despotism, but disapproved of the chance distribution of wealth. He wanted to divide property in a 'materially just' way, equally according to the service of each head of a family

---

[27] Rohr, pp. 153–4. For full references to articles by Welcker, Schulz and Abt, see pp. 61 and 65 above.

to general culture and relative to their proven needs. The fundamental safeguard lay in the eternal principles of justice and their application to the conditions of life [*RW2* IV, pp. 216–17]. Schulz thought that the right to property had to be defended, but was not absolute; individual property rights should not deprive others of the necessary means of education and life. But the acquisition of property was not a desirable over-riding aim in life, it was vulgar, evil, sinful. Many liberals, and not only intellectuals like Droysen, Arndt, and Welcker but also industrialists like Mevissen, valued work highly, but condemned it if it was directed to the mere amassing of wealth.[28]

III

'It comes down to this: the excessive riches and over-education of the privileged classes must be diverted in favour of the proletariat,' wrote Struve [*RW2* XI, p. 216]. If the liberals disagreed with the socialist solutions, they must have had some ideas themselves about the ways in which the social problem could be solved. Struve himself had some proposals to make, vague and mild as they were: general legal and constitutional reforms, and a 'just' system of taxation. Reform of the taxation system was certainly one of the solutions liberals put forward. Many articles in the *Staatslexikon* dealt with taxation and put forward schemes of reform, but practical answers were most clearly advanced in two parliamentary debates, the first on the abolition of the slaughtering and milling tax in the Prussian United Diet of 1847, and the second on Article 30 of the Fundamental Rights in the Frankfurt Parliament in February 1849.

Camphausen saw the abolition of indirect taxes on necessities of life as social progress [Valentin I, p. 77]. Many liberals, particularly Hansemann,[29] were in favour of replacing them by an income tax, perhaps even a progressive income tax. 'The capacity to pay taxes should be the basis of the tax burden', argued the *Deutsche Zeitung* which devoted some of its first leading articles to this question. These early articles went further than most liberals would go. The *Deutsche Zeitung* itself later feared [*DZ* nos 4, 5 and 15, 4, 5 and 15 July 1847, and no. 80, 20 March 1848, leading articles] that too high an income tax might reduce the incentive to economic activity and might even cause damage to those whom it intended to help. Its leading article on the Frankfurt debate mentioned with approval Moritz Mohl's rejection of a progressive income tax and his defence of some in-

[28] W. Hock, *Liberales Denken im Zeitalter der Paulskirche: Droysen und die Frankfurter Mitte* (Münster, 1957), pp. 108–10.
[29] See *Neue deutsche Biographie* (Berlin, 1953, in progress) VII, p. 628 and J. Hansen (ed.), *Rheinische Briefe und Akten ... 1830–1850* (Publikationen der Gesellschaft für Rheinische Geschichtskunde, 36, 2 vols, Bonn, 1919) II *passim*.

direct taxes. Yet it is clear from Mohl's speech, and from that of Georg Beseler, that their opposition was not to a just reform of the taxation system in the interest of greater equality, but to an incorporation of specific measures into the constitution [*DZ* no. 42, 11 February 1849, leading article; *St. B.* VII, pp. 5107–9, 5141].

Equality, that is legal equality, was one of the great remedies proposed. The *Deutsche Zeitung* included the principle in its programme, and returned to it in many leading articles [*DZ, Ankündigungsblatt*, 8 May 1847; no. 2, 2 July 1847, no. 1, 1 January 1848, and no. 230, 21 August 1848]. But legal equality was clearly not enough.

> The main thing is that each individual should be provided with the opportunity so to employ his energies, in accordance with his inclinations and ability, and to acquire so much money as would enable him to live a human life.[30] This aim will be achieved … by calling to life the idea of the state, by using the state structure not for private but for public interests, that is, for the well-being of all individuals, by guaranteeing to everyone his part in the administration of the state, and by counteracting, through appropriate laws, the inequality of property and the absolutism of money [*RW2* IV, p. 526].

The role of the state is emphasized in this quotation. This was not to be a night-watchman state, a *laissez-faire* state, a state which would confine its activities to a minimum. On the contrary, the state should take an active part in maintaining justice, including economic and social justice, it should protect the well-being of all its citizens. Many examples can be found of liberals wanting the state to play an active part. Rotteck wanted the state to set a limit to industrial development, Hansemann wanted the state to assist it. Robert von Mohl proposed a whole range of activities [Sheehan, p. 599; Rohr, pp. 123–5]. Moritz, Mohl and many others wanted economic well-being, including employment, to be safeguarded by the state's tariff policy [*St. B.* VII, p. 5109]. Even the more radical writers took this view: Oppenheim, writing about workers' riots, desired that the state should think about saving the greater part of its subjects' [*RW2* I, p. 615].

This state, however, does not appear to be a Hegelian state where impartial bureaucracy, the universal class, would be the safeguard against the self-interest and conflict inherent in civil society. I have not found reflections of Hegelian ideas in the literature I have surveyed. On the contrary, bureaucracy was attacked as a vested interest and as a disturbing factor which tended to divide society. It was seen as willing to increase the numbers of the proletariat in order to have a more effective ally against liberal reform [*DZ* no. 106, 14 October

---

[30] A leading article, *DZ* no. 105, 13 October 1847, qualifies this to 'as would satisfy his desire to enjoy life'.

1847, leading article; no. 182 (should be 183), 31 December 1847, p. 1461, [Heidelberg].

Such conflicts would disappear without the extreme means proposed by socialism and communism. In a liberal state 'the welfare of the fatherland would be based on the legal and organic unity of all classes and on their staunch, self-reliant co-operation'. The life of the new state would involve 'all classes of the nation, the poor and the rich, those who earn their living with the work of their hands, those who do so with intellectual labour'. 'Classes cannot be separated from each other, and their interests even less. They are linked together for ever.' All would work together, 'without regard to their class, birth, descent ... in the measure of their *Tüchtigkeit* [fitness, ability, competence—there is no exact English equivalent] and the confidence felt in them' [*DZ* n. 27, 27 January 1848, leading article; no. 101, 10 April 1848, p. 802; nos 283 and 226, 21 October and 16 August 1848, leading articles].

A state based on such social harmony and cooperation has its important tasks, but it need not interfere excessively. Much could be left to the self-regulation of society, and in this pride of place was given to the principle of association. Biedermann believed in self-help association, Mathy argued for trade associations in the organization of work—though by no means in Blanc's sense—and in poor relief [Rohr, p. 153; Angermann, 'Karl Mathy', pp. 521–2]. Many tasks of social policy should be divided between elected and self-governing local government bodies and voluntary associations. Voluntary associations should be formed to give interest-free loans to artisans and peasants who needed capital, to establish workshops where the unemployed could be gainfully occupied and looked after [*DZ* nos 25, 27 and 28, 25, 27 and 28 January 1848, leading articles]. Lette argued in the Frankfurt debate that the workers should use the right of association to discuss and improve their condition, and even to negotiate about their wages and conditions of work. Georg Beseler, in his speech, eulogized the 'old German institution' of the spirit of association [*St. B.* VII, pp. 5132, 5141–2].

Some state action, then, tempered and supplemented by free associations; generally free, and unselfish, economic activity; a spirit of harmony, of cooperation, of devoted unselfish work on the part of all—this is the picture of the future society. But even if we accept that such a society is possible, how can we reconcile it with the picture of the lazy and selfish worker who will not work unless he is forced to? The indolent and selfish worker occurs again and again in writings and speeches, some of which have been quoted above; he occurs again in the Frankfurt debates, in the attacks on the democratic amendment which provided for state unemployment benefits [*St.B.* VII, pp. 5104–5]. Clearly more was needed than the institutions and ideals so far discussed. To solve the social question, to gain the greatest benefit possible from the new free and popular institutions, the lower classes of the population had to be fitted for the task of fully fledged citizens. This is the point where we come up against the liberal concept of *Bildung*, which I shall translate as 'education', although the English word does not entirely cover the meaning of the German.[31]

Bildung could, and did, mean many things: higher education, vocational training, political and even ethical education. The liberals regarded all of them as important. Lack of education, because of lack of means, was regarded by Struve, Schulz, Oppenheim and others in the *Staatslexikon* as the greatest injustice of the social system. The *Deutsche Zeitung* repeatedly advocated the education of the masses and Schulz wrote of it as the main aim of the educational process of the time [Vierhaus, p. 545]. Not only general education was advocated, to limits to which one could profit by it, but also education in practical skills as, for instance, proposed by the economic committee of the Frankfurt Parliament.[32] It could also involve political education and the development of the moral qualities of the individual [*RW2* II, pp. 516–17; Vierhaus, pp. 542–3; *DZ* no. 117, 25 October 1847, leading article].

When the people at large had benefited from the process of education, they could not only improve their economic position but also play a full part in the self-governing activities of the state. Until then, however, the highly educated middle class would play the leading rôle. Two schemes of society by liberal writers make this quite clear. Hoffmann, in 1844, saw the educated middle class as the core of the nation; Welcker, in 1843, identified two main groups in the population, those who had higher education and those who had not, *Der Stand der Studirten* and *Der Stand der Nichtstudirten, der Bürgerstand*, the former being the leaders in state and society [Vierhaus, p. 544; *RW* xv, p. 131].

This emphasis on *Bildung* appears to have increased as time went on. To give one example: in the programme of the *Deutsche Zeitung* great stress was put on economic matters, education being only implied; even in writing about the future structure of society, Gervinus, who drafted the programme, put equal weight on 'external and internal property'. In October 1850 the paper published an article by Arndt in which we read of the class of the best-educated citizens, the class of the learned doctors, to whom one must listen if one is

---

[31] The most comprehensive recent discussion is by Rudolf Vierhaus, 'Bildung', *Geschichtliche Grundbegriffe*, hrsg. von O. Brunner, W. Conze, R. Koselleck (Stuttgart, 1972, in progress) I, pp. 508–51.

[32] *St.B.* VII, p. 5102; *Abschnitt* VI, Article 6, paragraphs 152–8 of the Frankfurt Constitution, in E. R. Huber, *Dokumente zur deutschen Verfassungsgeschichte* (3 vols, Stuttgart, 1961–6) I, p. 320.

to hear the voice of the people, the voice of the age, the voice of God, and no mention is made of property at all.[33]

IV

These best-educated citizens, we have seen, knew about the social question and were concerned with the problems it raised. Yet, when they met at Frankfurt, they did not attack such problems but turned to legal and constitutional ones. They wanted to discuss the political aspects of the reforms first. This was, of course, the purpose for which they were elected: they were to form a 'constituent National Assembly' and constitutions are political. They began their constitution-making by drafting the Fundamental Rights of the German People. Yet it is important to remember that, in spite of the many social demands incorporated in the fundamental rights section of the resolutions of the Pre-Parliament, the first drafts of the Fundamental Rights were kept entirely political, or were social only to the extent that they tended to abolish traditional privileges. This was true especially of the draft of the Committee of Seventeen. In the draft of the *Vorkommission* and the text proposed by the Constitutional Committee, we find more and more social demands intruding, largely because of pressure from the democratic elements in parliament.[34] Nevertheless, even in February 1849, in his speech at the close of the social question debate, Georg Beseler stated unequivocally, on behalf of the Constitutional Committee, that they held 'to the principle of including only the political aspects of the creation of German unity in the constitution and of leaving the social problems to find their solution in a different way' [*St.B.* VII, p. 5141], that is, through legislation to be introduced by the ministry to which many petitions on social matters were referred [for example, *St.B.* VII, p. 5103].

The instinct of the centre groups, which dominated parliament, might well have been right when they decided to give priority to political matters. Lorenz von Stein thought so. In his very interesting analysis published in 1852, he wrote that there was a possibility of creating a new state as there was unity of opinion on the *Staatsidee* or *Reichsidee*. The way to destroy this unity of opinion was to intro-

---

[33] *DZ, Ankündigungsblatt*, 8 May 1847; no. 276, 3 October 1850, Beilage. How far this increasing emphasis on the *Bildungsbürgertum* foreshadows the split with the *Wirtschaftsbürgertum* which W. Bussmann places in the late 1850s ('Zur Geschichte des deutschen Liberalismus im 19. Jahrhundert', *Historische Zeitschrift* CLXXXVI (1958), pp. 527–57 at pp. 541ff.) cannot be explored here but would merit attention.

[34] *Bundesbeschluss*, 7 April 1848 in Huber, *Dokumente* I, pp. 274, 273. For the successive versions of the Fundamental Rights draft, see H. Scholler (ed.), *Die Grundrechtsdiskussion in der Paulskirche: eine Dokumentation* (Darmstadt, 1973), especially pp. 51–5 and 62ff.

duce social questions on which there was no agreement, to begin by attempting to draft a constitution for the society of a yet non-existent state, that is, to enact a set of fundamental rights [*GW* VII, pp. 557–60]. Stein was probably right. The social question was a deeply divisive one. Yet its discussion could not be postponed or avoided, the distress and dissatisfaction of the lower classes was too great, their advocates too vocal. Biedermann foresaw the difficulty in 1847:

> It would be the greatest misfortune if the socialist movement overtook the political one, if the movement penetrated the lower classes before the middle classes are completely emancipated and fitted for participation in the life of the state . . . The more one promotes the political education and maturity of the people, the more it participates in the maintenance of order and the promotion of general interests through a free participation in the life of the state, through self-government, the surer one will be that the social movement can be steered into harmless and beneficial channels through gradual reform [Biedermann I, pp. 160–61.]

What Biedermann feared in 1847 came true in 1848. Political and social problems had to be solved at the same time. This was impossible. Here lies the tragedy of the German revolution.

V

A brief essay like this can do no more than raise certain themes, put forward some tentative explanations. It has to disregard many aspects of the question completely and cannot do full justice to the large problems discussed. Only a full-scale treatment of its subject could prove the validity of the views put forward. Much will depend on the features emphasized, on the acceptance of idealistic views as independent and genuine, not determined by economic class interest.

The crucial point seems to me whether a historian can accept the liberal philosophy of organic wholeness, of cooperation, of hostility to individual and class selfishness as genuine. I have certainly found no evidence of conscious economic class interest in my reading. But this does not necessarily disprove the existence of unconscious class interest, or the derivation from it of such views. The Marxian view holds that the ideological superstructure is determined by the economic sub-structure, without man being aware of such determination or even of its influence. The trouble with using such unconscious or sub-conscious influences in historical explanation is that, *ex hypothesi*, their existence, particularly in the case of individuals or small groups, is going to be extremely difficult—perhaps impossible —to establish.

6

'The Party of the Proletariat': Marx and Engels in the Revolution of 1848

Eugene Kamenka

I

The years of 1848 and 1849 were a high point—perhaps the high point—of the careers of Marx and Engels as revolutionaries. In the early 1840s, under the influence of Feuerbach and of the Young Hegelians, especially of Bruno Bauer, the young Marx had stood for a rational society in which man would be free and self-determined as a social being, cooperating rationally and spontaneously with his fellows, mastering nature, social institutions and social life instead of being mastered by them. As editor of the liberal *Rheinische Zeitung*, in 1842 and part of 1843—virtually until its suppression by the Prussian censorship—Marx had stood for democracy, the rights and needs of the poor and the claims of reason as against autocracy, censorship and privilege. Late in 1843 and in 1844, on becoming more seriously aware of French socialism and of Moses Hess's work on money, Marx proclaimed that such a transformation of society had for its prime targets the two fundamental conditions and expressions of human alienation: money and the state. The struggle against these required not only philosophy—'the lightning of thought'—but also 'a material weapon'. This weapon was the proletariat: the class outside existing society and its existing system of property which was fitted, by its very deprivation, to overcome the whole apparatus of social and economic coercion and to inaugurate the society of freedom.

The emphasis on a material weapon had both theoretical and practical consequences. Marx and Engels, who had previously met but not much liked each other, had both contributed to the *Deutsch-französische Jahrbücher* of 1844. Engels's critique of modern political economy there, as bearing on its brows all the revolting marks of avarice and resting on alienation and logical contradictions, attracted Marx's favourable attention. One of the most momentous literary partnerships in history began. In Marx's *Economico-Philosophical Manuscripts* of 1884 and, more concretely and less philosophically, in *The German Ideology*, which he and Engels wrote together in

Brussels in 1845 and 1846 after Marx had 'discovered' the materialist interpretation of history, the theoretical foundations for practical, material struggle began to be laid. The division of labour, accompanied by private property, they argued, made men the slaves of a social system of production instead of allowing them to be its masters; forced each man to play out a certain rôle, to subordinate himself to his needs and to the abstract economic rôle, or money, necessary to satisfy those needs; brought man into conflict with other men; forced men to live at each other's expense. This alienation was both monstrous and dehumanizing, but it was also a necessary step in the history of mankind. If the division of labour made men slaves to the process of production, it also enabled them to realize and perfect their powers. The process of production, developing by its own logic, was the great moulder and educator of mankind. The 'material' life of men, Marx discovered between the spring and autumn of 1845, shaped and explained their political institutions, ideas, conceptions, and legal systems. The history or 'pre-history' of man in the period of alienation and consequent class struggle was to be understood through economic history or, at least, through the history of material production.

By 1848, when Marx and Engels published the *Communist Manifesto*, they had worked out the outlines of the general view that has come to be almost inextricably linked with Marx's name. The introduction of tools, the division of labour and the rise of private property divide men into social classes, primarily into the class of exploiters who own and administer means of production and the class or classes of the exploited who actually work and produce. Each class of exploiters—slave owners, feudal lords, capitalist merchants and manufacturers—comes upon the arena of history as the bearer of economic enterprise, as a class developing new techniques of production and increasing human capacities. But the class relationships in a social system tend to be rigid, whereas the productive forces are constantly developing. There comes a time, at each stage, when the class which inaugurated and developed a given mode of production becomes a fetter upon further development and is swept aside by revolutionary change. Thus slave owners give way to feudal landlords and feudal landlords give way to the bourgeoisie. The state, which pretends to represent the *general* social interest is in fact a *sectional* interest, safeguarding the social and political conditions congenial to the ruling class.

The alienation and 'contradiction' expressed in the class struggles of history is oppressive and dehumanizing, but it is nevertheless *necessary* for the development of economic and human potentialities, for *progress*. Thus, in the *Communist Manifesto*, Marx and Engels recognize fully the historic rôle of the bourgeoisie in developing

human productivity and capacities, in tearing down privileges, superstitions and national barriers.

The bourgeoisie, however, is also doomed. The 'inner logic of
capitalism'—economic forces independent of the will of man—will
produce the breakdown of the whole system of private property and
production for a market; it will raise in its stead the socialist-
communist society of conscious cooperation and rational planning.
Then production will be *socially* controlled and directed toward use
instead of profit. Man will cease to be the *object* of history, the slave
of a productive process that he himself created, and will become master
of himself, society and nature. Human relations, instead of being
determined by forces beyond man's individual control, will assume
the aspect of rational and intelligible relations; they will no longer
be 'mystified'—concealed from the consciousness of the actors involved through their abstraction from their real context and their real
purpose. Men will act as conscious and cooperative members of a
community and will cease to live and act as individuals existing at
each other's expense. To make all this possible, the *Communist Manifesto* proclaims, the workers of the world must unite: only the
proletariat that is forming itself 'into a class and consequently into
a political party' can be the agent of this transformation. It must
overthrow the existing coercive state and the system of private
property and sectional privilege which that state protects; it must place
production under social control by abolishing private property and
nationalizing the means of production, distribution and exchange.
'The proletariat', says the *Communist Manifesto*, 'will use its political
supremacy to wrest, by degrees, all capital from the bourgeoisie, to
centralize all instruments of production in the hands of the state, i.e.
of the proletariat organized as the ruling class.' To do this, at least
in the conditions in which Marx and Engels were writing in the 1840s,
it must make a revolution.

The theory of revolution that Marx and Engels proclaimed in the
Communist Manifesto as a general theory was unquestionably a mile-
stone in the development of the concept of revolution as a category
in social thought. It may be called, and has been called, a *realist* theory
of revolution, synthesizing and correcting earlier naturalistic and
romantic conceptions of revolution. To the vast majority of social
thinkers and statesmen and politicians before 1791, social revolution
was a natural and therefore irresistible event, a turn in the wheel of
fortune that destroys one form of government and casts up another
with some of the inexorability of the revolution of the planets. It was
even governed, for many, by a cyclical law of *corsi* and *ricorsi*. With
the French Revolution came the romantic concept – revolution as an
act of will. Marx and Engels say it is both and neither. Revolutions
take place as part of the general laws of historical development; they

are inevitable and irresistible, they both rest upon and require objective conditions. But they do not take place by themselves: men make their own history and the history of men is a history of class struggles, of the conscious or unconscious pursuits of interests, of consciousness and political organization. Tools, knowledge and machines may make revolution inevitable, but the revolution itself is made by men, historically shaped into classes—by disciplined, conscious men, in modern conditions by the party of the proletariat.

To the music of nationalism, Marx and Engels were deaf. They recognized, as we shall see, that the world of the 1840s was a world of nation-states or nations, some politically independent and some in bondage. They pursued tactics and preached policies in relation to national conflicts and movements of national liberation. They thought some nationalities were culturally and historically superior to others. But their proletarian 'internationalism' was perfectly genuine: the only real conflict for them was the conflict between bourgeois and proletarian; everything else was subordinate, tactical, transitional. Mazzini was, in the Europe of 1848, a far more important and better known figure than either Marx or Engels, but for the socialist view of the world and the socialist perception of 1848, he is only an embarrassment. Political nationalism, I have argued elsewhere,[1] becomes important, even overwhelmingly important, as an energizing charge in the life of a society only where the transition from dynastic rule to political democracy cannot rest upon an independently defined and established political community. Oliver Cromwell, the men who made the great French Revolution of 1789 and those who sought the union or federation and independence of the American and Australian colonies could take for granted the existence of a national community, for geographical, historical and political reasons. In the German lands and the Austrian Empire of 1848, the revolutionaries could not. But precisely because that problem was a political problem—a precondition, in the eyes of nationalists and democrats for further social development—Marx and Engels saw it as distracting attention from the real problem, substituting political revolution for social revolution, the drive to unity for the war of classes. Revolution, not constitution-making, was their concern.

The year 1848 was the first, and ideologically as opposed to intellectually still the most important, culmination of Marx's theoretical endeavour. In the *Communist Manifesto*, we have not only a political pamphlet of great power and skill, which presents the aspirations of a particular class, or party, or even of the authors themselves, as the

[1] Eugene Kamenka, 'Political Nationalism—the Evolution of an Idea', in Eugene Kamenka (ed.), *Nationalism: the Nature and Evolution of an Idea* (Canberra, 1973, London, 1976), pp. 2–20.

irresistible and unquestionable demand of history; we have the first full yet simple statement of the great Marxian synthesis of widespread, familiar, but conflicting, socialist hopes and aspirations: the demands for freedom, for community, for social planning, for equality and for sufficiency; the romantic elevation of the face-to-face idealized organic community of the past and the acceptance of social planning and the welfare and organizational powers of the state; the hatred for the rich and powerful, and for the whole system of wage-slavery, coupled with the affirmation of social, political and industrial discipline and of the liberating effects of technological progress. Revolution is given the dignity and appeal of a historical categorical imperative and those who stray from the true path, whatever their motives, are shown to belong to the rubbish bin of history. The *Communist Manifesto* may be and has been embarrassing for those who want to find in Marxism a subtle and sophisticated science of society, recognizing complexity, coming to grips with the internal self-transformation of capitalism that became more evident from the 1860s onwards. But it is a document for revolutionaries. It has appealed to them and continues to appeal to them even though so much of the world has changed. It has appealed most, of course, not in the transformed centres of advanced capitalism of today, but in those countries—relics of empires, newly liberated areas, pre-capitalist societies—whose politics, traditions and problems are so much closer to the Europe of 1848 than to the United States or northwestern Europe today.

But the actual beliefs of men who are moved to act, and the theories of intellectuals about the springs of action and the purposes of actors, are separate and different things. The *Communist Manifesto*, as we shall see, was published in London in German in February 1848 as a leisurely prediction of a revolutionary storm that was in fact about to burst. As a pamphlet and as a programme of a group of exiles calling themselves a party, it had no direct influence on that revolution or the thoughts of the men who made it. Even those who stood closest in the political spectrum to Marx and Engels were, as we shall see, full of different, 'incorrect', thoughts and attitudes. There was in 1848 no important socialist spokesman at a national level, and no important popular group or party, that stood on the position of Marx or Engels. The *Communist Manifesto* lives, like all of Marx's writings, by its clarity and coherence, its incisiveness and its power, not by its impact on the minds of men at the time or by its correct perception of what it was that brought them to political revolt. That story was to be repeated in the Paris Commune of 1871, which did so much to revive the fortunes of the then long-forgotten *Communist Manifesto*. Reactionaries may have screamed that Marx was the *éminence grise* of the dreaded Commune. The historian knows better.

Even the French section of the First International in 1871, which did not direct the Commune but played a part in it, was not Marxist but Proudhonian. Even less did the workers who took to the streets in 1848 have in mind, or flourish in their hands, the *Communist Manifesto* of Marx and Engels. The importance of the pamphlet, and of Marx and Engels themselves as towering figures in socialist movements, was to lie in the future—above all, in the years after their death.

II

If the year 1848 was the culmination of the evolution of the young Marx and Engels into ideologists of revolution, it was also the consummation of their youthful careers as practical revolutionaries, displaying the mixture of unromantic clear-sightedness and quarrelsome intransigence, devotion to a cause and jealousy of rivals or actual and potential opposition, that was to remain characteristic of Marx especially. With the suppression of the *Rheinische Zeitung* in 1843 and his marriage to Jenny von Westphalen in June of that year, Marx rejected an offer of employment in the Prussian civil service and emigrated to Paris. There, in 1844, he attended an international democratic banquet with Leroux, Louis Blanc, Pyat and Bakunin present and formed contact with the leaders of the communist League of the Just and some clandestine French workers' associations. Soon he was in personal touch with Proudhon and Bakunin and collaborating with the radical socialist group publishing the German émigré newspaper, *Vorwärts*, in Paris. On 11 January 1845, the French ministry of the interior, after complaints from Prussia, ordered that Marx and other members of the *Vorwärts* group leave France. Marx with his wife and daughter settled in Brussels. There, later that year, he relinquished his citizenship of the Prussian Union and thus entered upon a lifelong exile that was to be interrupted only by the events of 1848 and 1849.

It was in Brussels in February and March 1846 that Marx and Engels embarked on their conspiratorial careers. They founded in those months a communist Correspondence Committee to engage in international propaganda and lay the foundations for an international communist organization that would continue the work of the League of the Just. Its members, almost entirely young German émigrés with a sprinkling of artisans, included Marx's wife Jenny and her brother, Edgar von Westphalen, Moses Hess, the poet Ferdinand Freiligrath, the simple Christian-communist Wilhelm Weitling, author of *The Guarantees of Harmony and Freedom*, who had suffered for the cause in Swiss gaols and whose name was then far better known than Marx's, and the revolutionary agitator Wilhelm Wolff ('Lupus') to whom Marx was to dedicate *Capital*. By the end of March, Marx was denouncing the sectarian 'artisan-communism' of Weitling, with its rejection of political struggle, and the philosophical communism of Karl Grün and the true socialists, and demanding a 'sorting-out of the party', as he called it. By May Marx, in the name of the Correspondence Committee, was writing to Proudhon in Paris asking for regular reports on France and warning an unimpressed Proudhon against Grün, denouncing the 'empty Communism' of Hermann Kriege and his New York German radical paper, *Volkstribun*, and demanding that a London Correspondence Committee be formed by the German émigrés there on the basis of the London League of the Just and its associated organization, the German Workers' Educational Association. London in reply complained about the 'academic arrogance' of the Brussels Committee and suggested that attitudes to so-called sentimental communism be discussed at the proposed communist congress in London. Meanwhile Marx and Engels and other members of the Brussels Committee established contact with communists in the Wuppertal and Silesia and sent an address to the Chartist Feargus O'Connor, congratulating him on his electoral victory in Nottingham.

The first Congress of Communists urged by the Brussels Committee took place in London in June 1847. Marx, in financial difficulties and unable to raise the fare, was represented by Engels and Wilhelm Wolff. The Congress resolved to reorganize the League of the Just as the Communist League, to draft a communist credo for the next congress and to expel the followers of Weitling. The Brussels Correspondence Committee two months later became the Brussels Chapter of the Communist League, with Marx as president and a German Workers' Association as a wholly controlled subsidiary. In October, Marx in a series of articles for the *Deutsche-Brüsseler Zeitung* emphasized the importance of a bourgeois revolution as a precondition for the proletarian revolution, but denounced his admirer, the revolutionary Karl Heinzen, for attacking princes instead of the bourgeoisie. In November, Marx was elected vice-president of the Association Démocratique—what we would today call a front organization—and travelled to London for the second Congress of the Communist League, held secretly in its Great Windmill Street premises over ten days. He and Engels were commissioned to prepare a statement of principles of the League now purged of Weitling and his utopian socialists, under the title *Manifesto of the Communist Party* (the term party here referring not to the League, but rather to the communist movement as such). Marx, in London, addressed a rally on behalf of Poland, proposed, in the name of the Association Démocratique, the holding of an international democratic congress in 1848, and had discussions with George Julian Harney (later known to Marx and Engels privately as 'Mr Hip Hip Hooray'), Ernest Charles Jones and other English Chartists. In January 1848, Marx, making little use of an earlier draft prepared by Engels, completed the manuscript of the *Communist Manifesto* and sent it to London, where it was published, originally without the names of its authors, a few days before revolution broke out in Paris on 21 February 1848. No copies arrived there until March. Engels, at the same time, was expelled from Paris and arrived in Brussels. With revolution in the air, Marx began to take an active part in preparation for an armed republican uprising in Brussels and encouraged similar preparations in Cologne. On 3 March, he received, virtually simultaneously, an invitation from the provisional government of France to return to French soil, and an order issued on behalf of the king of Belgium that he leave Belgium within twenty-four hours. He, his wife and two children (by now) left under armed escort.

The takeover of the old League of the Just by Marx, Engels and their followers was efficient, thorough and ungentlemanly. Marx's strength in these operations did not lie in his charm or in any capacity to inspire widespread loyalty and admiration for him as a person, nor did it rest on any gift of oratory (which he conspicuously lacked). He had, it is true, a certain taste for intrigue and a total lack of scruple or compassion in the matter of personal denunciation. Marx is a man who is diminished by his personal correspondence, just as Freud is a man whose stature is enhanced by his. But by and large Marx's penchant for intrigue, as in his correspondence with Proudhon, tended to be self-defeating: it produced revulsion rather than support. Marx's strength as a revolutionary activist was entirely intellectual: his mind was sharper, his thoughts were clearer, his knowledge was greater than that of any other person in the socialist movement, and he backed his capacity for brilliant analysis, cogent general theorizing and powerful pamphleteering with total intellectual self-confidence and intransigence. One contemporary after another, in letters and reminiscences, confirms this characterization of Marx, differing only on the relative importance they ascribe to his arrogance and his abilities. Years later, the émigré Carl Schurz recalled meeting Marx in Cologne in the summer of 1848 when Marx, as we shall see, was at the height of his rôle as a revolutionary activist. Schurz wrote:

> Karl Marx ... could not have been much more than thirty years old at that time, but he was already the recognized head of the advanced socialistic school. The somewhat thick-set man, with broad forehead, very black hair and beard and dark sparkling eyes, at once attracted general attention. He enjoyed the reputation of having acquired great learning, and as I knew very little of his discoveries and theories, I was all the more eager to gather words of wisdom from the lips of the famous man. This expectation was disappointed in a peculiar way. Marx's utterances were indeed full of meaning, logical and clear, but I have never

seen a man whose bearing was so provoking and intolerable. To no opinion which differed from his own did he accord the honor of even condescending consideration. Everyone who contradicted him he treated with abject contempt; every argument that he did not like he answered either with biting scorn at the unfathomable ignorance that had prompted it, or with opprobrious aspersions upon the motives of him who had advanced it. I remember most distinctly the cutting disdain with which he pronounced the word 'bourgeois'; and as a 'bourgeois'— that is, as a detestable example of the deepest mental and moral degeneracy—he denounced everyone who dared to oppose his opinion. . . . It was very evident that not only had he had not won any adherents, but had repelled many who otherwise might have become his followers.[2]

A finer and more sensitive person, the Russian P. Annenkov, had reached a remarkably similar judgement two years earlier:

Marx was the sort of man who is packed with energy, force of character and unshakable conviction—a type highly remarkable in outward appearance as well. In spite of the thick black mane of hair on his head, his hairy hands and his crookedly buttoned frock coat, he gave the impression of a man who has the right and the power to command respect, no matter how he appears before you or what he does. All his movements were angular, but bold and confident; his manners directly violated all accepted social conventions. They were proud and somehow contemptuous, while his sharp, metallic voice matched remarkably well the radical judgments he was continually passing on men and things. Marx never spoke at all except to pronounce judgments which permitted no appeal, and he said everything in a painfully harsh tone. This tone expressed his firm conviction that he had a mission to rule men's minds, to legislate for them, to compel them to follow him. Before me stood the personification of a democratic dictator, as one might imagine it in a moment of fantasy.[3]

Arriving in Paris in March 1848, in the period of revolutionary upswing and revolutionary hopes, Marx, as secretary, participated in a meeting of the four Paris sections of the Communist League and busied himself in founding a German Workers' Club and arranging for German exiles to return to Germany. Proletarian internationalism was one thing; Marx's particular work and possibility of exercising influence clearly lay in Germany. The democratic German poet, Georg Herwegh, had already formed in Paris a German Legion to return to the fatherland and promote the democratic revolution there.

[2] Carl Schurz, *Reminiscences* (3 vols, New York, 1918) I, pp. 138–9. For this and other contemporary characterizations of Marx, see Eugene Kamenka, *The Portable Karl Marx* (New York, 1980), Section I: 'Karl Marx The Man—in His Letters and in the Eyes of His Family and His Contemporaries.'

[3] P. Annenkov, 'A Wonderful Ten Years', in *Vestnik Yevropy*, no. 4, April 1880, p. 407. The last sentence with the words 'democratic dictator' is regularly omitted in Soviet citations.

'Bornstedt and Herwegh', Marx wrote on 16 March to Engels who was still in Brussels, 'behave like blackguards. They have founded a black, red and gold [the German republican colours] society directed against us. The former is to be expelled from the League today.' Marx, Karl Schapper, H. Bauer, Engels, J. Moll, Wilhelm Wolff and others of the Communist League, having clearly broken with Herwegh's Legion, drafted a leaflet, *The Demands of the Communist Party in Germany*, published in Paris on 31 March, reproduced in various democratic German newspapers in the beginning of April and reprinted in Cologne during the summer. The leaflet, after calling on proletarians of all countries to unite, presented seventeen demands. The whole of Germany was to be declared a single and indivisible republic, every German over twenty-one without criminal record was to be able to vote and be elected, representatives of the people were to be paid, the whole population was to be armed, so that there could be forces of workers and the army could organize labour and produce more than the cost of its upkeep. The exercise of justice was to be free of charge, all feudal dues, tributes, duties, tithes and so on were to be abolished without compensation, the estates of princes and other feudal lords, and all mines and pits were to become state property. Mortgages on peasant lands were also to be declared state property, with the interest going to the state. One state bank was to replace all private banks, issuing legal tender and regulating credit in the interest of the whole population. All means of transport were to be taken over by the state, transformed into state property and put at the free service of the needy. All civil servants were to receive the same payment without any distinction, except that those with a family, that is with more needs, would receive a higher salary. There was to be complete separation of church and state, restriction of the right of inheritance, introduction of severely progressive taxation, establishment of national workshops, state guarantee of the needs of their existence for all workers and care for those unable to work, and free education for all the people.

By April, Marx and Engels had also organized some 300 or 400 Germans to return to the fatherland in small groups and on 10 April Marx arrived in Cologne to take over the organization of the planned radical democratic newspaper, *Die Neue Rheinische Zeitung*. Its title deliberately pointed back to the first *Rheinische Zeitung*. Its first number, subtitled 'Organ of Democracy', dated 1 June, appeared on 31 May, listing Karl Marx as editor-in-chief and Engels and Wilhelm Wolff among the five editors. Cologne had been chosen for the scene of Marx's and Engels's activity on behalf of the revolution because Marx was well known there and because it possessed an active Communist League organization and, under the leadership of the socialist physician Andreas Gottschalk, had attracted some 5,000 followers into his Cologne Workers' Association. But before the *Neue Rheinische Zeitung* had even appeared, there had been sharp conflict between Marx and his followers on the one hand and Gottschalk's Cologne Workers' Association on the other hand over the latter's refusal to take part in the 'undemocratic' indirect elections for the Prussian National Diet. Gottschalk's followers, strong on principle and weak on tactics, and determined to reject all undemocratic united front causes that might be favourable to democracy, were more powerful than Marx's supporters in the local Communist League, though Marx controlled the central committee by virtue of his mandate from London. When Gottschalk refused League discipline, Marx dissolved the central committee, leaving the League headless, and made the *Neue Rheinische Zeitung* the centre and base of his operations. It was denounced by Gottschalk's followers for ignoring the workers' economic interests and concentrating on general democratic causes—what Marx regarded as the single-minded fight against autocratic regimes. 'The political programme of the *Neue Rheinische Zeitung*', Engels was to write later, 'consisted of two main points: a single, indivisible, democratic German republic, and war with Russia, which included the restoration of Poland.'[4] But if the *Neue Rheinische Zeitung* was insufficiently radical and proletarian for Gottschalk and his followers, it was certainly quite radical enough for most others. The first issue contained an article by Engels criticizing the National Assembly in Frankfurt. A number of shareholders withdrew. In June, the newspaper printed verbatim the decree of the French National Convention that had sentenced Louis XVI to death and hailed the news of the June uprising in Paris as indicating a revolution of the proletariat against the bourgeoisie. More shareholders withdrew. In July, when Gottschalk and others were arrested, Marx and Engels used the newspaper to attack the judicial authorities in Cologne and to call on the left in the Berlin National Assembly to act more energetically and to take part in an extra-parliamentary struggle. Interrogations, a search of the editorial offices and the claim that the *Neue Rheinische Zeitung* had insulted public officials were the result.

From May 1848 until May 1849 Marx and Engels contributed to the revolution in Germany almost exclusively by their work on the *Neue Rheinische Zeitung*. In the first optimistic flush of revolution, between February and June 1848, their tone was comparatively moderate, reminiscent in its rejection of demonstrative sectionalism of Marx's editorship of the *Rheinische Zeitung* of 1842–3, when he refused to frighten the liberal bourgeoisie by letting his paper become a vehicle for the 'Free [and Wild] Ones' from Berlin. With the onset of reaction after the June uprising in Paris and the Prussian emperor's

---

[4] F. Engels, 'Karl Marx and the *Neue Rheinische Zeitung*', Karl Marx and Friedrich Engels, *Selected Works* (2 vols, Moscow, 1950) II, p. 300.

recovery of will, Marx and Engels through the newspaper came to speak more frankly on behalf of revolutionary Germany—a revolutionary Germany that could only free itself and centralize itself internally by fighting externally against Russia in a great revolutionary war analogous to that of 1792. By August–September 1848, Marx had to protest against the refusal of the Cologne authorities to restore his citizenship and at the same time to try to raise money for the financially ailing *Neue Rheinische Zeitung*. The editors sponsored a mass meeting in Cologne, with delegates from other Rhenish cities to discuss the situation produced by the crises in Berlin and Frankfurt. The meeting, of over 6,000 people, declared itself for a 'democratic-social red republic', but on the same day the Frankfurt revolt was crushed. A further meeting expressed solidarity with those fighting on the barricades in Frankfurt and the *Neue Rheinische Zeitung* opened an appeal for the insurgents and their families. On 26 September, a state of siege was declared in Cologne, the *Neue Rheinische Zeitung* was suppressed and Engels, Wolff and other editors forced to leave Cologne to escape arrest. Marx remained and re-established the *Neue Rheinische Zeitung* under the same editorial committee together with Freiligrath when the state of siege was lifted on 11 October. Soon his newspaper was calling for the formation of a volunteer corps to aid revolutionary Vienna and for a refusal to pay taxes until the Prussian National Assembly was reconvened.

In November Marx was brought before the Cologne Investigatory Tribunal, in December before the Assizes, on a charge of insulting a procurator and a gendarme in articles in his newspaper; in February 1849, he, Engels and Korff were charged before the Assizes with printing material insulting officials; Marx spoke in his own defence. The accused were acquitted and the next day, Marx, Schapper and Schneider were charged before the Assizes with inciting to rebellion. Again, Marx spoke in his own defence. Again, the accused, who had considerable public sympathy in Cologne, were acquitted. But by now it was clear that the *Neue Rheinische Zeitung* could only hope to go down with its flags flying. In March it declared that it would not celebrate the anniversary of the March revolution but that of the June uprising; in May it attacked the German royal house of Hohenzollern and sympathetically reported the uprising in Elberfeld. Marx was promptly ordered to leave Prussian territory on the grounds that his paper had called for violent overthrow of the government. The last issue of the *Neue Rheinische Zeitung*, printed in red, appeared on 18 May 1849 in several editions. It contained a poem of Freiligrath, a call to the workers of Cologne warning them against any useless *putsch* in Cologne, and an editorial attacking the expulsion order against Marx and stressing that the *Neue Rheinische Zeitung* stood for a red democratic republic, for solidarity with the June uprising in Paris and for the emancipation of the working class.

Then Marx and Engels left for Frankfurt in a vain attempt to persuade the left delegates to the National Assembly to lead the uprising in southwest Germany by bringing in revolutionary forces from Baden and the Pfalz. Marx and Engels themselves went on to Baden, the Pfalz and Bingen, being arrested but then released on the way. On 3 June, Marx left for Paris as a representative of the German revolutionary parties while Engels took courageous part in the revolutionary campaigns in Baden-Pfalz, which were crushed by 13 June, when Engels escaped to Switzerland. By November 1849, they were both in London, to begin their lifelong residence in England; in 1850 they were writing on their recent experiences for the *Neue Rheinische Zeitung—Politisch-Oekonomische Revue*, published in Hamburg as a (short-lived) periodical.

Personally and politically this first great high point of the revolutionary careers of Marx and Engels ended at best ambiguously. Within a year of his arrival in London, Marx, besides being in great financial difficulties and personal distress, was involved in sharp conflicts with German émigrés in the Communist League and the German Workers' Educational Association, with the followers of Willich and Schapper. The League and its central committee split; Marx had its headquarters transferred to Cologne to end its effectiveness. In May 1851, the Cologne communists were arrested. Nasty allegations and counter-allegations of dishonesty and betrayal followed; they culminated in a series of slanders surrounding the trial of the Cologne communists in May 1852. In November, Marx dissolved the Communist League, noting that with the Cologne arrests it had in fact ceased to exist.

The first years of exile were hard and the total defeat of the European revolutions of 1848 and 1849 was not easy to accept. In the early months of 1850—in the March Address of the Central Bureau to the Communist League, for example—Marx and Engels still hoped that a new revolutionary upheaval in Germany would be sparked off by a renewed revolt of the French working class or by a counter-revolutionary military invasion of France. By the end of 1850, they knew better. Between July and December of 1850, Marx had undertaken a systematic examination of economic conditions, prices and economic crises over the preceding decade. He was led to the conclusion that the economic crisis that touched off the revolutions of 1848 had ended and that Europe would experience for a period conditions of general prosperity and rapid expansion of the means of production. The major appraisals of the 1848 revolutions and aftermath published by Marx and Engels—the series of articles 'Revolution and Counter-Revolution in Germany', written by Engels under Marx's name for the *New York Daily Tribune* in 1851, and

Marx's brilliant study of the rise of Louis Napoleon, *The Civil War in France*—inevitably bore the marks of a post-mortem.

III

When the United Diet was summoned in Prussia in 1847, that veteran of revolution and counter-revolution, Prince Metternich, warned that it would go the way of the French Estates-General of 1789, meeting to solve a financial crisis and ending by making a revolution. Certainly, the model of the French Revolution was in more minds than Metternich's. To begin with, before 1848, Marx and Engels believed that Germany still had to make its French, bourgeois revolution. In accordance with the national tradition, and as a result of its lateness, the German revolution might, in the end, be a more thoroughgoing one and it would be made with the much more conscious participation of the proletariat. It is thus that Israel Getzler, writing from the standpoint of a man deeply immersed in and conscious of the tensions between Mensheviks and Bolsheviks, minimalists and maximalists, in the Russian Revolution, has no doubt that Marx and Engels began as minimalists and began to strike a more maximalist note only in June 1848—a note reminiscent of the heresies they had so recently denounced. Before 1848, Getzler writes in his 'Marxist Revolutionaries and the Dilemma of Power',[5]

> Marx and Engels hoped and prophesied that the German revolution would be a *bourgeois revolution*. Marx, in his famous row with Wilhelm Weitling in Brussels on March 30, 1846, did more than ridicule Weitling's Utopian *Handwerkerkommunismus* as 'sentimental drivel'; he insisted that in Germany a bourgeois revolution was on the agenda. This, he stated, meant that 'there could be no talk of the immediate realization of communism—first the bourgeoisie must come to the helm.'[6] Yet Weitling had no time for the moderate counsel of scientific socialism which told impatient maximalists like himself to wait. To him 'mankind was always or never ripe [for communism]' and Marx's patient writing-desk analyses were developed 'in aloofness from the suffering world and the tribulations of the people.'[7]
> One reason why Moses Hess fell foul of Marx and Engels in 1847 was his insistence that in Germany, because of the cowardice and weakness of its bourgeoisie, a proletarian and not a bourgeois revolution was on

[5] Published in Alexander and Janet Rabinowitch (eds), *Revolution and Politics in Russia* (Bloomington, 1972), pp. 88–112 at p. 89.
[6] Wilhelm Weitling to Moses Hess, 31 March 1846, in Moses Hess, *Briefwechsel*, edited by E. Silberner (The Hague, 1959), p. 151.
[7] [Pavel Annenkov], 'Eine russische Stimme über Karl Marx', *Neue Zeit* 1 (1883), pp. 238–9; also see Max Nettlau, 'Londoner deutsche Kommunistische Diskussionen, 1845' in Grünberg's *Archiv für die Geschichte des Sozialismus und der Arbeiterbewegung* X (1922), pp. 368–70, 380, 382–3.

the agenda. However, thanks to the German *Misère*, that proletarian revolution would have to rely on an 'external stimulus', the 'approaching storm' of a French revolution.[8]

Karl Heinzen, who campaigned in 1847 for an immediate insurrection in Germany, was thus lectured by Engels and Marx: in a country like Germany, which 'industrially was so dependent and enslaved', the only possible change in property relations would be 'in the interest of the bourgeoisie and of free competition'.[9] To try to do more in a situation where the political rule of the bourgeoisie corresponded to the stage reached in the development of productive relations was futile. 'Even were the proletariat to overthrow the political domination of the bourgeoisie, its victory could only be transient, nothing but a passing moment in the service of the *bourgeois revolution* as in Anno 1794.'[10]

The *Communist Manifesto*, indeed, as Getzler goes on to remind us, diagnosed Germany as being on the eve of a bourgeois revolution and prescribed a revolutionary strategy of full support for the bourgeoisie 'whenever it acts in a revolutionary way against the absolute monarchy, the feudal squirearchy, and the petty bourgeoisie'. Engels had spelt this out in a typically more literary and less guarded fashion in a passage of his review of the year 1847, a passage which Getzler properly calls memorable:

> We need you for the time being; we even need your dominion here and there. You must remove for us the relics of the Middle Ages and the absolute monarchy; you must destroy patriarchalism, you must centralize; you must transform all more or less property-less classes into real proletarians, into recruits for us by means of your factories and trade connections; you must supply the basis for these material means which the proletariat requires for its emancipation. As your wage for this you may for a short time rule. You may dictate laws and bask in the majestic splendour which you have created; you may feast in the royal hall and wed the beautiful princess; but do not forget—'The executioner stands at the door.'[11]

No one reading the *Demands of the Communist Party in Germany*, with which Marx and Engels signalled their return to German politics, could think of their tone or their programme as conciliatory to feudalism or the big bourgeoisie. It was hardly likely to reassure even the small capitalists. Nevertheless, it is true to say that within the limits allowed by their communist principles, Marx and Engels began their activity on the *Neue Rheinische Zeitung* by emphasizing

[8] Moses Hess, *Sozialistische Aufsätze 1841–1847*, herausgegeben von Theodor Zlocisti (Berlin, 1921), pp. 229–30; Edmund Silberner, *Moses Hess, Geschichte seines Lebens* (Leiden, 1966), pp. 278–80.

[9] Karl Marx and Friedrich Engels, *Werke* (39 vols, Berlin, 1960–68) IV, p. 314.

[10] *Werke*, pp. 338–9.

[11] Getzler, p. 90, translating from Marx and Engels, *Werke*, IV, pp. 502–3.

a united democratic front, attempting to stiffen rather than frighten the republican democratic elements in the National Assembly in Frankfurt and the Prussian Diet in Berlin. Their concern, from the beginning, was to inject a realistic understanding of power and the importance of power. Marx and his followers in the Communist League, repudiating what a later generation of communists would have called Gottschalk's splittism, attempted to merge with the general democratic movement, playing down the specifically sectional, proletarian commitment of their ideology and using the Cologne Democratic Society as a base. The *Neue Rheinische Zeitung*, from the beginning, had an impressively international flavour, with frequent supplements and reports from Italy, France, Vienna, Brussels and Dublin. But while all five of its editors were communists, the *Neue Rheinische Zeitung* in its first issues made no reference to communism or to the seventeen demands of the Communist Party in Germany, which the reader had to find in other German papers.

When the *Neue Rheinische Zeitung* commenced publication, the revolutionary movement of March 1848 had succeeded in gaining initial democratic concessions in Prussia, Austria and the smaller German states; the All-German National Assembly had started its deliberations in Frankfurt and a Prussian National Diet was sitting in Berlin. But the victories were fragile—resting on the initial indecision of rulers rather than the power of the revolutionary movement—and by May in Germany, as in Europe as a whole, the revolutionary movement had spent its main force and was being put on the defensive. In Italy, Austrian troops were suppressing revolutionary Venice and Milan. In France, the April elections with universal male suffrage had resulted in a massive defeat of the provisional government of socialists and red republicans. In Germany, behind the concessions, the Prussian and Austrian monarchies stood secure in command of their armies and bureaucracies, supported by the power of Tsarist Russia watching from the sidelines.

It was in these circumstances that Marx and Engels, with the example of the French Revolution in mind, initially pursued a policy of supporting the democratic revolution but seeking to radicalize it and at the same time make its power secure. Centralization and war, they believed, were necessary for this end. War against Russia, for which the *Neue Rheinische Zeitung* consistently called in July, was not merely an attempt to pre-empt the threat of intervention or to restore Poland to its national sovereignty and thus create a bastion of 20 million heroes between Germany and Russia. Marx and Engels also believed that such a war would require an unprecedented marshalling of Germany's economic and military resources; it would require the centralization of power and thus favour the most decisive of the revolutionary parties, the party that understood about power.

During the summer which brought the news of the rising and renewed defeat of the Paris proletariat, the Berlin and Frankfurt Assemblies succumbed increasingly to the disease of 'parliamentary cretinism', as the *Neue Rheinische Zeitung* called it—the folly of being totally bogged down in constitution-making instead of seeking to build up a revolutionary movement and a strong executive arm. As the inability of the German bourgeoisie to consummate the bourgeois revolution became more evident, Marx and Engels began to strike a more aggressive, proletarian note. The bourgeoisie, Marx announced, in a series of articles on 'The Bourgeoisie and the Counter-revolution' published in the *Neue Rheinische Zeitung* in December 1848, was backsliding into the camp of reaction. It did not, like the French of 1789, represent the whole of modern society against the old society, the monarchy and the nobility. It was not the voice of the people, but a narrow, sectional class, so frightened of the proletariat that it dared not make a revolution. The bourgeoisie had gone over to the camp of reaction, he concluded, and from then on Marx and Engels no longer felt the need to play down the fundamental antagonism of the proletariat for the bourgeoisie. The only hope of real revolution in Germany, they believed by the beginning of 1849, lay in support from the more genuine revolutionaries outside Germany—in the revolutionary armies of France, Poland and Hungary defeating German and Austrian reaction.

The revolution in Germany, a number of historians have argued, was decisively lost by the inability of German liberals to support the national independence of Slavic peoples on 'German' lands, in particular by their failure to support the Czechs. Marx and Engels shared in this central failing. Like most of the radical left, they were strongly in favour of Polish independence, even if Marx could say seriously, in 1847, that Poland would best be freed by the victory of the working class in England, Germany and France. In their insistence that German democracy and Polish liberation were indissolubly allied, Marx and Engels did not waver throughout 1848 and 1849; they opposed strongly the Frankfurt National Assembly's claim to a share of Prussia and the former province of Posen (Poznan), with its Polish majority. They believed that the first condition for freeing both Germany and Poland was the overthrow of the monarchical regime in Germany and the withdrawal of Russia to the Dniester and the Dvina. But they distinguished sharply, as is widely known, between great historic nations, such as the Poles and Hungarians, and other central and southern Slavs who, according to them, had no history and had derived all their culture from the Germans. Thus they rejected totally Bakunin's call for pan-Slav coalition in favour of democracy, and the *Neue Rheinische Zeitung* shared in the universal

German opposition to Czech independence, which drove Czech nationalism on to a pro-Russian path and enabled the Hapsburg monarchy to crush revolutionary Vienna with Croatian troops.

7

The View from Britain
I: 'Tumults abroad,
stability at home'

F. B. Smith

Lord Brougham, aspiring to become the Burke of 1848, remarked in his essay on the Revolutions that his fellow countrymen were 'Pharisaical' about tumults abroad and complacent about stability at home.[1] They appeared oblivious of the 'pace of mob progress under [the] revolutionary tuition' of France, which had convulsed Europe and left no nation safe. My reading of the evidence accords with Brougham's sensing of the public mood about the Continental revolts, but the servant-employing classes in Great Britain did share, more than he realized, his alarm about mob progress at home for a brief period towards the end of March and during the first ten days of April 1848.

Paris, which encapsulated France in the imagination of Britons, was a dream-object on to which British commentators projected their desires and fears. They were reassured by the French response. French intellectuals held Paris to be the cultural headquarters of France, adding that France was the guiding nation of Europe and that French civilization as exemplified in Paris epitomized European civilization. British spokesmen readily allowed the claim; they liked to believe that their history lay outside the European pattern of unbridled passion, revolution, war, and reaction, and that Britons never shared the moral deficiencies so signally displayed by the French.

In 1848, at least, France monopolized British concern with Continental events. The preceding Sonderbund crisis in Switzerland in 1847 and the rising in Palermo were apparently forgotten, and British historians writing about 1848 continue to overlook them. The historians accurately follow the contemporary public mood by starting with the Paris banquet crisis in mid-February 1848. The drama in the French capital also obscured events in the Austro-Hungarian

[1] H. Brougham, 1st baron Brougham and Vaux, *Letter to the Marquess of Lansdowne, K.G., on the Late Revolution in France* (4th edn, London, 1848), p. 151.

Empire. The daily bulletins from Paris retailing speeches from the tribune, demonstrations, the beating of the *rappel*, rumours about the clubs, arrived by telegraph and express train and always exceeded the five-day-old paragraphs of rather generalized, disjointed narrative that came from central and eastern Europe.

Cracow, Prague, Pesth, Blaj and Islaz seem to have existed in a limbo of geographical and linguistic confusion that deterred commentators, editors and readers alike. Kossuth stood out as a Byronic hero almost universally admired but there were apparently very few who professed to know about his comrades.[2] Among such a hotch-potch of outlandish aristocrats and students behaving so uncharacteristically as revolutionaries, Kossuth, in British eyes, was a recognizable middle-class liberal. His rôle in Austro-Hungarian politics passed unanalysed in the standard newspapers and reviews.

Informed analysis of what was passing in the German states was also rare. Commentators, editors and diarists seem to have agreed in seeing the struggle for liberal constitutions, for free trade and reformed taxation as eminently British and reasonable.[3] The Germans seemed to be a naive, unpractical people, keen to progress and therefore deserving of sympathy. Unlike the French, the Germans had not attacked property.

The chief defect of the French, British speakers and writers agreed in 1848, was their want of moral courage. The public manifestation of this defect was a lack of what the *Economist* called 'the habit of municipality'.[4] The ruling classes had no sense of duty to their nation and *département*, to their class, or to their inferiors. The lower orders had no sense of that 'deference of the heart' which bound British classes and institutions together. Unconstrained by altruism, the French grabbed at power, grabbed at money, followed demagogues at a moment's notice, and equally at a moment's notice, grabbed property. The seizure without compensation of railway property owned by British shareholders figured largely in the respectable daily press. The moral deficiencies of individual Frenchmen, the eminent Tory historian Archibald Alison explained, were the outcome of centralization. Louis XIV, that power-mad lascivious king, had forced on the process and it had grown ever since, especially under Napoleon. Centralization had sapped the spirit of personal independence in

[2] Matthew Arnold, 'Sonnet to the Hungarian Nation', mid-July, 1849.

[3] 'Fermentation in Europe', *Economist*, 1 April 1848; Charlotte Bronte to Miss Wooler, 31 March 1848, in E. Gaskell, *Life of Charlotte Bronte* (London, 1971), p. 286; Rev. Dr Massie, Speech to Anti-State Church Meeting, Finsbury Chapel, *Nonconformist*, 11 October 1848.

[4] *Economist*, 1 April 1848, p. 10; cf. 'The Reaction, or Foreign Conservatism', *Blackwood's Edinburgh Magazine* (hereafter *BEM*) LXV (1849), pp. 529–41; 'Organisation du travail', *Westminster Review* (hereafter *WR*) XLIX (April 1848), p. 119.

politics and destroyed the notion of obligation to the municipality and national polity, which the British landowning classes possessed and almost invariably acted upon. And as the spirit of duty and deference weakened, centralized arbitrary administrative power took its place. From want of class mutuality, coexistent with arbitrary power, came revolution. Revolution in its turn worsened the disunity.[5]

The great revolution of 1789 had broken the landholding backbone of the country. Primogeniture and entail had been abolished and estates were fragmented. Landholders in France were now too poor, or too new and too selfish, to sustain that visible proof of class duty and dependence in Britain, the poor law. In this respect as in many others, France resembled that other tumultuous land, Ireland. The revolution had also broken the authority of the church. France languished between a labouring class riddled with infidelity and an aristocracy and intelligentsia which scoffed at religion. The country was bereft of that faith in the providentially ordered hierarchy of being and resignation under suffering which it was the function of Christianity to inculcate. Moreover, such remnants of religion as the French retained were popish: popery necessarily involved a slavish abnegation of personal responsibility and that abnegation of responsibility removed the basis for the modern mixed constitution. The confessional and superstitious practices associated with Mariolatory and worship of saints also nurtured moral cowardice. And moral cowardice in turn, Alison, Lord Ashley, and the radical Baptist minister, Mr Aldis, agreed, issued in licentiousness and corruption. The recent Teste, Cubières and Duchâtel ministerial scandals were notorious and vice was proved, Alison noted, by the fact that the French read George Sand's novels and *La Réforme*, and that one in two babies born in Paris was illegitimate (a roughly comparable figure —for Middlesex in 1830—was one in thirty-eight). Such governmental scandals had been banished from the British polity by the Reform Act and such vice, while not unthinkable, was undoubtedly less prevalent.[6] Baseness, Alison remarked, always bred its opposite. Frenchmen were peculiarly given to dreams of instituting, by force if need be, the perfectibility of man.

Corruption, Alison and James Wilson of the *Economist* agreed, also pervaded French commerce. The issue of *assignats* in the first revolution and their subsequent dishonouring had destroyed such little probity as the French had shown in financial affairs and in recent

[5] Archibald Alison, 'The Revolution in Europe', *BEM* LXIII (1848), pp. 638–52 at p. 640.
[6] A. Alison, 'Lamartine's Revolution of 1848', *BEM* LXVI (1849), pp. 219–34 at p. 224; Edwin Hodder, *The Life and Work of the Seventh Earl of Shaftesbury, K.G.* (London, 1888), p. 391, quoting diary, 2 March 1848; Rev. J. Aldis, speech at meeting of Baptist Home Missionary Society, Finsbury Chapel, *Nonconformist*, 26 April 1848.

years every British businessman, and indeed in 1848 every railway
shareholder, had personal experience of their untrustworthiness
[*Economist*, 1 April 1848, p. 10; Alison, 'Lamartine', pp. 222–4].
The moral cowardice and perfidy displayed by Louis Philippe lost
him public sympathy in Britain. Tories such as Croker, Kirwan, the
informed commentator on French affairs in *Fraser's Magazine*, and
Alison, each disposed to uphold monarchical institutions, explained
the sudden collapse of the court and the inauguration of the Republic
as the result of a failure of nerve—an interpretation which Dr Zeldin
revives in his recent work. Louis Philippe had no claim to join
Louis XVI as a royal martyr. His crown had been won on the
barricades and possessed no legitimacy. As a contributor to *Fraser's
Magazine* remarked: 'A throne won by treachery has been lost by
folly.' Only the redoubtable J. W. Croker sought to exonerate the
king by emphasizing the harsh necessities which forced the abdica-
tion.[7] These Tory explanations are impressive. They link the long-
term dimension of the breaking and erosion of religious belief, the
breaking of the legitimacy of the monarchy, centralization growing
through the centuries, with immediate causes in the frailties of Louis
Philippe and his ministers, recently demonstrated yet again in his
perversity about the Spanish marriages.

Ultra-conservatives like J. W. Croker went beyond the immediate
political explanations and produced the usual ultra-conservative plot
theory—familiar to them, as in Croker's case, from their own political
activities. Croker asserted that a '*third party*' had captured the ban-
queting movement and turned it to violence. The proof, and here
Croker prefigures French historians such as Crémieux, was the rapid
building of the barricades and the early appearance of the red flag.
This conspiracy theory of revolution is linked with a determinist pro-
jection of the course of the violence, based on the 'natural law of
revolutions' derived from the model of 1789. Curiously, the July
Revolution, the Three Days and its outcome, a more exact analogue,
passed unremarked by nearly all British commentators. Before the
end of February, John Austin, the jurist, was predicting a collapse
of the economy that would follow from the extravagant demands of
the newly empowered poor. Gold would be sent out of the country;
and it was. The parlous state of the economy, employment and public
order that must ensue would engender a committee of public safety.
The committee, in order to control the armed populace and to pre-

[7] Anon. [A. V. Kirwan?], 'The Revolution in France', *Fraser's Magazine* (hereafter
FM) XXXVII (1848), pp. 368–70; A. Alison, 'The Year of Reaction', *BEM* LXVII (1850),
pp. 1–15 at pp. 4–6 and 'Results of Revolution in Europe', *BEM* LXXI (1852), pp. 242–
258; Theodore Zeldin, *France 1848–1945* (2 vols, Oxford, 1973–7) I, pp. 467–70; J. W.
Croker, 'French Revolution of February—Escape of Louis Philippe', *Quarterly Review*
(hereafter *QR*) LXXXVI (1850), pp. 526–85 at pp. 545–52.

serve itself, would have to use force against its rivals and eventually there must be massacres. The massacres in turn would breed reaction and out of reaction must come dictatorship. Dictators needed to divert the populace in order to survive and the only practicable diversion that would engage the whole population was a European war. During the unfolding of the revolution, Austin predicted, the press would be gagged worse than before, the economy damaged beyond repair, and there would be massive loss of life.[8]

The opinions of conservatives were further complicated by their hatred of the perfidious democratical Pope Pius IX. Lord Ashley and Dr John Cumming, the Presbyterian millennialist, saw the fulfilment of prophecy in the fall of Rome in 1848. Ashley exulted in his diary: 'Marvellous, marvellous accounts from Rome! ... Are not all the powers preparing to "eat her flesh, and burn her with fire?"' The Protestant Alliance convened a special meeting to condemn the democratical pope and the engrafting of a slavish mobocracy on to degenerate popery. Popery had sapped personal conscience: now Europe was reaping the whirlwind with the spread of democracy. Radicals, on the other hand, welcomed an unexpected ally. The *Northern Star*, among the best-selling papers in Britain in 1848 at about 21,000 copies, was offering free portraits of the people's pope, along with those of Feargus O'Connor and Ernest Jones.[9]

Straightforward class interpretations are rare. The most arresting is that of John Ruskin, whose observations on his journey through France in the autumn of 1848 closely prefigure Marx's analysis of the class struggle in France. Ruskin noted that the revolution had developed into 'a simple fight of the poor against the rich' and that the bourgeoisie had broken with the poor as 'common sense views had been forced upon them.' Ruskin's two letters to his friend, W. H. Harrison, contain vivid descriptions of the pervasive bitterness and distrust in the aftermath of the June Days and offer a penetrating social commentary.[10]

Liberals writing in the *Economist* and *Westminster Review*, Lord Brougham and journalists contributing to *The Times*, adduced a set of economic causes. The French government had been insecure because French trade was weak. Too much money had gone into wild

[8] J. A. [Austin], 'Paris 27 February', *The Times*, 1 March 1848; J. S. Mill to Sarah Austin, [March?] 1848, in J. S. Mill, *Earlier Letters ... 1812–1848*, ed. F. E. Mineka (Collected Works, XII, Toronto, 1963), p. 734.

[9] G. F. A. Best, *Shaftesbury* (London, 1964), p. 72; *Nonconformist*, 11 May 1848; George Croly, 'The Italian Revolution', *BEM* LXX (1851), pp. 431–47 at p. 447; Donald Read and Eric Glasgow, *Feargus O'Connor: Irishman and Chartist* (London, 1961), pp. 59–60; *Northern Star*, 1 April 1848.

[10] *The Works of John Ruskin*, edited by E. T. Cook and A. Wedderburn (39 vols, London, 1903–12) VIII, pp. xxxii–iii; cf. 'France: Another Insurrection in Paris', *FM* XXXVIII (1848), pp. 121–5.

speculation and French industry was directed to producing luxuries and not to supplying that morally and financially rewarding market that lay in the real wants of the people. It was yet another proof of French licentiousness. The weakness of the French economy showed how the system had been 'rotted by protection'. France needed free trade. The banquets had promised to develop along the lines of the Anti-Corn Law triumph, and indeed Cobden had been associated with them, but unfortunately France had no Peel.[11]

Explanations of the revolts in Italy and the Austrian Empire were simple, out of ignorance. In each case respectable middle-class patriots appeared to be seeking from despotisms their ordinary privileges as citizens. Demands for a balanced constitution, a free press, less expenditure on the aristocracy, army and bureaucracy, and the abolition of passports—this last an especially sore point with letter-writers to *The Times*—were all matters British observers could comprehend. Everyone, from writers in the *Economist* to that stern old Tory, Charlotte Brontë, approved the noble work, especially the romantic revolution in Italy. The discussions in the *Economist* also, interestingly, involve the notion of the revolts as necessary steps to modernizing the economy and progressing towards British-style industrial capitalism. More distinctively, the young George Eliot rejoiced in the vision of free nations entering upon their spiritual destiny and throwing off despotism. She had feared, she told her friend Sibree, that their epoch was merely a *'critical'* one in the Saint-Simonian sense but she exulted in the realization that they were to experience a new age of 'organic' change which signalled the beginning of the end of the gross materialism engendered by 'decayed monarchs' and the 'brute sensuality' of the lower orders.[12]

These diverse hopes and fears have their fullest expression in the two major essays on 1848 by Lord Brougham and John Stuart Mill. Brougham, the seventy-year-old Whig and former lord chancellor, had spent a lifetime teaching the British working classes respect for the exclusive polity. He had been prominent in the Society for the Diffusion of Useful Knowledge and had written volumes for them presenting Whig views of the progressive, popular, balanced British constitution and definitions of its opposites, democracy and despotism. Like Burke before him, and Alison and Croker, he was a marginal

---

[11] *Economist*, 1 April 1848; Brougham, *Late Revolution*, pp. 267–8; *The Times*, 5 April, 27 June 1848. There is an amusing skit on Cobden in France by W. E. Aytoun, 'How We Got Possession of the Tuileries', reprinted in his *Stories and Verse* (Edinburgh, 1964).

[12] George Eliot to John Sibree Jr [8 March 1848] and to the Brays [8 June 1848] in *The George Eliot Letters*, edited by G. S. Haight (7 vols, London and New Haven, 1954–5) I, pp. 253–4, 267.

man whose self-made success gave him a sharp eye for threats to established hierarchy. Brougham also had strong French associations through his intimacy with the Orléanist court and his ownership of Château Eleanor Louise at Cannes, the prospective confiscation of which by the Republic worried him exceedingly. (He had had to defend his English estate against seizure in 1843.) Moving to avert confiscation he applied to the provisional government to become a French citizen and deputy in the National Assembly. The provisional government adroitly offered him citizenship provided he surrender his British nationality, titles and perquisites: Brougham, who was receiving a civil list pension of £5,000 a year, refused. Unkind contemporaries, including Lord Lansdowne—the addressee of the *Letter on the Late Revolution*—hinted that he attacked the Republic out of spite.[13]

Brougham, indefatigable as usual, took pains to verify his prejudices. He applied to Guizot, Molé and Mignet to fill out his knowledge of Parisian affairs and he sought details on Germany from the British minister at Berlin, the earl of Westmorland.[14] Despite some reassuring advice from Lord and Lady Westmorland, Brougham emerged as distinctive among critics of the revolution in strongly denouncing the Germans. For him, the European revolution was of a piece, a 'catastrophe . . . having no parallel in the history of nations' which made all social order, all governments, especially 'popular' ones, insecure. In Germany, the danger of anarchy, confiscation and bloodshed was acute precisely because the Germans were inexperienced in revolution. Prefiguring much British historiography of the twentieth century, Brougham asserted that they were a 'childish' people, prone to 'exalted fancies' which they carried to extremes. Given their inexperience and the absence of a national polity to shape their political ambitions, the Germans would have full play for their fancies and they were likely to end with more empty allegiances and bloody excesses than anything the French had perpetrated [*Late Revolution*, pp. 1, 15, 77–85].

The German tumults were the more dangerous because they were inflamed by nationalism. Brougham is distinguished among his conservative contemporaries in perceiving the 'newfangled notion of nationalism' as a force in the events of 1848. Nationality broke the sacred rights of treaties and this boded ill. The empires and nations of Europe had remained at peace since 1815; the peace had been uneasy but it had been peace. Nationality would unleash passion

---

[13] Lansdowne, *Parl Debs.* 3 XCVIII, cols 138, 151–2, 11 April 1848; *The Life and Times of Henry Lord Brougham Written by Himself* (3 vols, London 1871) III, pp. 511–517; *The Times*, 18 April 1848.

[14] *The Correspondence of Priscilla, Countess of Westmorland*, edited by R. Weigall (London, 1909), p. 134.

among linguistic and religious minorities, lead to internal upheavals and thereby abridge central sovereignty and control and end, inexorably, in bloodshed. Internal upheaval also would induce interference from foreign powers and alien groups. The United Kingdom, as the Irish showed by taking their deputation to the provisional government and receiving vague promises of help, could not remain immune from the nationality problem. Irish demands for independence threatened an abridgement of British sovereignty and on that ground, quite apart from reasons of defence and protection of property, must be opposed. Italy posed a different question. There was no ground for Italian national claims because Italy had never been a single sovereign state. On the other hand, these claims exacerbated the pretensions of the Austrian Catholic despotism and provoked the threat of French intervention, all of which portended a European war and an end to Palmerston's long struggle for peace and reform on the Continent [*Late Revolution*, pp. 126–7].

The Thomas Paine *redivivus* who answered these reflections was John Stuart Mill. He did so with a combative panache that makes his essay exceptional among his work. Mill included the article in *Dissertations and Discussions*, but it has not, to my knowledge, been reprinted and modern students of Mill have disregarded it. Yet the essay is of a piece with his reconsiderations of socialism and the working classes in the second and third editions of the *Political Economy* and it vividly illuminates this phase of his mental evolution. Mill was forty-two in 1848; his writings about the revolution constitute a declaration of independence from his father's friend, Brougham, and his Benthamite mentor, John Austin. Several of the issues Mill raised in his essay were to preoccupy him to the end of his life.

For Mill, as for Brougham, the February revolution was a world historical event. 'There never was a time', he told H. S. Chapman, 'when so great a drama was being played out in one generation.'[15] Given our hindsight of the aftermath, it is difficult to recapture the excitement that gripped them. Apart from spitting Brougham on several minor errors of fact, Mill opposed nearly all Brougham's assumptions about the causes and impact of the revolution and rejected the logic of his gloomy prognostications about the outcome of 1848.[16] Brougham, foreseeing attacks on the House of Lords, deplored the abolition of the second chamber because it removed the surest barrier to radical legislation and exposed political conflict with-

[15] J. S. Mill to H. S. Chapman, 29 February 1848, to Sarah Austin, 7 March 1848, *Earlier Letters*, pp. 732, 733–4.
[16] J. S. Mill, 'Vindication of the French Revolution of February 1848, in Reply to Lord Brougham and Others', *WR* XLIX (April 1848), reprinted in his *Dissertations and Discussions* (2 vols, London, 1859) II, pp. 335–410.

in the ruling classes to pressures from the masses. Mill cautiously
approved the abolition. Political contained within ruling
circles or vented only as disagreements between legislative bodies
failed to educate the people in the principles at stake in the conflict
and thereby failed to win their understanding and support for the
laws which finally emerged. It was, moreover, from a conservative
viewpoint, needless to insulate aristocratic legislatures from the populace because the populace was conservative anyway. Brougham denounced the provisional government's attempts to move towards
social equality as infringements of the providential order. Mill welcomed equality as a moral good: it increased personal individuality
and thereby enlarged diversity and creativity in the community.
Brougham ridiculed the provisional government's efforts to foster
cooperative production on the grounds that private interest alone
motivated work and improvement. Mill admitted that cooperation in
France had been ineffective, although it was not the utter failure that
Brougham depicted; but Mill argued, as he was to do in the second
edition of the *Political Economy* which he was preparing in late 1848,
that cooperation was both economically feasible and socially possible
and it was yet unproved that many men would not work for objects
higher than their private interest. In this essay, consonant with his
other writings, Mill did not argue that the February revolution or
any revolution would perfect human nature, but that it opened the
possibility, by altering social relations, of diminishing personal
malignancies.

Like other Francophiles back to Paine and including Monckton
Milnes and A. H. Clough among his contemporaries, Mill was
fascinated by French inventiveness, zest and humanity in human
relations.[17] The debate on 1848 forms a vivid moment in that continuing schism in British life between 'Europeans' and 'Little
Englanders'. Brougham ascribed the collapse of the provisional
government ultimately to tensions inherent in revolutionary situations, on the analogue of 1793–9. Mill, more subtly, argued that the
failure to solve the economic depression and unemployment crisis,
which produced the June Days, was an 'accidental' result of long-
term difficulties and not the necessary outcome of the provisional

---

[17] Mill, 'Vindication', pp. 394–5; James Pope-Hennessy, *Monckton Milnes* (2 vols,
London, 1949–51) I, pp. 278–92. I have been unable to obtain a copy of Milnes's actual
pamphlet, *The Events of 1848, Especially in Relation to Great Britain: A Letter to the
Marquis of Lansdowne* (London, 1849), but the lengthy controversy about it in the
Morning Chronicle indicates its tone and contents. See also A. H. Clough to A. P.
Stanley, 28 May [1848], to R. W. Church, 30 May [1848] and to T. Arnold, 16 July
1848, in *The Correspondence of Arthur Hugh Clough*, edited by F. L. Mulhauser
(2 vols, Oxford, 1957) I, pp. 211, 212, 214.

government's meliorist efforts. The provisional government had come to power 'accidentally' and was unready for it. The miscarriage of its 'experimental legislation' neither demonstrated the inherent frailty of such projects nor proved the incompetence of the revolutionary law-makers. Amidst such unpropitious circumstances, they showed imagination, diligence and courage in even making the attempt. Mill also noted, unlike Brougham who prophesied a quick return to anarchy, that the June Days had destroyed the possibility of an early renewal of radical republicanism in France. Like Marx, he recognized the importance of the split between the republicans and socialists and the divisions among the populace.

Mill also accepted nationality, mainly because existing anti-national empires were illiberal. The Austrians played off one linguistic group against another. This tactic closed advancement in administration and centres of learning and thereby stifled the development of a strong critical public opinion and civic concern. The end result, as was shown by sending the Croatians into Italy, was bloodshed and stagnation. The law of nations and treaties, which Brougham held so sacrosanct, was open to alteration like any other laws as the world changed, as 1815 had proved.

This debate has less brilliance and memorable rhetoric than the clash between Burke and Paine, but it builds to a resonant review of factors leading to the present age. Curiously, the Brougham–Mill encounter appears to be the last worthwhile debate about revolution by two British intellectuals; the academic confrontations engendered by the Russian and Chinese revolutions look callow beside it.

All the commentators in my sample, except Mill who relied on the contingent and unforeseen, show uneasiness about the chains of causes they adduce—personal frailties in monarchs, economic crises in France in 1847, student unrest and Lola Montez alike seemed puny triggers of the convulsion that had shaken almost the whole continent. The pattern of cause and result lacked that convincing symmetry which Victorians believed to be inherent in physical laws. Writers ended their reports on 1848 with admissions that the greatest upheaval in European history seemed fundamentally inexplicable. This inexplicability and the obscurity of the laws governing social movements obsessed British commentators, both conservatives and radicals: it meant that until 10 April at least, no one could predict with certainty that revolution would not happen in Britain. Meanwhile they expended much hard work and thousands of words in probing the mystery across the Channel.

In face of the inexplicable, Alison, Palgrave Simpson (Acton's friend and fellow Catholic who knew the Continent well and wrote for the *Edinburgh Review*) and Brougham agreed that while providence might propose, man disposes.[18] By transgressing the providential order of ranks and property, the faithless Europeans were provoking a terrible vengeance. All that Britain could do, as a God-fearing nation, was to hold the faith, strengthen the laws against sedition and keep the dragoons ready. God's laws were as manifest in the natural laws of society as they were in the physical universe and any infringement of them was strictly blasphemy. From February onwards Chartist spokesmen, led by Ernest Jones, G. M. W. Reynolds, and W. J. Vernon and the Irish Confederates, were preaching armed rebellion. The conservatives responded with increasingly strident demands that government do its duty to God and the nation and suppress the dissidents.[19]

The rhetoric of providential intervention was not the monopoly of conservatives. The faithful among Nonconformists, Chartists and radicals also readily claimed that God had moved in Europe. The *Nonconformist* (1 March 1848) asserted that, if providence could use a 'street row ... to prick the gorgeous bubble' of monarchy, popery and army in France, God equally might move to eradicate the 'hollow ... pretence' of the Church of England. Chartists and radicals rejoiced that the hand of God had levelled despotism in Europe, and thereby reified moral force. The slogan most quoted on the banners carried to Kennington Common on 10 April was 'Man to be free has only to will it', coupled with another favourite, 'The voice of the people is the voice of God.' By contrast, the Irish wagons were festooned with 'If liberty is good enough to live by it is good enough to die by.' Sacrificial fantasies were never central to British Chartist aspirations. The Chartists quickly assimilated into their everyday rhetoric the toppling of seemingly impregnable foreign autocracies. W. P. Roberts told the participants in a demonstration at Manchester on 10 April that 'the finger of God might be seen in the revolutions ... and ... the same power might be extended to the people of this country, who were threatened with a despotism such as they had never groaned under before [cheers].' Meetings of Chartists and 'democrats' summoned at Halifax, Burnley, Wigan, Derby, Lincoln, Dumfries, Merthyr Tydfil and elsewhere to adopt congratulatory

[18] Alison, 'The Year of Revolutions', *BEM* LXV (1849), pp. 1–19 at p. 3; 'A Few Congratulations and Warnings', *FM* XXXVII (1848), pp. 474–6; Brougham, *Late Revolution*, p. 89. An unidentified writer in *WR* remarked: 'The revolution was incredible. We seem to have stood as witnesses to the opening of the seventh seal' (XLIX, April 1848, p. 138).

[19] *Northern Star*, 8 April 1848; *Nonconformist*, 15 March 1848; *Morning Chronicle*, 16 March, 7 April 1848; *The Times*, 6 April 1848; J. W. Crocker, 'Democracy', *QR* LXXXV (1849), pp. 260–312; 'Chartism', *FM* XXXVII (1848), pp. 579–92; Sir D. L. Evans, *Parl Debs.* 3, XCVIII, cols 17–18, 7 April 1848.

addresses to the French Republic acclaimed speeches involving providence and likely providential intervention in Britain [*The Times*, 12
April 1848; *Northern Star*, 1 and 8 April 1848]. The European
republics proved that the people could win. 'God-given fraternity',
a newly revived word in English radical usage, was quickly incorporated in the set of arguments against authority. The proprietors
of the *Northern Star* made a special attempt to define the word for
their readers: it meant, they explained, the opposite of 'exclusiveness',
class government and 'patronage and sectionalism', equal opportunity
rather than altruism or good feelings toward others. The *Nonconformist* put in a counter-bid for the new word. Fraternity allied to
physical force could mean only 'fratricide', but 'true fraternity and
the millennium [would] come only through the triumph of spiritual
Truth' and brotherhood under God.[20] But to the common people
fraternity, liberty and equality came seemingly as new rallying calls
in their resistance to authority.

In early June two tipsy Irish workmen sought to exemplify the
lessons of the French Republic by shouting 'liberty, equality, fraternity' and the points of the Charter, and trying to embrace passers-by
in the Blackwall Tunnel. The passers-by avoided them. While they
were being arrested, one Irishman called on the people 'to fraternize',
knock out the policemen and release them. The plea was ignored.
His friend struggled free, tried to break the gaslamps and declared
'he should like to see all the police and special constables extin-
guished as well as the gas.' This incident recalls Mayhew's reported
interview with the costermonger who said that 'numbers of costers
... were keen Chartists without understanding anything about the
six points, whose notion of fraternity consisted of sticking more
together in any "row"' and provoking an immediate showdown with
the police who harried them.'[21] At Chartist meetings between March
and July women draped themselves with the tricolour, speakers often
invoked the tree of liberty, the cap of liberty was hoisted as an
emblem and proceedings usually ended with the *Marseillaise*, sung
in a newly prepared 'Chartist' translation. During the summer in
Edinburgh, Aberdeen, Ashton-under-Lyne, Bradford and elsewhere
in the north, there were attempts to form corps of 'National Guards'.
Only the Finsbury group of respectable moral force Chartists surrounding James Watson, Richard Moore, William Lovett and W. J.
Linton glimpsed the implications of the 'social and democratic

---

[20] *Northern Star*, 1 April 1848; *Nonconformist*, 5 July 1848. *Punch*, January–June
1848, p. 109, also recognizes the newness of 'fraternity' and the uncertainties about
its meaning.

[21] Henry Mayhew, *London Labour and the London Poor* (4 vols, London, 1864) I,
p. 22; *The Times*, 6 June 1848.

republic', but their expositions passed almost unheard amidst the O'Connorite and Irish tumults.[22]

The collapse of the July monarchy supplied the spark to an already combustible situation. During 1847 there had been severe distress throughout the United Kingdom. The collapse of the railway share-market, dozens of major company failures and a bad harvest had worsened unemployment, especially in London and the north, quite apart from the terrible situation in Ireland. In January 1848, according to police returns, half the labouring classes of Manchester were un-employed and another third were on part time. In Glasgow the magistrates found that beyond 100,000 'poor casual labourers and Irish' in severe distress, 14,000 railway workers had been dismissed and were in distress, 7,000 other workers were on short time and 11,000 more were unemployed. Misery bred widespread expressions of unrest. In 1847 there were food riots in Cornwall, Devon, East Anglia and the Highlands.[23]

During the winter of 1847–8 the duke of Wellington lent his authority to a scare story about French invasion plans and the scare had intensified after the revolution. The duke wanted the army enlarged and forts built along the south coast. This demand, and other foreshadowed government spending, presaged a rise in the income tax from three to five per cent (seven pence to one shilling in the pound). The threat aroused the urban middle class and revitalized the Anti-Corn Law League. In January 1848, in their new guise as 'financial reformers' and peace men, the middle-class radical forces looked strong and ready to return to action. In January–February there were enthusiastic demonstrations against the proposal in almost every town in Britain.[24] Historians have underestimated the force of this reaction. The O'Connorite junta was also busy during the winter organizing a new national petition. They were now almost un-challenged as spokesmen for the masses. The older generation of experienced moral-force Chartists were removed from leadership, some by emigration, others broken by imprisonment or the onset of ill-health. Hetherington was 56, Watson 49, Lovett 48, O'Brien 44.

The crowd was open to capture and younger more histrionic men were making bids: Ernest Jones aged 29, H. R. Nicholls 34, G. J.

[22] *The Times*, 13 March, 21 April 1848; *Northern Star*, 1, 15 April 1848; *Noncon-formist*, 7 June, 19 July 1848; *Annual Register* (1848), pp. 59, 150. F. B. Smith, *Radical Artisan* (Manchester, 1973), pp. 71–81.

[23] *The Times*, 4 May 1848, quoted by Alison in 'How to Disarm the Chartists', *BEM* LXIII (1848, pp. 653–73 at p. 655; *Parl. Debs.* 3 LXXXIX, cols 608–9; XC, col. 952.

[24] *The Times*, 1 March 1848; *Republican*, 1848, pp. 5–6; *Northern Star*, 5 February 1848; *Nonconformist*, 1, 8 March 1848; John Morley, *The Life of Richard Cobden* (2 vols, London, 1903) II, pp. 16–18.

Harney 31, G. M. W. Reynolds 34. In Birmingham, under the impetus of the income tax and war threat, Joseph Sturge and the Attwoods were reactivating the old middle-class Chartist alliance [*Nonconformist*, 8 March 1848]. In London the hero of the crowd initially was Charles Cochrane. From early February he had been leading demonstrations of the unemployed against the income tax. Cochrane, aged about forty-one, was the illegitimate son of Colonel the Honourable Basil Cochrane. He had travelled the kingdom in the 1820s in Spanish costume, singing folk and patriotic songs to his own accompaniment on the guitar. From 1842, in opposition to the poor law, he conducted the National Philanthropic Institute, a soup kitchen in Leicester Square, and stood colourfully if unsuccessfully for Westminster in 1847. His meetings in Trafalgar Square were very large and noisy.[25] Meanwhile Ireland was smouldering and Irish Confederates in England and Scotland formed new alliances with O'Connorite Chartists. Thus agitation was already running hot before the February Revolution erupted.

The great figurehead, Feargus O'Connor, had temporarily lost momentum in the movement in early 1848. He had spent time securing his election for Nottingham in 1847, his land company was in trouble and he had lost support from the vocal physical-force men who envied his arrival in parliament. Their alliances with the Irish in Manchester, Glasgow, and Liverpool also threatened his own position as Irish Chartist patriot. He was caught, too, in a new struggle for control of the *Northern Star*.[26] O'Connor's two most immediate rivals in London were Ernest Jones and G. M. W. Reynolds. Jones was a gentleman who had come down in the world in 1845, after having been presented at court in 1841. He wrote wildly romantic novels about disguised gentlemen who had come down in the world who, at intervals between winning the hearts of the common people and leading them to a better life, saved maidens of high but disguised lineage from wicked aristocrats. G. M. W. Reynolds had also come down in the world a little: he had been withdrawn from Sandhurst and had taken to journalism and writing novels after the manner of Eugène Sue and Paul de Kock. In the winter of 1847–8 he lost his place as foreign editor of the *Despatch* and clearly was looking for a new audience for the popular journal he was planning. On 6 March he captured an income tax protest meeting in Trafalgar Square from Cochrane and thereafter rose quickly in the Chartist leadership.

[25] *Northern Star*, 11 March 1848; *The Times*, 24 April 1848. See also Celina Fox, 'The Development of Social Reportage in English Periodical Illustration during the 1840s and early 1850s', *Past & Present*, no. 74 (1977), pp. 90–111.
[26] Alfred Plummer, *Bronterre: A Political Biography of Bronterre O'Brien, 1804–1864* (London, 1971), pp. 189–92.

In 1849 *Reynolds's Political Instructor* swept the radical periodical market with sales of 30,000 per issue.[27]

The want of secure leadership in London and the other great cities allowed demonstrations to get out of hand. At the Cochrane/Reynolds meeting on 6 March the crowd of about 15,000, armed with stones and pieces of the fence around the Nelson Column, drove the police back to Scotland Yard. In the evening, after the police regrouped and retook the square, a crowd of 200 set off 'for the Palace', led by John White, aged eighteen, 'of no trade', 'of a small size', sporting a jacket with epaulettes. The mob broke street lights as they went. At the Palace they were turned by troops with bayonets and on their return to Trafalgar Square via Westminster, amidst occasional shouts of 'Vive la République', they looted a bakery and a beer shop. When arrested White burst into tears, said he meant no harm and swore he knew no Chartists. Intermittent riots—mostly by youths aged thirteen to twenty, it would appear from the persons arrested—continued around the strand for several days [*The Times*, 8 March 1848; *Annual Register* (1848), pp. 35–6]. In Glasgow on the same day the riots were much more formidable. The crowd attacked gunsmiths' shops, armed themselves and then proceeded to loot over thirty food shops and the silversmiths. The sheriff summoned the soldiery and 10,000 special constables were sworn. A band of pensioners fired into the crowd and two or three were killed. Again there were isolated cries of 'Vive la République' and 'Down with the Queen', but onlookers agreed that the crowd, like the London one, was essentially without 'a political object'. Smaller riots, without loss of life, occurred in Edinburgh, Liverpool, Manchester and Newcastle.[28] On the succeeding Monday, 13 March, the first of the great meetings at Kennington Common was called by Ernest Jones. Rain broke up the meeting but as the crowd of about 14,000 dispersed, bands attacked the provision dealers' and bakers' carts ringing the gathering and then went on to sack a baker's and a pawnbroker's shop. The latter lost £1,000 in goods. This meeting, the first real attempt to attach the unrest to a revolutionary programme, also saw the first posting of troops at strategic points in London. The meeting for the next Monday was confined to the John Street Institution. Ernest Jones was again prominent and W. J. Vernon emerged for the first time as a fiery advocate of direct action. Reports of these speeches heightened the anxiety that had begun to grip the London shopkeepers, merchants and gentry after the raids on the pawnbroker's

[27] John Saville, *Ernest Jones, Chartist* (London, 1952), pp. 14–16; *DNB* 'Reynolds'; *Reynolds's Miscellany*, 1 April 1848.

[28] *Annual Register* (1848), p. 37; Joseph Irving, *Annals of Our Time* (London, 1880), p. 240; 'The French Revolution, *WR* XLIX (April 1848), p. 149.

shop on the thirteenth.[29] Recruiting and drilling of special constables continued apace. This month of training was to be the foundation of their remarkable control on 10 April.

Soon after 6 March, probably, O'Connor decided to cut his triumphal tour of northern towns, summon a convention in London and prepare a mass demonstration to accompany the presentation to parliament of the national petition. The arrangements were made in haste: presumably O'Connor was bent on reasserting his chieftain-ship and reimposing control in London. Rumours of the projected meeting reached the government about the sixteenth and plans to combat the Chartists began in earnest. The respectable press first published the rumours on 28 March. The government, which had capitulated on raising the income tax on 29 February, and then had been buffeted by what Earl Grey privately called a 'storm in the City and the whole House of Commons' over continuing the existing 'temporary' tax at its current level, now had to deaden the issue by referring it to a select committee. The majority of the House of Commons, fearful of the agitation that had erupted throughout the country, gladly accepted the manoeuvre on 17 March. This had its effect in taking the now alarmed middle classes out of contention. Their protests subsided. Meanwhile the delegates to the convention, many of them Irish and hitherto unknown in the Chartist movement, began to make their mark by calling for pikes and blood. The rump of old Chartist campaigners at the sessions was outshouted and out-numbered. News of the growing crisis in Ireland heightened the excitement.[30]

The swearing of specials also gathered momentum. Those sworn for the meeting on 13 March had to be re-sworn, as their warrants ran only for a month. Together with fresh recruits they queued by the hundred at police stations in London, Manchester, Bradford, York, Glasgow, Edinburgh, Dumfries and many other towns.

> Rouse, ye lovers of Peace and of Order,
> Of true freedom with honour united,
> Rally round the old banner of England,
> And its glory shall never be blighted.
>
> Shame the brawlers who trade in Sedition,
> Base misleaders who traffic in lies
> And beware lest these self-seeking martyrs,
> Would-be lions, prove wolves in disguise,
> Viva Victoria!!
>
> [Charles Jeffreys, 'The Throne and the Queen']

[29] R. G. Gammage, *History of The Chartist Movement 1837–1854*, facsimile of 1894 edition (London, 1969), p. 298; *The Greville Memoirs 1814–60*, edited by L. Strachey and R. Fulford (8 vols, London, 1938) VI, pp. 43–7.

[30] Gammage, p. 296; Henry Grey, 3rd earl Grey, 'Journal', 21, 29 February 1848 (University of Durham, ms.); *Parl. Debs.* 3 XVI, col. 1414.

In each case the volunteers included a wide cross-section of the population, excepting the Irish, although in London at least many 'respectable repealers' offered themselves. Their ranks comprised 2,500 Thames coal-whippers, who ended the oath-taking ceremony with three cheers for the queen, 'great numbers of merchants and tradesmen', all 800 men from highest to lowest at the Bank of England, all the residents of the Temple, 500 Bermondsey tanners and wool sorters, the members of the University Club (this also became— shades of 1926—a main assembly and communications post), many Thames lightermen, nearly all the members of the House of Lords and their sons, all clerks at government offices. The entire work-forces of establishments considered particularly vulnerable were instructed to volunteer. Thus the railway companies, bankers, distilleries and breweries, the post office, the 1,200 labourers on the Houses of Parliament, even Collard's piano factory, were enrolled to defend their workplaces. In Manchester, 11,000 men were sworn, including 600 clerks and porters from workhouses, and hundreds of 'tradesmen'. In Glasgow volunteers came from among the students and the Western Club. Students were also sworn in Edinburgh. Captained by aristocrats, they were drilled in the evenings by the police.[31] The warrants were still being renewed in June when, upon entering a government office in Whitehall, Feargus O'Connor was nearly sworn by mistake [*The Times*, 10 June 1848]. In all about 170,000 specials were enrolled in London alone. More importantly, contemporaries put the total up to 250,000.[32]

The specials were mobilized on the clear understanding that they were to prevent pillage. They were armed only with batons. Each group of twenty was to patrol its own premises. Messrs Maudsleys, for example, refused to encourage their men even to volunteer until they were assured that they would not have to leave the works. Those who wished to parade the streets, and very many did, had to offer for extra duties. Although the gentry and the respectable press acclaimed the specials as a mighty rebuff to the Chartists, and historians have accepted that version, the intentions of the working-men specials were more limited. The 2,000 Eastern Counties Railway specials called a meeting to declare themselves 'willing to protect the Company's property' but also to proclaim that they 'would never consent to uphold the existing order of things, or to resist the people in their efforts to obtain political enfranchisement . . . [because] they sympathized too much with the movement going forward—with

[31] *Northern Star*, 1 April 1848; *The Times*, 14, 15, 17 March, 4, 6, 7, 10, 12 April 1848; Henry Labouchére, *Parl. Debs.* 3 XCVII, col. 459; A. Alison, *Some Account of My Life and Writings* (2 vols, Edinburgh, 1883) I, pp. 577–8.

[32] *Morning Chronicle*, 11 April 1848; Lady Palmerston to Mrs Huskisson, 14 April 1848, in *The Letters of Lady Palmerston*, edited by T. Lever (London, 1957), p. 300.

Europe at large—to do that' [*Northern Star*, 15 April 1848]. The employees of the Lancashire and Yorkshire Railway objected to being 'marshalled to be sworn as specials' and instead carried a motion deploring 'class legislation' as the real source of civil disturbance. The leaders of the men at Robert Gordon's millwright shop at Lancashire Hill were dismissed for organizing the refusal of the men to be sworn. In Manchester, many of the specials were Chartists. They held two meetings chaired by Abel Heywood at the Corn Exchange in support of the Charter. At Bradford the specials were sworn at a Chartist gathering before the speeches commenced [*Northern Star*, 25 March, 1, 15, 22 April 1848; *Nonconformist*, 12 April 1848]. The governing classes may have thought differently, especially during the first weeks of April, but the working-men and the shopkeeper specials saw themselves essentially as preventing pillage and street violence and not as combating an almost unimaginable social revolution.

The military preparations and events of 10 April are well known and need no repetition here. The Chartists' fantasies of half a million people marching on parliament, a collapse of government and transfer of power to themselves, of death or glory, were shattered. Had O'Connor, Jones and other spokesmen possessed clear ideas of their aims or real ambitions of challenging authority they would never have consented to gather south of the river and they would never have repeated the old Chartist failure to check, however cursorily, the signatures of the national petition. The bands of marchers taking their various routes to the bridges and thence to Kennington Common possibly amounted to 20,000. They walked quietly in the mild sunshine, along silent thoroughfares, shadowed by closed shops and houses bare of the Chartist tricolour of red, green and white. Barred from Whitehall, they shuffled apprehensively over the bridges 'by permission' of the police and specials. Even before they reached the Common, they were broken. Momentarily, the crowd roused itself when O'Connor was approached by a police inspector. They thought O'Connor was to be arrested. But the inspector merely warned O'Connor that the meeting was illegal and that the gathering should disperse. O'Connor immediately turned to pacify the people. He had made his will the night before and had convinced himself that his martyrdom was at hand. But one informed participant recalled that O'Connor's secretary, Thomas Martin Wheeler, had secretly agreed with the police that if trouble erupted O'Connor was to be spirited away in a cab kept at the ready.[33] The demonstration fragmented as the orators on the waggons (built from timber from the Land Company's estates) squabbled about their order of speaking. Jones and Reynolds left to find an audience at the separate meeting of the

---

[33] William Stevens, *A Memoir of Thomas Martin Wheeler* (London, 1862), pp. 43–4.

Irish Confederates, while Cuffay, after shouting that his colleagues were 'cowardly humbugs', climbed out of the waggon and harangued another clutch of hearers. O'Connor's speech hardly alluded to the Charter. He denounced the wild talk at the Convention and remarked that had he been the government he would have banned the procession too. The only motion put to the meeting was a plea against the gagging bill (extending the sedition law of Great Britain to Ireland) then before the parliament. France was not mentioned. By midday the meeting had collapsed and the crowd ebbed back across the bridges, where scuffles broke out as the police controlled the flow. Before the afternoon was out terrified citizens like W. M. Thackeray and the shopkeepers, prepared with red hot pokers behind their shutters, learned that the threat had passed. The simultaneous demonstrations and rising threatened in Glasgow and Manchester evaporated as the news was telegraphed from London.[34]

The exposure during the following weeks of the four million bogus names and obscenities among the alleged six million signatures to the petition further demoralized the Chartists. Six million equalled the total adult male population of Great Britain in 1848. Rather than weighing five and a half tons, the petition was only three and a half hundredweight. One Gradgrind took 'the trouble to ascertain exactly how many [legible] signatures [could] be put on an area of a square yard', and found that the greatest number was 1,440. If the national petition contained at least 5,700,000 signatures, then 5,700,000 divided by 1,440 equals 3,958 and 'therefore the whole petition must be 3,958 square yards, or, if it be three feet in width, it must be 2 miles in length' [H.G.W. in *The Times*, 17 April 1848]. The fear that gripped respectable people before 10 April turned into vicious ridicule of the 'contemptible catastrophe of humbug'. The remarkable finding that two million signatures, that is, twice the electorate of the House of Commons in Great Britain, were 'genuine', was masked by derision as it has been ever since; but the methods by which the parliamentary clerks performed their miracle of counting in under three days and the tests by which they established the authenticity of signatures remain mysterious. Even so, the Chartists were indubitably tapping enormous reserves of disaffection: two million signatures works out at roughly one signature among every six of the total population of Great Britain over nineteen.

Some unbalanced souls, like Henry Smith speaking to a Chartist rally in Liverpool, clung to make-believe by ignoring criticism and chanting over and over the old numbers for 10 April and the signatures; others like Richard Pilling at Ashton-under-Lyne, or O'Connor in the *Northern Star*, gloried in the 'prodigious preparations' made

---

[34] Charles Knight, *Passages of a Working Life*, facsimile of 1864–5 edition (3 vols, Shannon, 1971) III, p. 36; *The Times*, 4 April 1848; Alison, *Some Account* I, pp. 580–81.

by 'the bloody and brutal Whigs', thereby proving their own innate strength and righteousness [*The Times*, 22 April 1848; *Northern Star*, 15 April 1848]. The final pathetic London demonstration occurred on 12 June. The authorities renewed their precautions, but heavy rain intervened and only about 8,000 trudged to the Common, thence to drift away, leaderless. Meetings in other parts of Great Britain, in late May and early June, failed similarly. The Chartists' faith in the power of public gatherings was smashed. Thereafter a few desperate individuals were to turn to insurrectionary conspiracy. The government readily used troops, police, spies and *agents provocateurs* to pick off the leaders and crush the conspiracies and remaining demonstrations. Jones, Vernon, Williams, Sharpe, Looney and Fussell were arrested in early June and charged with sedition, unlawful assembly and riot. All received two years' imprisonment. They were treated as common criminals, although Jones at least gained exemption from oakum picking. Williams and Sharpe died in gaol and Vernon soon after his release, while Jones's health was said to have been broken by his sentence. But the *Nonconformist* reporter noticed that each looked broken and ill during their trial. It seems likely that prison only completed the deterioration that began with the collapse of their fantasy world on 10 April [Saville, pp. 31–4; *Nonconformist*, 14 June 1848]. Over thirty more Chartists and Confederates were arrested in London in August upon information from Powell, a psychopathic *agent provocateur* who had supplied them with weapons, including 'combustible balls'. Four men, including Cuffay, were transported for life; thirteen others were imprisoned for up to two years. At Ashton-under-Lyne on 14 August men armed with pikes and a few fire-arms suddenly emerged into the streets, but were put down by a 'great force' of specials, and a detachment of soldiers. A policeman, possibly by premeditation, was shot dead in the fracas. The actual murderer was alleged to have escaped to America, but six accomplices were convicted of treasonable conspiracy and sentenced to transportation for life on the evidence of eight of their mates who became crown witnesses (including the probable actual murderer).

Other rioters were gaoled for up to a year.[35] Men and youths were

[35] *Annual Register* (1848), pp. 121–37, 165–6; *Revolution in Europe: A Monthly Record . . .*, edited by Percy St. John (nos 1–4, Glasgow, 1848), June, p. 2. Intimations of the nature of the leadership of the Ashton riot can be gleaned from the report of the enquiry into the behaviour of some ringleaders during expatriation to New South Wales. The group comprised the eight so-called Chartist crown witnesses and two other witnesses, and their families. The 'Chartists' were William Broadbent, William Eckersley, John Latimer senior, Thomas Latimer, John Latimer junior, John Platt, William Macklin, Thomas Winterbottom. The two others were: James Winterbottom (no relation to Thomas), Joseph Armitage.

also imprisoned for seditious conspiracy and riot in Birmingham, Bradford, Bolton, Liverpool and Edinburgh. The European revolutions and the massive disaffection among the middle and labouring classes had opened a marvellous opportunity to the Chartist leadership to break through on the Six Points and build an enduring movement at a time when even extreme conservatives were admitting the necessity for parliamentary, financial and philanthropic reforms. The madmen at the top spoiled that opportunity. There was to be no second chance for nearly twenty years. The respectables turned to rebuilding local moral force associations and through them, in alliance with middle-class radicals, to work in municipal politics. Others occupied themselves with trade unions, secularism, advocating temperance and vegetarianism, selling life assurance, helping refugees, abolishing newspaper stamps, public hanging and other par-

---

During the train journey from Lancashire to London a fight developed and Eckersley was taken from the train and arrested, but then apparently restored to the group. At their hotel in London the police were called to another fight among them. One policeman was 'hit by a missile', variously described as a knife, plate or jug. A second policeman was beaten by John Latimer senior and another man.

The group embarked as assisted emigrants on the *Mary Bannatyne*, together with a 'collection of respectable farm servants'. The Ashton group soon terrorized the other passengers. The captain considered putting them in irons but apparently feared an assault on the brig if he did so. But he doubled the night watch. The ship's surgeon recorded: 'The Latimers are a curse ... the old man beats his wife and the children beat their father.' Eckersley pushed to the front of a mess queue waiting for hot water and when the man at the head of the queue remonstrated, Eckersley grabbed him by the testicles and tried to throw him into a hold. Another passenger grabbed the victim's arm and a tug of war ensued. On arrival in Sydney, Eckersley was convicted of this assault, fined and moved to Bathurst. John Platt was also a problem on board. The surgeon employed him as an assistant. When the *Mary Bannatyne* went to assist another ship requiring medical supplies, the surgeon discovered that Platt had sold large quantities of equipment and medicines. Platt also smashed and threw overboard a navigation lamp after lighting his pipe from it.

In Sydney the group lodged together and quickly became known to the police. 'The language of these people was blasphemous and indecent and their conduct was disgracefully riotous and insubordinate.' Finally they were evicted after Latimer senior in 'a drunken fit' had nearly burned the house down. He set up as a chiropodist—'Late chiropodist to the Duchess of Kent'—and was last recorded as a labourer in the Botanic Gardens.

Macklin and the ship's mate deposed to the enquiry that the actual murderer of the policeman was John Latimer junior. Macklin and James Winterbottom also alleged that Eckersley, who had been an organizer of the violence, had been a police spy in 1848–49.

The enquiry resulted from demands in the Colonial Legislative Council that the £304 18s expended on the assisted passages be refunded to the colony's emigration fund. The Colonial Office refunded £354 18s (Colonial Office Despatch No. 257, 19 December 1849). I owe this reference to Dr Janet McCalman of the Australian National University. Powell also ended up in South Australia, at the public expense.

ticular abuses and cruelties, and promoting education. Their new object was to permeate local authority and justify their respectable rôle in the social order, rather than challenge the national hierarchy. In the long run they were to effect major ameliorations in British life, but through 1848–9 and the early 1850s their cry of 'the Charter and Something More' was a sad acknowledgement of their disenchantment with the mass movement of the previous twenty years and their current impotence.

The collapse of the 10 April demonstration nerved the British ruling classes and renewed their faith in their polity. It was a revelation, the *Morning Chronicle* remarked, of 'how deeply and solidly are the foundations laid upon which the vast fabric of our social state silently reposes. . . . Commerce and shopkeeping have not taken the manhood out of us.' A country gentleman, W. S. Dugdale, of Merevale Hall, Warwickshire, exulted in his diary on 11 April:

> Never was so grand and glorious a Demonstration of loyalty of feeling. All ranks from the Duke to the artificer were associated together in this imposing Band of Special Constables. No French fraternity here. At no period in our history have the upper and middle class been more united. . . . Why have we been so wonderfully preserved while Europe has been convulsed to the centre? By the comparative soundness of our social system.[36]

The crisis and its aftermath fostered a new concern, a new imaginative approach to the lower orders. Mrs Gaskell's *Mary Barton*, which was almost completed before the spring of 1848, was acclaimed in this spirit.[37] It undoubtedly contributed to the Luddite subject matter in *Shirley*. The assumptions about social order and class mutuality which underlie Mayhew's questions suggest that he knew his middle-class readers would receive his testimony in that context. Possibly the situation in which Le Play did his work is similar. There are also hints in *The Germ* and Ford Madox Brown's diary that the Pre-Raphaelites turned to realism in the early 1850s to illustrate the lessons of class mutuality exemplified by 1848. In 'Christ in the House of His Parents' ('The Carpenter's Shop'), 'The Awakening Conscience', 'Found', 'The Irish Vagrants' and 'Work', they sought to teach the middle classes their duty by showing, unflinchingly and whole, the working classes and the ways to social salvation. The furious denunciations of 'The Carpenter's Shop' and the debate about

---

[36] *Morning Chronicle*, 11 April 1848; Dugdale is quoted in Norman Gash (ed.), *The Age of Peel* (London, 1968), pp. 178–9.
[37] Mrs Gaskell to Edward Chapman, in *The Letters of Mrs Gaskell*, edited by J. A. V. Chapple and A. Pollard (Manchester, 1966), p. 58.

'Work' suggest that respectable opinion realized what they were at and did not like it.[38] This subject needs exploration, along the lines of Timothy Clark's brilliant work on Courbet and French opinion in the same period.

The setbacks to the Cobdenites that came with the withdrawal of the income tax grievance, French threats to peace, and rioting among their working-class allies, were accompanied by a revival of Tory protectionism and its bonds with the Chartists. Their meetings from late 1848 through 1849 were large and enthusiastic, with numerous Chartist speakers. The gatherings were living demonstrations of aristocratic bonhomie and working-class deference. The tenth of April and the débâcles of the European revolts showed that if Britain could isolate herself from the Continent and build up a protected stable agriculture, the nation could rebuild the medieval ideal of a ranked, mutually responsible community'.[39]

The United Kingdom was more dependent upon the Continent than the protectionists imagined. By May 1848 the Bank of England was reported to have sent £700 million of special funds to Ireland to thwart the threatened run on the savings banks [*Nonconformist*, 26 April 1848]. Had the banks collapsed, O'Brien, Meagher and the Young Irelanders might have found considerably greater support for their revolt. Certainly the authorities would have had much more difficulty in controlling the situation. Yet bullion stocks in England fell only marginally. It appears that these were replenished by gold from the Continent.[40] This, together with a fairly good harvest, the recovery of railway shares after 10 April (some rose by three pounds almost overnight to the highest price since 1846) and the recovery of the three per cent consols (which had fallen from 89 and three-quarters on 19 February to 81 on 6 March—coinciding with the first riots—and to 80 and five-eighths on the eve of 10 April, but which then rose in the next week to 84 and one-eighth and to 84 and a quarter by the end of May) laid the foundation of mid-Victorian middle-class prosperity. The new confidence expressed itself in the resumption of railway building and the industrial arts exhibition of 1849 and culminated in the Great Exhibition of 1851, when the High Victorian age is normally said to have begun. If Britain became 'the

---

[38] The young Holman Hunt and J. E. Millais had joined a Chartist protest march in 1848 and according to family tradition had narrowly escaped arrest. See D. Holman-Hunt, *My Grandfather, His Wives and Loves* (London, 1969), p. 41. See also the extracts from Madox Brown's diary for 13 July, 7 August 1854 in W. M. Rossetti, *Ruskin: Rossetti: Preraphaelitism*, reprint of 1899 edn (New York, 1971), pp. 38–41, and John L. Tupper, 'The Subject in Art', *Art and Poetry (The Germ)*, March 1850.

[39] 'The Great Protection Meeting in London', *BEM* LXVII (1850), pp. 738–82.

[40] 'Panic and Party', *FM* XXXVII (1848), pp. 608–9.

rock on which the counter-revolution [built] its church', that rock was largely made of continental gold.[41]

The new concern for class mutuality emerged also in Ashley's work for the Milliners' and Dressmakers' Association, formed to persuade ladies of the upper classes to buy only non-sweated goods, after the notorious suicide of Catherine Brooks, an exploited seamstress.[42] A similar concern, to draw classes together, to mitigate competition in production and to counter infidel social nostrums, drove Charles Kingsley, F. D. Maurice and Thomas Hughes to create the misnamed Christian Socialist movement, based on vague ideas of Christian fraternity, small property rights, and the providential order. The Evangelical Alliance also strengthened its support of city missionaries and began *The Working Man's Charter: or The Voice of the People* to defend the Sabbath. Two notable radicals, R. G. Gammage and J. A. Langford, launched their respective careers by the surprising expedient of submitting essays on the Sabbath which won prizes from Prince Albert.[43]

John Ruskin was moved to bring his aesthetic closer to society and embarked on the *Seven Lamps of Architecture* (1849) in order to preach—so far as one can determine from what Ruskin himself called a 'mist of fine words'—that style in architecture and politics depended on knowing not only 'what is right' but upon ascertaining 'what is possible'. Man had to discover, 'aided by Revelation', his right relations with his fellows, that is, as in good architecture, to establish the supremacy of the 'higher part' over the 'lower', to assert the integrity of the 'constructive' and the necessary contribution from the pure 'reflective element'.[44] Carlyle also set out in his *Latter-Day Pamphlets* to inculcate in 'captains of industry' a sense of responsibility expressed through 'fair' dealing with their workmen and the community. He had been rather bemused and depressed by the 'gallop' of revolutions and at the time wrote nothing about them for publication; but his letters betray a nasty preoccupation with Thomas's scheme of work under military discipline for the unemployed. Carlyle saw in it a model for 'proceeding with our own Paupers'.[45] The recovery of the economy after April reinvigorated the liberals' faith in free market political economy. Harriet Martineau

---

[41] Karl Marx in the *Neue Rheinische Zeitung*, 23 June 1848, reprinted in *The Revolutions of 1848*, edited by D. Fernbach (Harmondsworth, 1973), p. 128.

[42] 'Work and Wages', *FM* XL (1849), pp. 522–30 at p. 522.

[43] *The Working Man's Charter*, edited by J. Jordan (3 pts, London, 1848–9), pp. 31–2.

[44] J. Ruskin, *The Seven Lamps of Architecture* (London, 1903), pp. 2–12; see also chapter 7, 'The Lamp of Obedience'.

[45] T. Carlyle to Rev. Alexander Scott, 5 August 1848, in his *New Letters*, edited by Alexander Carlyle, photographic reprint of London 1904 edition (2 vols, Hildesheim, 1969), p. 61.

and Charles Knight began, under aristocratic patronage, yet another *Voice of the People* to propagate the laws of political economy among the lower orders. Mrs Grote, the friend of John Austin, wrote on the same theme, as did dozens of other condescending pamphleteers.[46] Historians refurbished their comparisons between the secure British polity and the tumultuous condition of France. The Regius Professor of Modern History at Cambridge, Sir James Stephen, advised by John Austin and Dr Whewell, decided in 1849 to lecture on the history of France, in order to draw out the moral advantages enjoyed by England:

> To improve, not to subvert—to adapt our institutions to the successive exigencies to which Time has given birth—to encounter and subdue evils, real and remediable, not evils imaginary, or inherent in the indestructible conditions of all human society—to abandon to the schools all Utopian reveries—to regard the constitution of the realm ... as a sacred trust for which each generation is in turn responsible.[47]

Alison's history of Europe during the French Revolution enjoyed a revival and went through four editions between 1848 and 1853, and epitomes of the vast work flowed from the press for several years. Above all, Macaulay broke the design of his *History of England* in the summer of 1848 to write the great third chapter extolling rational progress and the popular mixed constitution. Like Burke in the *Reflections*, he saw the need to neutralize the Revolution of 1688 and defend the Revolution Settlement. Macaulay succeeded brilliantly and imposed a vision of the British past which has lasted to our own day. Contemporaries perceived his aims immediately. Halifax told him, 'I have finished your second volume and I cannot tell you how grateful all lovers of truth, all lovers of liberty, all lovers of order and of civilized freedom, ought to be to you for having so set forth before them the History of our Revolution of 1688. It has come at a moment when the lessons it inculcates ought to produce great practical effects.'[48] This recognition of the purpose of the *History* surely accounts in part for its popularity: 6,000 copies were bought within six months of publication.

[46] Knight III, pp. 87–92; [Harriet Grote] *The Case of the Poor against the Rich Fairly Considered. By a Mutual Friend* (London, 1850); G. Poulett Scrope, *The Rights of Industry or the Social Problem of the Day, as exemplified in France, Ireland and Britain* (London, 1848).

[47] Sir James Stephen, *Lectures on the History of France* (2nd edn, 2 vols, London, 1852) II, pp. 494–5.

[48] Sir G. O. Trevelyan, *The Life and Letters of Lord Macaulay* (Nelson's Shilling Library, 2 vols, London, 1913) II, p. 215. Macaulay's speech in March 1849, upon his installation as Lord Rector of the University of Glasgow is also illuminating in this respect. *Speeches of Lord Macaulay* (London, 1860), especially pp. 498–501; see also the review of Macaulay's *History*, Thiers's *Rights of Property* and Caussidière's *Memoirs*, *WR* L (January 1849).

By the autumn of 1848 the ruling classes had eschewed other ways of reinforcing traditional authority. Their interest in extending the suffrage quickly ebbed and 'Christian Socialism' and cooperation never became fashionable. The only safety valve which offered no threat to rank and property in Britain and which promised only economic, social and political advantage was emigration. Talk about emigration, which had been neglected by the upper classes in the later 1840s, intensified after 10 April. Ashley, who had been instrumental in arranging the emigration to South Australia of British artisans expelled from France, introduced his motion for a new emigration scheme in the House of Commons on 6 June.[49]

The emigration cause never became urgent. The reassuring knowledge of the strength of the constitution, the failure of the French Republic, the discredit brought on the Chartist and Cobdenite movements by the riots and the revolutionary collapse in Ireland, all eased the pressures on the ruling classes. In mid-April a committee headed by the archbishop of Canterbury, Lord John Russell, Sir George Grey, Viscount Hardinge, Lord Stanley and Sir Robert Peel had launched a subscription to build a monument in the form of a free hospital or baths and workhouses, to express 'deep gratitude to Almighty God' and thanks to the specials for their 'brilliant and admirable example to Great Britain and the world'. All London banks agreed to act as agencies. The royal family led off with £1,000. But the project flopped. A month after the launching the committee quickly disbanded and the little money it had collected was returned to the donors [*Nonconformist*, 26 April, 16 May 1848].

Respectable opinion considered even the cholera, which also infected Britain from the Continent in late 1848, with equanimity. There is no trace in the press of that terror which was loosed in 1831. 'Cholera is ... not the frightful scourge which was depicted in our imagination sixteen years ago,' the editor of the *Nonconformist* remarked; it only threatened 'the infirm and intemperate'. *The Times* recommended calm: 'If we are scared out of our national propriety by any precipitate alarm on the subject, we shall be doing ourselves no less discredit in the eyes of Europe than damage in our own proper fortunes.... We now know [alleging Board of Health advice] that it is not contagious, that its attack is neither sudden nor irresistible, that its devastations, in a well-ordered state, are not such as to warrant a panic.' The weakness in the 1848 Public Health Act, the laxity of public precautions as compared with those of 1831, and Chadwick's struggles in the next few years and his eventual defeat, owe much

---

[49] *The Times*, 27 April 1848; *Nonconformist*, 31 May, 26 July 1848, Alison, 'How to Disarm the Chartists', *BEM* LXIII (1848), pp. 653–73 at p. 654; *Parl. Debs.* 3 C, col. 1172, C1, 1–50.

to the complacency fostered by the political outlook of the ruling classes in the summer and autumn of 1848. In fact the mortality rate of the 1848–9 outbreak was almost twice that of 1831–2: in 1831–2 there were 16,437 deaths or one in 250 of the population of England and Wales and, in 1848–9, 72,180 or one in 151.[50]

The motifs of the ruling classes' success—providence, Little Englandism, recognition of status, the continuance of the exclusive polity—were brought together in the verdict on 1848 in the *Annual Register*:

> The security which under the protection of Providence this country derives from its free and popular constitution was never more signally exemplified than during the year of political agitation and disorder.... While almost every throne on the Continent was emptied or shaken by revolution, the English monarchy, strong in the loyal attachment of the people, not only stood firm in the tempest, but appeared even to derive increased stability from the events that convulsed foreign kingdoms.... A loyalty, based on reason and conviction, and an enlightened appreciation of the benefits derived from well-tried institutions, proves a sure bulwark in the hour of trial against the machinations of conspirators and anarchists.... [In Britain], awed by the overwhelming strength and imposing attitude of the friends of order the mischief subsided almost as soon as it appeared. [*Annual Register* (1848), p. 124.]

This panegyric and the editorials and speeches of 11 April found their ironic apotheosis nearly twenty years later, towards the end of the period of High Victorian prosperity and ruling-class confidence, when Mr Podsnap informed the foreign gentlemen that the British constitution had been bestowed by providence. 'This island was Blest, Sir, to the Direct Exclusion of such Other Countries as—as there may happen to be.'

[50] *Nonconformist*, 23, 30 August, 4, 11 October 1848; *The Times*, 4 October 1848; see also Richard A. Lewis, *Edwin Chadwick and the Public Health Movement 1832–1854* (London, 1952), p. 213.

8

The view from Britain II: the moralizing island

J. H. Grainger

A review of British reactions to the Year of Revolutions can hardly be other than an exercise in what Professor W. L. Burn once called 'selective Victorianism'. The historian turns from 'blind elections' and instinctive rejections in an uncharted and mysterious history of opinion to acknowledge hierarchies of mind and sensibility within a given tradition of discourse. And for yet another French Revolution, England was replete with touchstones, pent-up arguments and long-harboured moralizings. It is among so many rehearsed responses that the historian discriminates.

The English middle classes were briefly alarmed by events in Europe in 1848, especially in France. There was indeed something to be alarmed about. Even without the last tremors of Chartism from Kennington Common, the rumblings from a mobile, club-ridden and excited Paris, open for weeks to the republican eloquence of Lamartine, the socialist earnestness of Louis Blanc, the insurrectionary persistency of Barbès and Blanqui, were deeply disturbing, clear threats to peace, property and authority.

But not even the sudden emergence of 'a democracy without a throne' across the Channel could impair England's long-cultivated sense of political superiority. England remained the moralizing and editorializing island confident within her insular immunity of her own political and social achievements. It was a confidence and superiority which went back through Burke, Locke, Halifax, Hooker and More to Sir John Fortescue, who first identified the *dominium politicum et regale* in the fifteenth century.

England had the accidental uncoerced *patria*, unobtrusive sea-borne *Macht*, quiet civilization. To Englishmen it seemed that the country could always redeem herself within her own tradition of practical reason, to which all had contributed and in which all had a stake. England was the country where political power had been humanized, the country which had created the durable constitution of liberty celebrated throughout Europe in the eighteenth century and still deeply respected in the nineteenth, not least by liberals in France and Germany now making their revolutions.

Cut off from the rest of the world, she was yet ahead of the world. England had all the things other countries sought: a freely elected parliament, responsible government, an independent judiciary and generous political freedoms. Celebrated by others, the English also celebrated themselves. According to Brougham, in his *Letter to the Marquess of Lansdowne* (1848), eight centuries had given Englishmen the benefits of free government, stability and order. 'Our position is in all respects the envy of every other nation in the world, with *perhaps* the exception of America.' The French envied the English their happiness. As Carlyle despondently admitted, the English constitution was now the model of the world—even solid Germany had broken out into 'Frankfort parliamenting and palavering'. And those German conservatives who could not enthuse over England's liberal institutions could nevertheless admire, as had Ranke, historiographer of Prussia, its aristocratic culture and middle-class religion, its Protestant vigour and manliness in the world.

By comparison France was the country of convulsion, of political saturnalia. This was the price it paid for having a *political* working class. The extruded Guizot told Greville with some pride that 'you English cannot conceive what our lowest class is; your own is a mere mob without courage or organization, and not given to politics; ours on the contrary, the lowest class, is eager about politics and with a perfect military organization, and therefore most formidable.' George Eliot, suddenly glad to be living in a Saint-Simonian 'organic epoch', agreed that the English working classes were 'eminently inferior to the mass of the French people. In France the *mind* of the people is highly electrified; they are full of ideas on social subjects; they really desire social *reform....* Here there is so much larger a proportion of selfish radicalism and unsatisfied brute sensuality.' She regretted that there was nothing in the British constitution 'to obstruct the slow progress of *political* reform'. She longed for barricades and dreamed of the day 'when there will be a temple of white marble, where sweet incense and anthems shall rise to the memory of every man and woman who has had a deep *Ahnung*', such as 'poor Louis Blanc'.

England may well have been short on *Ahnung*, 'a presentiment, a yearning, or a clear vision'. It was obviously not one of those Mazzinian nations 'arising from the dust to reclaim their rights, and call their rulers to account for the injustice and oppression of ages'. But what England undoubtedly had—even John Stuart Mill had to admit this—was a long tradition of practical civic duty. And instead of all those 'damned men of genius' or even Hamiltonian or Lincoln-

ian statesmen to harvest the fields of glory (*vide* Lincoln's speech on
'The Perpetuation of our Political Institutions' in 1838 at the Young
Men's Lyceum in Springfield, Illinois), England had what Bagehot
called *hommes de caractère*: men like the duke of Wellington and Lord
Palmerston (not Lord John Russell), capable of acting within the
tradition.

Not only had England *hommes de caractère* but, so editorialized the
pre-Bagehot *Economist* in a Bagehotian way, it was also a country
with a sound *national* character. The English, flanked by 'savage Celt'
and 'flighty Gaul', could congratulate themselves that they had neither
the 'flowing fancy' of the one nor 'the brilliant *esprit*' of the other.
Nor were they likely, Brougham tells us, to become, like the honest,
kindly and industrious Germans, the slaves of fantastic theory, the
victims of ideologists. Greville dismissed the whole of the year 1848
as one of theory and crotchet. And for both Bagehot and Mill, the
one approving, the other deploring, the English were a people resistant
to theory. For Bagehot unreceptivity to theory had become by 1852
a political virtue. What a people really needed was a kind of obtuse-
ness, a well balanced national character. And Queen Victoria, who
thought that constitutions were 'a sad mistake in these Southern
countries', agreed.

It was easy then, from this fastness, for Palmerston to defend
England's 'perpetual interests' and to discriminate among and even
patronize continental revolutions. He might be at one with Disraeli
about 'the dreamy and dangerous nonsense' of *German* nationalism
but support worthy aspirations to constitutions (and national freedom)
in France, Italy and Spain. He was insufferable. He could support
the Austrian Empire, but also enrage Schwarzenberg with his liberal
promptings and protests against military rigour in Italy, with his
'eternal insinuations'. Palmerston was the remote moralizer who could
afford to offend. And because he was not disciplined by land frontiers
and peasant armies he could also afford to make mistakes.

It was easy for Lord Brougham, with all the authority of one who
had helped to bring about the exemplary changes of 1832 in
England, to write a Burkean pamphlet. His *Letter to the Marquess
of Lansdowne* is of course not comparable with the *Reflections*. Burke
had passionately and brilliantly articulated the whole of the island's
concrete political experience against French rationalism and French
abstraction. Brougham merely played a tune on the old fiddle, expressing alarm at the suddenness of the revolution, the power that it had
given to untried, obscure men many of whom had never done anything more than write for the newspapers. Once more the French
patria had been dissolved in general ideas—this time of an ephemeral
'off-hand' republic. The calculus of revolutionary benefits, the
constitution-making, would fail again. You know what you have: you

cannot know what is not yet. France had suddenly and arbitrarily created a strange unpredictable new order, given over her destiny to a 'handful of armed ruffians headed by a shoemaker and a sub-editor'. This was and was not France. Frenchmen saw it all as a stage-play, as mere soap-bubbles. But in the meantime there would be anarchy, confusion and bloodshed; in the future, as after 1789, military despotism.

Brougham's may well seem a characteristic English stance. But hardly for Bagehot, who would sense a 'mischievous excitability' in him, detect a glare in his eye. 'If he were a horse, nobody would buy him.' Writing after the *coup d'état* of Louis Napoleon, Bagehot had solidified into an impregnable self-confidence. Within Bagehot there is a brisk, reassured, even philistine Burke, encased in clubman mail of proof. He need be no more than mildly dismissive of enlightened continental oratory, newspaper liberalism and written constitutions: 'Parliaments, liberty, leading articles, essays, eloquence—all are good, but they are secondary.' And 'Paper is but paper, and no virtue is to be discovered in it to retain within due boundaries the un-disciplined passions of those who have never set themselves seriously to restrain them.' Politics were made of time and place and institu-tions, were but shifting things 'to be tried by and adjusted to the shifting conditions of a mutable world'. Politics were, in fact, 'but a piece of business', a world away from all those clever axioms of Parisian newspaper statesmen. The French have too much 'celerity of intellectual apprehension', too much levity, too little stupidity, to be a free people. 'Their habitual mode of argument is to get hold of some large principle ... to begin to deduce immediately; and to reason down from it to the most trivial details of common action. *Il faut être conséquent avec soi-même*—is their fundamental maxim; and in a world the essence of which is compromise, they could not well have a worse.' He saw France forever plagued with lean, gesticulating deputies, Montagnards, 'sallow, stern, compressed ... gloomy fana-tics, *over*-principled ruffians'. In all, France suffered from an excess of political sensibility. The only cure for this was civilized auto-cracy and the assurance of private happiness.

Bagehot was more sceptical about the durability of liberal political institutions than Brougham but both exhibited their Englishry in their distaste for excessive political ardour and contempt for con-stitutions that were but 'painted sticks', planted in the ground like trees of liberty. There were three other reactions that were perhaps not so characteristically English.

Thomas Carlyle thought that 'the universal dungheap' had caught fire again. Like Brougham, like Bagehot, like Guizot (like Burke sixty years before), he blamed 'the Public Haranguer, haranguing on barrel-head; in leading article; or getting himself aggregated into a National Parliament to harangue'. Only a thin 'earth-rind' lay between 'Society with all its arrangements and acquirements' and 'the universal powder mine' of democracy. Society was immediately at the mercy of the wild, inflammatory words and deeds of a paedocracy, the passions of 'students, young men of letters, advocates, editors, hot inexperienced enthusiasts, or fierce and justly bankrupt desperadoes'. It was a mad world in which experience had not taught and age had failed. 'In these days, what of *lordship* or of leadership is still to be done, the youth must do it, not the mature or aged man; the mature man, hardened into sceptical egoism, knows no monition but that of his own frigid cautions, avarices, mean timidities; and can lead nowhither towards an object that even seems noble.'

Carlyle was glad to see the 'histrio-kings' of Europe capitulating or absconding. Unlike Bagehot he could not appreciate shams. But he did not want kinglessness; it was after all an *ungoverned* world. Rather he wanted real kings without sanctification. They alone could take men from the delusive to the real. The task of statesmanship was for Carlyle enormous: no less than 'how decipher, with best fidelity, the eternal regulation of the Universe'. Neither ballot-box nor parliament was the method. Enfranchisement would merely free men of one another, cut all human relations asunder (it might be Marx), 'loosen by assiduous wedges in every joint, the whole fabric of social existence, stone from stone'. If England was to show the nations how to live, it would not be through her parliament. Despite ineluctable 'black' democracy, England must produce her Saint-Simonian captains and kings, not least in order that she might organize her labour, 'bring these hordes of outcast captainless soldiers under due captaincy'. He saw the organization of labour as the problem for all governments, one that they must solve or themselves disappear.

Carlyle was unprepared for 1848. For most of the year he simmered and glowered but could say little that he had not said before and said better. 'There is no established journal that can stand my articles, no single one they would not blow the bottom out of.' There was a book in him but he could not write it. He could not hiss up enough steam. He had his ambience, Christian Socialist, eccentric Tory and eccentric radical but no definable audience. No one really knew to whom Carlyle was speaking. He himself did not know.

Disraeli was, if less vehement, as illiberal as Carlyle. Mingling with Guizot, Louis Philippe and Metternich, he picked up gossip and characteristically blamed the 'confederations', the secret societies, ranged against property, against the Jews, against Christ, which now covered Europe like a network. But fortunately there was not, as in 1789, a great movement for them to ride. Like Brougham he considered that the French disturbance of 1848 had required nothing more than a change of ministry. But although he could see nothing ordained in what had happened, he was prepared to take up a clear anti-Jacobin line and condemn Palmerston's sentimental liberal politics which had gratuitously created factions in every country from Greece to Spain.

> You looked on the English Constitution as a model farm. You forced this Constitution in every country. You laid it down as a great principle that you were not to consider the interests of England, or the interests of the country you were in connection with, but that you were to consider the great system of Liberalism which had nothing to do with the interests of England, and was generally antagonistic with the interests of the country with which you were in connection.

Disraeli also mocked that ingenuous domestic liberalism which so readily recognized and applauded worthy moral causes in the remote and ill-understood politics of Europe. On the danger of the 'modern newfangled sentimental principle of nationality' in foreign policy, he followed both Metternich and Brougham whose *Letter to the Marquess of Lansdowne* he approved: 'He says what we all think, but he is the first who has said it so completely.' He had never praised the 'old harlequin' before. It is as a sedulous English Metternich that Disraeli in *Lord George Bentinck* makes one of his grand statements. The people of England, he maintained, 'will, perhaps, after due reflection discover that ancient communities like the European must be governed either by traditional influences or by military force'. The ardent renovators must be preoccupied with controlling 'outraged tradition in multiplied forms': princely pretenders, dispossessed aristocrats, plundered churches and displaced corporations. 'In this state of affairs after a due course of paroxysms, for the sake of maintaining order and securing the rights of industry, the state quits the senate and takes refuge in the camp.' Disraeli was still very much a literary man in politics.

John Stuart Mill's *Vindication of the French Revolution of 1848* was a direct response to Brougham's 'outpourings of desultory invective'. As such it was an exculpation of the French political mind. It was an occasion for rejoicing in the possibilities of clear, rational and *elevated* politics. For this was the most disinterested revolution that had ever been. 'It stands almost alone among revolutions, in having placed power in the hands of men who neither expected nor sought it, nor used it for any personal purpose—not even for that of maintaining, otherwise than by opinion and discussion, the ascendancy of their own party; men whose every act proclaimed them to be that almost unheard-of phenomenon—unselfish politicians.' France had been blessed with public men who 'strove to make their tenure of power produce as much good as their countrymen were capable of receiving and more than their countrymen had yet learnt to desire'. The singularity of the revolution lay in this 'disinterested zeal' and not in its inexplicability or irrationality. Those who had brought it about were neither ruffians nor obscure. The seven original members of the provisional government had all had distinguished service in the Chamber of Deputies; the four popular nominees were 'acknowledged leaders' of the republican press.

George Eliot had seen in the February Revolution intimations of better politics to come—but not in England. Mill too moralized against England but, more strenuously, drew from the revolution a lesson for England. At home he saw earthy, interest-ridden, practical politics. In France he welcomed a 'government of improvement', one not merely reforming a political order which had rested upon a coalition of all the sinister interests in France but also imbuing it with political virtue. Mill recalled de Tocqueville's prophetic address to the Chamber of Deputies of 27 January 1848, in which he had deplored the decline of public morality under Louis Philippe. The old government had worked through the interests, the passions and vices of men. It had achieved ascendancy by cultivating men at their worst, not as bearers of civic rights and duties but as pursuers of self-interest. 'In Heaven's name', de Tocqueville had urged, 'change the spirit of the government, for, I say it again, that spirit is hurrying you to the abyss.'

For Mill the success of Lamartine and his associates was a triumph of the spirit, of the public spirit, in a desert of material interests. Like Carlyle, Mill sought 'nobility'; unlike Carlyle, he could find it in words as well as action. Without soldiers, without police, the politicians of the provisional government had ruled by 'fair words'. They had in fact kept the frame of government in existence by haranguing on the barrel-head, by using reason to republicanize the public mind. These were 'the better and the wiser few', the unbound yet responsible élite uttering the truths that would disperse or vanquish evil counsellors, evil means, vulgar and low moralities and vested interests. They showed the way; they represented a liberal and intellectual ascendancy; they were the creative, romantic energies prescribed to lead men out of what Mill was later to call a period of 'weak energies and weak feelings'.

And were such men, 'the noblest spirits and most enlightened minds in the country, to employ an opportunity such as scarcely occurs once in a thousand years, in simply waiting on the whims and prejudices of the many?' How could they when they were so aware of the political indifference, the want of education, 'the absence of habits of discussion and participation in public business' among the majority of the population? Serious, abstinent, dedicated, the new men were entitled to take initiatives, to strike the fetters from the slave, to hold out the hand of friendship to those in other lands seeking to free themselves from foreign yoke, to declare the *droit au travail* (to Mill nothing more than the Elizabethan poor law—in practical matters the French might still be trailing), to cooperate with the working class and their leaders in socialist experimentation, in just 'distribution of social advantages'—even if success there and then were unlikely.

Lamartine and his associates had also been truth in action, empirical truth, *in accordance with the fact*. The English refused to convert practice into theory. Mill defended the lucid unaccommodating French against the inexplicit dissimulating English who considered it 'unnatural and unsafe, either to do the thing which they profess or to profess the thing which they do'. Mill was identifying what another and more persistent Francophil, Hilaire Belloc, seventy years later called 'the aristocratic instinct for laying by on the shelf dead institutions and preserving them under continuity of name'. The English, maintained Mill, could not accept the consequences of theory, 'could never feel themselves safe unless they [were] living under the shadow of some conventional fiction'. The could, with 'sincere feeling', accept a 'so-called sovereign' who 'does not govern, ought not to govern, is not intended to govern, but yet must be held up to the nation, be addressed by the nation, and even address the nation as if he or she did govern'. To the French this could only be simulation. 'A constitutional monarchy, therefore, was likely in France, as it is likely in every other country in Continental Europe, to be but a brief halt on the road from a despotism to a republic.'

A Parisian revolution was now a recognized occasion for what Tom Arnold called the English propensity for external and mechanical moralizing. Whether the opportunity was for self-congratulation or self-criticism, it was clear that the English moral base had not been worn away. Whatever predominated in the minds and temperaments of Bagehot, Brougham, Carlyle, Eliot or Mill, earth, water, air or fire, each of them spoke for the whole of the English community as each saw it. The communal 'we' rolled easily through Greville's self-reassurance:

> In the midst of the roar of the revolutionary waters, that are deluging the whole earth, it is grand to see how we stand erect and unscathed. It is the finest tribute that ever has been paid to our Constitution, the greatest test that ever has been applied to it, and there is a general feeling of confidence, and a reliance on the soundness of the public mind.

The island plural continued to roll untroubled through the relaxed cultural self-criticism of Monckton Milnes, poet, *littérateur*, politican and gentleman. For Milnes, who had only just resigned from the Carlton Club but whose republican and democratic sentiments were well to the left of those of Russellite Whigs whom he joined, the revolution was not only a triumph of the spirit and of letters but also a romantic spectacle to be enjoyed.

There was the *Fête de la Fraternité*, Rachel singing the *Marseillaise*, lively political debate in the *salons*, in the streets and in the proliferating radical clubs, piquant dinner parties and, above all, the living theatre of 15 May when, before Milnes's very eyes, a real Parisian mob, *enragés*, *ouvriers* and *gamins*, swept through the *Assemblée* in the Palais Bourbon like a sea. It was all very entertaining but his old friend de Tocqueville, who had himself in the early February Days felt that his countrymen were merely staging a play, indeed warming themselves at the hearth of their fathers' passions, thought it necessary to warn Milnes about the bad impression his apparent levity was creating. He had a fine time and, when he returned to England, he too felt it necessary to write his letter to the Marquess of Lansdowne [*The Events of 1848, Especially in their Relation to Great Britain. A Letter to the Marquess of Lansdowne*, 1849]—this time from a new Whig to an old one:

> Our disregard of the political condition of other nations is always liable to be proud, selfish, and unjust. At one moment we reprobate every disturbance of social order in foreign countries, just as if our own order and freedom had not been won by civil war, by resistance to power, and by the punishment of evil-doers in high places; at another we exhaust our indignation and scorn against the meanness and effeminacy of men who submit to be under the terror of brute force, or still more, under the oppression of an alien rule, and justify the tyranny by the nature and the habits of a slave. Forgetful of our own ancestors, who in the field of battle, on the scaffold, in exile or captivity, have raised, stone by stone, the edifice of our civil life, we mock at the sacrifices, the labours, and the martyrdoms of other patriots who have not succeeded in realizing at once all their hopes and aims, but those whose blood and tears may be just as fruitful as those of our progenitors.

For George Smythe, writing in the *Morning Chronicle*, this solemn lest-we-forget Whiggery was too much:

> After the levity of Lord Palmerston's characteristic defence of his peculiar foreign policy, there was wanting nothing more than a pamphlet in its eulogy from Mr Monckton Milnes. The professional jester has a prescriptive claim to break his bulrush (after the danger has passed away) where the lance of the knight has been ruefully shivered.... Immethodic, absurd and illogical as is this pamphlet of Mr Milnes, it is occasionally, and by involuntary glimpses, so unwittingly true, that it is not without a purpose that we propose to gibbet him, in front of every country of which he has written with universal ignorance and omniscient-pretensions.

Milnes demanded satisfaction from the man who, three years later, was to fight in the last duel on English soil. This time the matter was settled peacefully with honour to both sides. There could be no doubt. The island was blessed.

9

Conclusion: communist revolution and the model of 1848

Eugene Kamenka

History, the young Ernest Barker wrote, has 'a way of numbing generous emotions. All things have happened already; nothing much came of them before; and nothing much can be expected of them now.'[1] The revolutions of 1848, as this volume has perhaps brought out, produced no great heroes and no stirring triumphs, no person and no class in whose hands one would wish to place the future. There has been, among radicals and the democratic left in France and Germany, a certain emphasis on 'the spirit of 1848' as a climate of opinion and style of living—the courage and generosity of the revolutionary masses, the devotion that could be inspired by the ideals of democracy and internationalism or at least of a liberal, internally and externally unaggressive nation-state. Not all of this is a myth. Nor is the suffering that became evident in revolt; in 1846 in Cologne, for instance, every third family was on relief and only Gottschalk seemed to care, personally and directly. But if, as Marx insisted, the proletariat is either revolutionary or it is nothing, then the little people of 1848 were not a Marxist proletariat destined to become the dynamic class in a period of reactionary stagnation. They could smash machines as being responsible for their poverty and degradation as enthusiastically as they jeered at monarchs and the rich. Their leaders in Paris seemed to subsequent generations romantic incompetents, unable to cope with the new trend toward mass democracy; their leaders in Germany, as national figures, did not exist and the middle classes who talked on behalf of democracy had neither the power nor the will to action. The degradation and suffering and lack of liberty against which they revolted were real, but immediate history was not of their making. For it is true that states are not built and autocracies are not destroyed overnight by argument and majority vote and that nations and classes are dramatically freed, united or broken by blood

[1] Ernest Barker, *Political Thought in England from Herbert Spencer to the Present Day* (London, 1915), p. 167.

and iron, not by a generous application of liberty and tomato sauce. But those who are at home with blood and iron are themselves not generous and do not usher in the republic where swords are beaten into ploughshares and the wicked do not flourish. If a country needs a revolution it is not likely to have its problems solved by one.

Marx and Engels themselves, in a curious way, recognized this in their role as scientific socialists, emphasizing the importance of objective conditions, of the historical process that had its own logic that might produce, but was not derivative from, the political act of revolution. They paid less attention to the legacy of the spirit, to the extent that a defeated revolution could be a carrier of values, a symbol of a free, egalitarian and democratic tradition which might well be destroyed—as it later was in Petrograd and Moscow—by success in grasping the reins of power. Such an accolade of a defeated revolution —that it was writing the poetry of the future—Marx was later to heap upon the Paris Commune of 1871; in 1848 and 1849 he was preoccupied with the problem of power. In that sense he was a revolutionist. For him the record of 1848 was above all a record of shameful weakness, indecision, incapacity to grasp or hold power on the part of the German bourgeoisie and the intellectuals generally. In France, the events of June 1848 proved the total irreconcilability of class interests. It was Ludwig Feuerbach, whom Marx by then scorned as still stuck in the theological phase of human thinking, who believed from the first that the revolution in Germany was premature because Germans were not yet emancipated from religion, because they were not yet scientific democrats or republicans. Feuerbach believed that a real revolution was a slow but steady conversion of the hearts, minds and lives of all men, a democratic upsurge and not a matter of cunning and manipulation, of shifting tactics and hypocritical alliances, decisive blows and strategic retreats. The Marx who stressed the revolutionary power of the process of material production could see this point and lay some of the foundations for a democratic socialism. Marx the revolutionist could not, and he bequeathed to the communist movement that arose in his name the ruthless single-minded concern with power that has led so many millions to their graves without furnishing the utopia they were promised.

In the revolutions of 1848, it has often been suggested, Marx and many others conflated the strains and crises that accompanied the beginnings of industrial capitalism with its death pangs. Marx and Engels came to see their mistake and to recognize that the laws of revolution and the laws of historical materialism might not be the same. For the revolutionary, the backwardness of the regime he faces might, contrary to the claims of the materialist interpretation of history in its simple form, be positively an advantage. This is why the world's first successful communist revolution broke out in the ramshackle, tottering state of the tsars—a state weakened by two disastrous wars with industrially much more advanced nations, saddled with an antiquated and backward-looking bureaucratic machine, unable effectively to take a leap into the modern world. This is why the next major successful communist revolution of world-historical importance broke out in that other ruin of a once-great empire, the Middle Kingdom of China. For the revolutionary in those countries, and many smaller ones like them, the social conditions of 1848 in Europe were astonishingly like their conditions in the present. Democracy, national liberation, the overthrow of feudalism, modernization, centralization and the demands and miseries of a newly emergent working class were all on their agenda. The *Communist Manifesto* and the *Neue Rheinische Zeitung* spoke to them, across the years, with an urgent and contemporary voice. Above all, in situations of stagnation or collapse, it taught them contempt for those who would not act, with confidence and ruthlessness, with the people or without them, recognizing that revolution was above all a struggle for the state and that states rose and fell with blood and iron. Between 1917 and the present day the basic tactics that Marx and Engels instictively worked with in 1848, but had not elaborated into a revolutionary manual, were to be copied time and time again: the democratic alliance, the purging of opponents, the constant pressure for radicalization and centralized control and the belief that war and the fear of war do much to promote both. Marx's theories are certainly not unequivocally Bolshevik; his temperament was.

Marx and Engels themselves, in 1848 and 1849, did not work out a theory to justify their shifts of emphasis and changing stances between 1846 and the defiant last issue of the *Neue Rheinische Zeitung*. To quite some extent, they followed their instinct and their emotions. But in the important 'Address of the Central Committee to the Communist League' in March 1850, Marx did elaborate a principle of permanent revolution that has emerged from time to time in the theory and constantly informed the practice of communist revolutionaries throughout the world. In the conditions of a bourgeois revolution, where the bourgeoisie is not strong enough to make its own revolution and hold power confidently, a revolutionary workers' party should give its support to the petty bourgeois democratic forces struggling against reactionary governments. It should even allow them to seize power. But it must prevent these democrats from consolidating power and freezing the revolution, reverting from a revolutionary enthusiasm that necessarily gives a universalizing aspect to their narrow class interest. The task of the revolutionary party is to make the revolution permanent until the proletariat has conquered state power. It must therefore take an attitude of unconcealed mistrust to the new democratic government, harass it and dictate such conditions as will bear within them the seeds of the bourgeois democrats' downfall. Revolutionary excitement must be maintained. While the temporary inevitable dominance of bourgeois democracy has to be accepted, the revolutionary workers should establish their own governments simultaneously with and alongside the new official government, whether they do so in the form of municipal committees and municipal councils or by way of workers' clubs or workers' committees. These would represent an irreconcilable revolutionary opposition, whose task was to push as many radical social objectives as possible and thus to undermine the position of the official government. But that story belongs to our twentieth century, to the struggle between the Petrograd soviet and the provisional government.

The concern with power, with infiltrating or capturing the state, and the tactics suggested by Marx and Engels on the basis of 1848 have remained the stock-in-trade of communist revolutionaries as disciplined political activists everywhere. Many a revolution now has been successfully captured and consolidated on that basis. The theory of permanent revolution, it is true, has been and can be converted into a weapon against the new communist dictatorships themselves: that was in part the message of Trotsky and clearly the message of the ageing Mao, who proclaimed that revolution is a continuous protest, restructuring and reappraisal lasting over centuries after the initial successful communist assumption of power. But Mao is becoming a prophet without honour in his own land, and its Communist Party has reverted to the principal message of Marx—that the working-class revolution is a seizure of state power and a development and reorganization on the basis of state control of the whole system of production, distribution and exchange for rational social ends. It is in the comparatively affluent countries of the West that radical revolutionaries have continued to maintain an interest in the Marx of the permanent revolution and in another, later Marx, who saw in the Paris Commune a possible model for the most developed of socialist revolutions—the revolution in advanced industrial conditions which would no longer seek to capture the state and keep its coercive machinery intact, but which would instantly instil new vigour and energy into society by dismantling the centralized bureaucratic machinery of state as opposed to municipal control. That Marx—or that mood of Marx—lasted about as long as the Paris Commune itself.

Chronology of events leading up to and during the revolutions of 1848–9

Compiled by E. Y. Short

1812	Democratic constitution proclaimed in Spain. Liberal constitution proclaimed in Sicily. General Diet meets at Warsaw.
1814	Democratic constitution establishes Norway as free and independent state under king of Sweden.
1815	Treaty of Vienna restores pre-Napoleonic *status quo* in Europe, but secures independence and neutrality of twenty-two Swiss cantons. Sicilian liberal constitution abolished. Polish central provinces constituted as Kingdom of Poland under Russian rule; Cracow declared a free republic. Radical agitation in Britain follows passing of Corn Laws.
1816–20	Liberal constitutions proclaimed in Nassau, Bavaria, Baden, Württemberg, Hesse-Darmstadt.
1817	Habeas Corpus Act suspended in Britain. Wartburg demonstration in favour of German unity.
1819	Peterloo Massacre in Britain. Society of Carbonari established at Naples. Federal reactionary measures in Germany.
1820	Military *coup détat* in Spain restores 1812 constitution. Revolution in Portugal. Polish Diet opens. Cato Street conspiracy to assassinate ministry in Britain. Rising in Palermo (Sicily) suppressed.
1820–21	Revolution against Austrians in Piedmont crushed at defeat of Novara. Carbonari lead successful insurrection in Naples and force king to swear to new liberal constitution, but he summons Austrian troops to suppress revolt.
1821	Insurrections against Turks in Moldavia and

	Wallachia joined by Greeks. Start of Greek War of Independence.
1822	Greek declaration of independence. Portugal granted liberal constitution similar to Spanish one of 1812.
1823	Daniel O'Connell founds Catholic Association in Ireland. Provincial Estates created in Prussia.
1824	In Britain Combination Act repeals law against associations of workmen.
1825	Hungarian Diet (of Pressburg) reconvened after lapse of many years, marking resurgence of Hungarian (Magyar) nationalism. Beginning of great Czech cultural revival, inspired by German thinkers, notably Herder, up to 1848.
1827	Election riots in Paris; Blanqui active on barricades.
1828	Buonarroti, Tuscan revolutionary and Carbonarist, publishes *Histoire de la conspiration pour l'égalité dite de Babeuf*, which greatly influences French radicals. Béranger imprisoned for political songs. Insurrection of Carbonari in Naples suppressed. Panhellenion, or Grand Council of Greek States, established.
1829	Catholic Emancipation Act passed in United Kingdom. Turkey acknowledges Greek independence. Greek National Assembly meets at Argos. Wallachia and Moldavia placed under Russian protection. Civil war in Portugal, to 1835.
1830 26 July	Ordinance restricting freedom of press in France.
27–9 July	Leads to 'The Three Glorious Days' revolution in Paris; Charles X forced to abdicate and Louis Philippe chosen as the 'people's king'. Revolution at Brussels is followed by declaration of Belgian independence from the Netherlands. Risings in Saxony and Brunswick lead to abdication of king of Saxony and flight of duke of Brunswick. In years 1830–39, secret societies active in France, led by Buonarroti, Blanqui, Flocon, Barbès and others.
November	Revolt of Poles against Russian rule.
1831 25 January	Polish declaration of independence.
September–October	Warsaw taken by Russian forces, the insurrection savagely suppressed and the Kingdom of Poland

made integral part of Russia. Risings in Modena, Parma and Papal States suppressed by Austria. Mazzini founds the Young Italy party at Marseilles. Silkweavers of Lyons riot. Heine settles in Paris. Belgian independence from the Netherlands recognized by allied powers in Treaty of 24 Articles.

1831–2   Russia gives Moldavia and Wallachia identical constitutions.

1832   Hambach (Palatinate) demonstration for German unity; new federal reactionary measures. Acts for parliamentary electoral reform passed in United Kingdom. Kollár's sonnet cycle, *Slava's Daughter* (2nd edn) extols Slavic life and Slavs' mission as leaders of Europe. Drasković urges Croat delegates to Hungarian Diet at Pressburg to resist Magyar domination and work for a Greater Illyria. Polish Democratic Society founded to prepare for insurrection against Russia and to support revolutionary movements of other peoples.

5–6 June   ABC (*abaissés*) Paris workers' insurrection, in support of a republic and Polish independence, suppressed.

1833   Act abolishing slavery and Shaftesbury's Factory Act passed in United Kingdom.

1834   Mazzini founds Young Europe at Basle, and Mazzinian groups spread in Europe from 1834–1845. *Hessischer Landsbote* founded by Georg Büchner, who joins the *Gesellschaft für Menschenrechte* founded by Weidig. In Britain the Poor Law Amendment Act is passed. In Paris German political exiles form the *Bund der Geächteten* (League of Outlaws). Carlist wars in Spain, to 1839.

April   Workers' insurrection in Lyons, led by the Society for the Rights of Man, is suppressed by troops. A rising in sympathy by Paris workers is suppressed in the massacre of the rue Transnonain.

1835   Gaj founds the Croat nationalist paper, the *Croat Gazette*, at Agram (Zagreb).

1836   Weitling, Schapper, Moll and others form the *Bund der Gerechten* (League of the Just) in Paris. Louis Napoleon's attempted revolution in Strasbourg fails. Revolutions in Lisbon. Palacký's *History of the Czech People* begins publication,

	giving Czech nationalism a political bias and sense of mission.
1837	Chartist movement founded in England. Reactionary policies in German states, press censorship. Seven liberal professors dismissed at University of Göttingen (including the brothers Grimm, Gervinus and Dahlmann). Vörösmarty publishes his *Appeal to the Hungarian Nation*.
1838	Ruge founds the *Hallesche Jahrbücher*. In England Cobden and Bright and friends found the Anti-Corn Law League.
1839	Louis Blanc publishes his influential pamphlet *Organisation du travail*. 'Insurrection of the seasons' in May at Paris, led by Barbès and Blanqui, who are imprisoned until 1848. Treaty between the Netherlands and Belgium, recognizing independence of latter, finally signed. Revision in constitution of the Swiss cantons leads to Catholic–Protestant strife.
1840	Accession of Frederick William IV as king of Prussia. Rhineland crisis between France and Germany. N. Becker's *Der deutsche Rhein* has great popular success. Hess, Herwegh, Venedey and many others publish their views. Reaction to French demands marks turning-point in German nationalist movement. Louis Napoleon's attempted revolution in Boulogne fails. Revolution in Madrid suppressed and Cortes dissolved. Young Ireland party formed.
1841	Ludwig Feuerbach's *The Essence of Christiantity* published. Ruge publishes his *Deutsche Jahrbücher*. The *Hülferuf der deutschen Jugend*, edited by W. Weitling, published in Geneva. Kossuth founds *Pesti Hirlap* in support of Hungarian political autonomy.
1842	Marx becomes editor of the *Rheinische Zeitung*, Cologne. Engels's first visit to England. *The Nation* founded at Dublin. Revolution in Barcelona where the National Guard joins the people.
1843	A revolutionary junta established at Barcelona, which is gradually successful throughout Spain, and the regent Espartero flees. Great Repeal movement, led by O'Connell, in Ireland; formation of 'Molly Maguire', a secret society. In

Brussels the abbé Gioberti publishes *The Moral and Civic Primacy of the Italians*. Marx arrives in Paris, where he becomes friendly with Heine. Bloodless revolution in Athens establishes new constitution, national representation and ministerial responsibility. Rumanian liberal secret society, Fraternity, founded to work for Polish–Rumanian alliance against Russia.

1844   Ruge and Marx publish the *Deutsch-französische Jahrbücher* in Paris; Marx quarrels with Ruge, joins editorial board of *Vorwärts*. Excitement about Ronge, the Catholic reformer. Workers' riots in many parts of Silesia, weavers' riots in Langenbielau and Peterswaldau attracting most attention. O'Connell tried for political conspiracy and convicted.

1845   Engels publishes *Condition of the Working Class in England*. Marx writes his *Theses on Feuerbach*, is expelled from Paris, moves to Brussels, gives up Prussian citizenship. Feuerbach publishes *The Essence of Religion*. The Sonderbund, an association of Catholic cantons, is founded in Switzerland. Foundation of the *Prague Gazette* marks growth of Czech democratic movement. *Slovak National Gazette* founded by Stúr in opposition to both Czech and Magyar claims to represent all Slavs. The Agram Diet adopts Croat as its official language. Foundation of Society of Rumanian Students in Paris, inspired by Michelet and Mickiewicz and under patronage of Lamartine, to propagate radical doctrines of democracy and nationalism.

1846   The liberal Pope Pius IX is elected, declares political amnesty. Potato famine in Ireland; O'Brien and Young Ireland party secede from Repeal Association. Repeal of Corn Laws in England. Communist Correspondence Committee formed in Brussels. Schleswig-Holstein crisis. First *Germanisten* Congress in September. Ruthene peasant risings against Polish overlords in Galicia savagely suppressed. Republic of Cracow annexed by Austria after unsuccessful rising. Kossuth founds Radical Party pledged to political emancipation of Magyars. Insurrection in north Portugal. Louis Napoleon escapes from imprisonment at Ham. Society of Rumanian Students in Paris translates and distributes chapter on nationality from Michelet's *The People* (1846).

1847   Portuguese insurgents enter Oporto, later capitulate to Spanish forces. Espartero restored to power in Spain. Kossuth's Magyar Radical Party dominates Hungarian Diet, antagonizes Croats and Slavs. Havlíček, editor of *Prague Gazette* and great admirer of Daniel O'Connell, founds Czech Repeal Club for peaceful constitutional reform. Young Serbia Society founded by students returned from German universities, to promote liberal and democratic ideas. Irish Confederation founded. O'Connell dies at Genoa. Kingdom of Poland declared a Russian province. Swiss radical victory over the Sonderbund; Jesuits expelled and monastic property secularized. Austrian troops occupy Ferrara. Cavour founds newspaper *Il Risorgimento* at Turin. People's International League founded in London, 28 April, under aegis of Mazzini; it publishes his *Address* on national self-determination which is widely read and reprinted in Europe. Liberal party gains at Belgian elections. Prussian General Diet (*Vereinigter Landtag*) meets from April to June. *Deutsche Zeitung*, organ of pro-Prussian moderate liberals, begins publication on 1 July. In September German Democrats meet at Offenburg in Baden. Heppenheim meeting of moderate liberals in October to concert political activity. In December Gottschalk founds a section of the Federation of Communists at Cologne. 'Campaign of the banquets', for electoral reform, in Paris. Louis Blanc's *History of the Revolution* published. The Chartist leader O'Connor returned to parliament in England. At the end of the year the Communist Congress, meeting in London, commissions Marx and Engels to prepare the Communist Manifesto.

1848
12 January   Insurrection at Palermo: great towns of Sicily demand restoration of 1812 constitution.
20 Jan.   Danish radicals demand constitution.
27 Jan.   Tocqueville's speech in Paris Chamber of Deputies, 'The storm is brewing.'

28 Jan.	Rescript of king of Denmark incorporating duchies into Denmark.
29 Jan.	Threatened insurrection at Naples.
February	*Communist Manifesto* published in London (in German).
10 Feb.	New liberal constitution at Naples. Insurrections in Turin, Tuscany, Lombardy.
12 Feb.	Motion in Baden chamber proposing German parliament. John Mitchell calls for insurrection in Ireland.
14 Feb.	Pius IX creates commission of reform.
17 Feb.	Liberal Tuscan consititution proclaimed at Florence.
21 Feb.	Reformist banquet at Paris banned.
22–4 Feb.	Revolution in Paris; barricades, Red Flag, Tuileries ransacked, prisons thrown open (Blanqui and Barbès among those set free). Louis Philippe abdicates; provisional government formed.
25 Feb.	Blanqui founds Central Republican Society. Louis Blanc draws up decree guaranteeing work for all citizens.
26 Feb.	French Republic proclaimed from steps of Hôtel de Ville.
27 Feb.	People's assembly at Mannheim in Baden demands popular representation, freedom of press; followed by disturbances throughout Germany.
March	During first weeks of March, liberal policies and ministers introduced in Hesse-Darmstadt, Nassau, Württemberg, Hesse-Kassel, Hanover, Saxony, Mecklenburg-Schwerin.
1 March	First session of Louis Blanc's Luxembourg Commission, Paris. Revolution at Neuchâtel (Switzerland). Declaration for German unity.
2 March	Reduced working day decreed in Paris.
3 March	Kossuth's speech to Hungarian Diet calling for independence from Austria. French provisional government invites Marx to return to Paris. German *Bundestag* decrees freedom of press.
4 March	Lamartine's manifesto in Europe.
5 March	Charles Albert of Sardinia and Piedmont promulgates constitutional statute. Riots in Berlin, Düsseldorf, Aachen, Cologne. Liberal congress at Heidelberg decides to summon a parliament.

6 March	National workshops organized in Paris. King of Prussia promises regular meetings of *Landtag*.
8 March	German *Bundestag* decides on black, red and gold as national colours.
11 March	Reformist assembly in Prague.
13 March	Viennese revolution; dismissal and flight of Metternich.
14 March	Windischgrätz military governor of Vienna; civic guard crushes working-class risings. Constitutions granted in Rome and Rumania. *Landtag* convoked in Prussia.
15 March	Revolution in Budapest. At Vienna the Emperor promises a constitution.
16 March	Paris: demonstrations of the 'bearskins' (bourgeois supporters).
17 March	Counter-demonstration by revolutionary party for postponement of elections. King of Prussia declares support for federal Germany.
18 March	Berlin revolution. Declaration of independence by Schleswig-Holstein.
18–22 March	Five-day rising in Milan.
20 March	Ludwig of Bavaria abdicates.
21 March	Danish provisional government, including radicals, formed after riots in duchies. Barbès founds Club of the Revolution. King of Prussia claims leadership in revolutionary Germany.
22 March	Spanish Cortes suspended to check spreading radical agitation. Revolution in Venice.
24 March	Charles Albert of Sardinia grants constitution and openly supports cause of Italian regeneration against Austria.
26 March	Riots in Madrid quickly suppressed.
27 March	Reformist demonstration at Jassy in Moldavia. King of Prussia supports revolutionary movements to promote unification of Germany.
30 March	German Diet declares in favour of constituent assembly.
31 March	*Vorparlament* meets at Frankfurt, until 13 April.
3 April	Deputation from O'Brien and his associates to Lamartine and provisional French government.
4 April	Great meeting of 'Young Irelanders', Dublin.
8 April	Bohemia promised a constitution.
10 April	Chartist demonstration in London collapses.
11 April	New Hungarian constitution ratified.
12 April	Hungarian Diet calls for reconstitution of Poland.

12–20 April	Republican rising in Baden; suppressed.
13 April	Bourbons deposed in Sicily.
16 April	Demonstrations in Paris demanding postponement of elections, state organization of labour, renewed confrontations of bourgeois and revolutionary parties.
17 April	King of the Netherlands agrees to political reform and new constitution.
23 April	General elections for Constituent Assembly in France produce setback for extreme radicals. Elections in Poland.
25 April	Projected constitution published in Vienna. Insurrection at Cracow suppressed by Austrian troops. German Legion, formed in Paris and led by Herwegh, crosses the Rhine.
27 April	Parisian German Legion defeated at Dössenbach (Baden).
29 April	Pope Pius IX condemns war in Italy.
2–9 May	Polish rising in Posen led by Mieroslawski; suppressed.
4 May	Opening meeting of French National Assembly at Paris.
5 May	Rising in Naples.
7 May	Rising in Madrid. Central Committee for National Guard formed in Vienna.
9 May	Paris: Commission of Executive Power instituted, elected by National Assembly.
13 May	Mitchell, editor of *United Irishmen*, sentenced to fourteen years transportation.
15 May	Demonstration in Paris for Polish independence. Riots in Vienna; Emperor grants universal suffrage. Fresh risings in Naples where liberals and National Guard almost wiped out by royal troops helped by *lazzaroni*. Demonstration of Transylvanian Rumanians at Blaj.
18 May	Frankfurt parliament opens in church of St Paul. Insurrection in Vienna; Emperor flees to Innsbruck.
22 May	Opening of Prussian *Landtag*.
26 May	Barricades in Vienna; Committee for Public Safety formed. Danes invade north Schleswig.
31 May	First number of *Neue Rheinische Zeitung* published at Cologne by Marx and his associates.
2 June	First Slavonic Congress opens at Prague; Bakunin takes part.

9 June	Rumanian peasants assemble at Islaz in Wallachia and decide to march on Bucharest.
10–11 June	Integrity of Kingdom of Hungary confirmed. Provisional Rumanian government formed at Bucharest.
11–12 June	Radetzky's counter-offensive in Italy begins.
12 June	Second proposed Chartist mass meeting collapses.
12–16 June	Riots in Prague; Windischgrätz breaks up the Congress, ending Czech democratic movement.
14–17 June	First Democratic Congress, Frankfurt.
21 June	Dissolution of national workshops, Paris.
23–6 June	'The June Days': Parisian workers' insurrection (Red Republicans) against troops and National Guard. Suppressed by Cavaignac and Lamoricière. Garibaldi arrives in Nice from South America. Carlist civil war breaks out in Catalonia.
28 June	Prague Congress finally dissolved. Cavaignac becomes President of the Council, Paris. Law on provisional central power enacted by Frankfurt Parliament.
3 July	Venice incorporated with Sardinia under Charles Albert.
4 July	New Hungarian Assembly meets.
8 July	Habeas Corpus suspended in Ireland.
12 July	German Diet (*Bundestag*) abolished.
Late July	*Reichstag* Constitutent Assembly opens in Vienna. Frankfurt Parliament claims most of Posen for the *Reich*.
25 July	Charles Albert of Sardinia defeated at Custozza by Austrian troops under Radetzky.
July–August	O'Brien's Irish insurrection suppressed; leaders arrested and sentenced to transportation.
August	Students of Heidelberg invite Feuerbach to lecture to them.
5 Aug.	Austrians occupy Milan.
7 Aug.	Venice proclaims loyalty to king of Sardinia.
9 Aug.	Austro-Sardinian armistice.
12 Aug.	Manin restored as dictator of independent republican Venice. Imperial court returns to Vienna.
21–3 Aug.	Workers' riots in Vienna.
23 Aug.–3 Sept.	Berlin: congress of workers' associations, and democratic agitation led by Stepan Born.
11 September	Jellaćic, restored as *ban* of Croatia, invades Hungary with Austro-Croat troops.

12 Sept.	New Swiss federal constitution.
18 Sept.	Republican riots at Frankfurt: barricades, street fighting. Abortive republican insurrection in Baden by Struve.
25 Sept.	Transylvanian Rumanians rise against Hungary.
26 Sept.–11 Oct.	State of siege in Cologne.
Sept.–Oct.	Hungarian insurgents defeat Austrian troops.
3 October	Emperor dissolves Hungarian Diet which refuses to be dissolved; it appoints a provisional government under Batthyány and Kossuth.
6 Oct.	Revolution begins in Vienna.
26–30 Oct.	Second Democratic Congress, Berlin.
30 Oct.	Austrian troops defeat Hungarian forces.
31 Oct.	Austrain troops under Windischgrätz defeat Viennese revolutionaries. Demonstrations of support for Viennese revolution in Berlin and Cologne.
4 November	Constitution accepted in Paris.
9 Nov.	Robert Blum, socialist leader, executed in Vienna.
12 Nov.	French constitution promulgated in front of Tuileries.
13–14 Nov.	Marx before Cologne investigatory tribunal: harangues crowd.
15–16 Nov.	Revolution in Rome: the people demand a democratic ministry and proclamation of Italian nationality. Pope, under complusion, accepts popular ministry.
18 Nov.	Berlin declared in state of siege.
20 Nov.	Free constitution published in Rome.
22 Nov.	Austrian *Reichstag* transferred to Kremsier in Moravia.
25 Nov.	Pope Pius IX flees from Rome to Gaeta.
27 Nov.	*Zentralmärzverein*, in favour of German unity, founded at Frankfurt, rallying moderates to constitutional cause.
1 December	Feuerbach delivers his first lecture to students of Heidelberg.
2 Dec.	Ferdinand I of Austria abdicates in favour of nephew, Francis Joseph.
5 Dec.	King of Prussia dissolves *Landtag* (National Assembly) and grants a liberal constitution.
11 Dec.	Louis Napoleon elected President of the French Republic.
28 Dec.	Publication of *Grundrechte*.
1849	
5 January	Imperial troops enter Budapest.

28 Jan.	Frankfurt Assembly's proposed constitution for unified Germany submitted to goverments of states.
8 February	Roman National Assembly divests the Pope of all temporal power. Tuscan Republic proclaimed.
9 Feb.	Roman Republic proclaimed.
15 Feb.	Frankfurt: the 'great Germany' group formed, supporting a decentralized *Reich*, to include a part at least of Austria.
17 Feb.	Frankfurt: the 'little Germany' group formed, supporting a *Reich* dominated by Prussia and fanatically opposed to the Hapsburgs and the Roman church.
2 March	Feuerbach's last lecture at Heidelberg.
7 March	Austrian *Reichstag* at Kremsier dissolved and new constitution granted to the Empire, taking no account of Hungary's constitutional rights.
9 March	Austria proposes central European federation; by these moves alienates its supporters in 'great Germany' group.
20–23 March	Complete defeat of Sardinian forces by Austrians at Novara. Charles Albert abdicates in favour of son, Victor Emmanuel II. Former governments restored in Parma, Modena, Florence.
28 March	Frankfurt National Assembly elects Frederick William of Prussia 'Emperor of the Germans'. Publication of German constitution and electoral law.
5 April	Austrian deputies to Frankfurt recalled by government in Vienna.
6 April	Hungarian nationalist forces defeat Austrians.
14 April	Hungarian independence proclaimed at Debrecen; Kossuth named as head of state.
28 April	Frederick William IV refuses imperial crown.
1 May	Russian troops enter Cracow.
May	Revolution in Baden; Wilhelm Liebknecht among revolutionaries.
3–9 May	Republican rising in Dresden, in which Bakunin and Wagner are active; riots at Elberfeld.
12 May	Secession of Rastatt garrison, Baden.
13 May	Revolutionary congress of Baden. Democratic associations at Offenburg. Conservatives successful in French legislative assembly.
14 May	Frederick William IV cancels mandate of Prussian deputies to Frankfurt.

15 May	Reoccupation of Palermo by forces of Ferdinand II signals end of Sicilian revolution.
18 May	Treaty of alliance between Palatinate insurgents and Baden revolutionaries.
19 May	Last number of *Neue Rheinische Zeitung* appears. Marx, banished from Cologne and Paris, goes into exile in London, where Engels follows him.
21 May	Warsaw Convention.
30 May	Frankfurt National Assembly transfers to Stuttgart.
4 June	Government of Kossuth returns to Pest. All cultural societies banned in Finland.
5 June	Denmark adopts liberal constitution and universal suffrage.
18 June	Final remnants of the National Assembly, presided over by Uhland, dissolved by government of Württemberg.
26–8 June	Gotha meeting of former members of Frankfurt Centre.
1 July	Roman republican forces capitulate to French troops. Roman assembly dissolved and Pope's authority re-established.
23 July	Baden revolutionaries capitulate at Rastatt.
6 August	Austro-Sardinian peace treaty.
13 Aug.	Hungarian forces capitulate to Russians at Vilâgos; end of Hungarian War of Independence. Kossuth and Andrassy escape to Turkey.
22 Aug.	Venice capitulates. Manin exiled.
September	Bavaria declares support for imperial constitution under king of Prussia.
6 October	Thirteen Hungarian revolutionary leaders, among them Batthyány, tried and shot at Arad.
December	Martial anarchy in Naples; liberal leaders arrested.
1850	
1 January	All associations banned in Finland.
21 Jan.	Pseudo-liberal constitution granted in Prussia.
21 March	Erfurt parliament meets to plan constitution of German Confederation.
9 May	New electoral law in France, after successes by democrats and socialists in March elections.
2 July	Peace signed between Prussia and Denmark.
1 October	Customs barriers removed between Austria and Hungary.
29 November	Austro-Prussian treaty of Olmütz. First English translation of the *Communist Manifesto* published

in *The Red Republican*, London. Marx's articles on 'Die Klassenkämpfe in Frankreich' appear in *Neue Rheinische Zeitung—Politisch-ökonomische Revue*, Hamburg.

1851

31 May   German *Bundestag* meets at Frankfurt.

13 November   Universal suffrage refused in France.

2 December   Louis Napoleon's *coup détat* in France, followed by street rioting, wins popular consent (Dec. 20).

31 Dec.   Austria's constitution suppressed; return to complete absolutism.

Suggested Reading

E. M. Acomb and M. L. Brown (eds), *French Society and Culture since the Old Regime* (New York, 1966), especially papers by Langer, Girard, Droz, Moody.

P. H. Amann, *Revolution and Mass Democracy: The Paris Club Movement in 1848* (Princeton, N.J., 1975).

A. Denholm, *France in Revolution: 1848* (Sydney, 1972).

F. Engels, *Revolution and Counter-Revolution in Germany* (often attributed to Karl Marx), numerous editions.

G. Fasel, *Europe in Upheaval: The Revolutions of 1848* (Chicago, 1970).

F. Fejtö (ed.), *The Opening of an Era: 1848* (London, 1948).

J. Godechot, *Les Révolutions de 1848* (Paris, 1971).

Oscar Hammen, *The Red '48ers* (New York, 1969).

L. C. Jennings, *France and Europe in 1848* (Oxford, 1973).

Eugene Kamenka (ed.), *Paradigm for Revolution? The Paris Commune 1871–1971* (Canberra, 1972).

Eugene Kamenka (ed.), *The Portable Karl Marx* (New York, 1980).

Karl Marx, *The Revolutions of 1848, Political Writings Volume 1*, edited by D. Fernbach (Harmondsworth, 1973).

Sir Lewis Namier, *1848: The Revolution of the Intellectuals* (London, 1946).

R. Pares and A. J. P. Taylor (eds), *Essays Presented to Sir Lewis Namier* (London, 1956), paper by Hugh Seton-Watson.

R. Price, *Revolution and Reaction* (London, 1975).

R. Price (ed.), *1848 in France* (London, 1975).

R. J. Rath, *The Viennese Revolution of 1848* (Austin, Texas, 1957).

M. Richter (ed.), *Essays in Theory and History* (Cambridge, Mass., 1970), paper by C. Tilly.

P. Robertson, *Revolutions of 1848: A Social History* (Princeton, N.J., 1952).

O. Rühle, *Die Revolutionen Europas* (3 vols, Dresden, 1927), III.

J. Sigmann, *Eighteen Forty Eight* translated from French (London, 1973).

R. Stadelmann, *Soziale und politische Geschichte der Revolution von 1848* (Munich, 1948).

J. Strey and G. Winkler, *Marx und Engels 1848/9* (Berlin, 1972).

V. Valentin, *Geschichte der deutschen Revolution, 1848–49* (2 vols, reprint of Berlin 1931 edn, Aalen, 1968).

G. Woodcock, *A Hundred Years of Revolution: 1848 and After* (London, 1948).

Contributors

Lesli Bodi is Professor of German at Monash University. Born in Budapest in 1922 and educated at the Universities of Budapest and Vienna, he gained his doctorate in Budapest in 1948, and was a tutor and lecturer there until emigrating to Australia in 1957. He did some high school teaching in Melbourne and lectured at Newcastle University College. Since 1961 he had been in charge of the Department of German at Monash University, first as a senior lecturer, then as professor. He has edited German texts in Hungarian (H. Heine, G. Forster, J. W. Goethe, G. Weerth, B. Brecht, A. Seghers) and English (Th. Huber-Forster) and has written numerous articles in the field of German studies, mainly concerned with the interrelationship of literature and politics in German and Austrian writing from the eighteenth to the twentieth century. He is the author of a Hungarian book on Heinrich Heine (1951); his latest book is *Tauwetter in Wien* (Frankfurt, 1977), a study of absolutism and enlightenment in Austria.

Anthony Denholm is Senior Lecturer in History in the University of Adelaide. Born in 1936, he was educated at the Universities of Wales and London. He was a regular RAF officer from 1959 to 62. After teaching at Manchester Polytechnic and the University of Hong Kong, he moved to the University of Adelaide in 1968. He is the author of *France in Revolution: 1848* (1972) and of several articles on aspects of the life of Lord Ripon (1827–1909). He is at present engaged on a full scale political biography of Ripon.

J. H. Grainger has recently retired as Reader in Political Science in the Australian National University. In 1976 he was a Visiting Fellow at Clare Hall, Cambridge, and a visiting lecturer at the Universities of Sheffield, Johns Hopkins, William and Mary, Maryland, and St John's, Annapolis. He was born in Cumberland, England, in 1917 and educated at Carlisle Grammar School and St Catharine's College, Cambridge. During the war he served with East African troops in Kenya and the Middle East. After appointments in the Colonial Service in British Somaliland, as a schoolmaster in Surrey, as an extra-mural tutor in Cornwall and as lecturer in government and politics at the Welsh College of Advanced Technology, Cardiff, he moved to the Australian National University in 1962. He is the author of *Character and Style in English Politics* (1969) and contributed the chapter on Bonar Law and Austen Chamberlain to *The Conservative Leadership*, edited by D. G. Southgate (1974). He has written articles on politics, government and literature for many journals and is at present engaged on a study of aspects of the ideology of British politics in the twentieth century.

Eugene Kamenka is Foundation Professor of the History of Ideas in the Institute of Advanced Studies of the Australian National University and in 1978–9 Visiting Fellow in Trinity College, Oxford, and in the Max-Planck-Institut für ausländisches und internationales Privatrecht in Hamburg. He is a Fellow of the Academy of the Social Sciences in Australia and Fellow and Secretary of the Australian Academy of the Humanities. His books include *The Ethical Foundations of Marxism* (1962), *Marxism and Ethics* (1969) and *The Philosophy of Ludwig Feuerbach* (1970); he has edited *A World in Revolution?* (1970), *Paradigm for Revolution? The Paris Commune 1871–1971* (1972), *Nationalism: the Nature and Evolution of an Idea* (1973), with R. S. Neale, *Feudalism, Capitalism and Beyond* (1975) and *The Portable Karl Marx* (1980). He is general editor of this series, 'Ideas and ideologies', in which he has co-edited and contributed to *Law and Society* (1978), *Human Rights* (1978) and *Bureaucracy* (1979).

George Kertesz is Senior Lecturer in History at Monash University. Born in Budapest in 1925, he emigrated to Australia in 1949. He read history at the University of Melbourne, and, after working for some years as a librarian in the University of Melbourne Library, he moved to Monash University as a lecturer in 1963. In 1968 he published a volume of *Documents in the Political History of the European Continent 1815–1939*. He is now engaged in writing a monograph on the Frankfurt Centre group of liberals in the years 1847–50.

R. B. Rose is Professor of History in the University of Tasmania. Born in England in 1929, he was educated at the University of Manchester and was Senior Research Fellow at that university during 1970. He was lecturer, senior lecturer and reader in the Department of History in the University of Sydney until his move to the

University of Tasmania in 1972. His publications include *Enragés: Socialists of the French Revolution* (1966); *Bibliographic Essay on Publications in Modern European History in Australia Since 1958* (1967); *Russian Revolution* (1970); and *Gracchus Babeuf: The First Revolutionary Communist* (1978).

F. B. Smith is Professorial Fellow in the Department of History of the Institute of Advanced Studies in the Australian National University, and a Fellow and former Secretary of the Australian Academy of the Humanities. Educated at Melbourne University and Trinity College, Cambridge, he is the author of *The Making of the Second Reform Bill* (1966) and *Radical Artisan* (1973), a study of the Mazzinian republican William James Linton, and of articles on British and Australian history. His latest book is *The People's Health*.

Index